RESOLVE
A New Model of Therapy

Dr Richard Bolstad

Crown House Publishing
www.crownhouse.co.uk

Crown House Publishing
Limited
Crown Buildings
Bancyfelin
Carmarthen
Wales
SA33 5ND
UK

Crown House Publishing
Limited
P.O. Box 2223
Williston
VT 05495-2223
USA

www.crownhouse.co.uk

British Library Cataloguing-in-Publication Data
A catalogue entry for this book is available
from the British Library.

International Standard Book Number
1899836845

Library of Congress Control Number
2002107640

Printed and bound in the UK by
Bell & Bain
Glasgow

Dedication

Dedicated to my late partner and lover Margot, the one person who knew all of this, and knew the importance of it, before me.

Table of Contents

The Author iii
Foreword v

Chapter 1   **How You'll be Able to Use This Book** 1
              The Need for Effective New Models 1
              NLP and the Context of Psychotherapy 3
              How Well Does NLP Work? 5
              The RESOLVE Model 8
              Choosing How You Use This Book 11

Chapter 2   **A User's Manual for the Brain** 13
              The Use of Neurology 13
              Perception is Not a Direct Process 14
              Colouring the World 16
              Modalities and Submodalities 18
              Higher Levels of Analysis 20
              Remembered and Constructed Images Use
                  the Same Pathways as Current Images 22
              Cross-referencing of Modalities 23
              Sensory Accessing and Representational Cues 24
              Research on the Eye-Movement Phenomenon 28
              Strategies 30
              The TOTE Model 31
              Meta-Levels in Strategies 32
              States that Regulate States 35
              How Emotional States Affect the Brain 35
              Neural Networks Are State-Dependent 37
              The Brain and State-Dependent Strategies:
                  A Summary 40

Chapter 3   **Choices for Change** 43
              A Range of NLP Intervention Choices 43
              Anchoring 45
              Installing a New Strategy 51
              Changing Submodalities 56
              Trancework 66
              Parts Integration 72
              Time-line Changes 82
              Linguistic Reframing 90

Changing Interpersonal Dynamics 96
Changing Physiological Contexts 102
Tasking 106

Chapter 4 **RESOLVE** **111**
The RESOLVE Model and the Relationship
of Changework 111
How People Change on Their Own 113
The RESOLVE Model 122
Summary: Using the RESOLVE Model 184

Conclusions **193**

Bibliography **197**

Index **213**

The Author

Dr Richard Bolstad is a certified trainer with the International NLP Association and five other international training organisations. He has a doctorate in clinical hypnotherapy and is a member of the New Zealand Association of Psychotherapists. His previous book, *Transforming Communication*, co-written with Margot Hamblett, is a required text in a number of degree-level programmes, training counsellors, health professionals and teachers. His articles have appeared in numerous journals, and he has taught the RESOLVE model to psychotherapists and counsellors around the world, including in post-war Bosnia-Herzegovina. His book *The Structure of Personality*, co-written with Bob Bodenhamer, Michael Hall and Margot Hamblett, introduces the RESOLVE model in the context of working with "Personality Disorders".

Foreword

It is a pleasure for me to introduce this book. There are lots of books on NLP, and a good many of these are about NLP therapy. *RESOLVE* deals with both in a broad, insightful and in the very best sense, a cultured way. This is a book that will leave you with a deeper knowledge of NLP and therapy whether you are already familiar with the field or not. Although not written as an introduction to NLP, it is a good one in its own right.

Let's start with the title of the book. Neuro-Linguistic Programming is about words, and to the skilled writer, words are the materials they play with, spinning threads into patterns of meaning that stay in the listener's mind long after the book is put down.

Take the word 'resolve', it has at least four meanings. First, it can mean to break down into constituent parts, to separate out or analyse something. This book does that to the field of NLP and therapy. It takes the elements of NLP, separates them out, explains them and then weaves them into a model of therapy. A model in NLP terms is something that works, and this model has been developed in very testing circumstances, working with Bosnian and Kosovar survivors of a horrendous war. It is heartening for me to know that NLP has been taken to exactly the places where it is needed and can help the people in the most need of comfort, resources and peace. There can be no synthesis into a good model, unless you have first done a good analysis, and Richard has done that. And, as with any systemic synthesis, the whole is greater than the parts.

The second meaning of the word 'resolve' is to make a firm and final decision about something. We talk about resolving an issue in the sense of being clear of it. I believe that NLP therapy can do this. It leads to sustainable change, not a quick fix, and this realisation is an important part of this book.

Third, 'resolve' can be a noun meaning firmness of purpose. This is an important part of any healing. Resolve or determination on the part of the therapist to do their best. Resolve and determination on the part of the client to deal with the issue. This determination is a crucial part of healing, but is seldom taught.

Fourth, 'resolve' can be taken to mean 'solve again'. In this sense I think the good therapist helps the client to find better and better solutions to the problems that life puts before them. No issue is ever completely solved, living means having to deal with problems, it means always bridging gaps between what we have and what we want. Some issues are more painful than others. I believe Freud said something to the effect that his goal was to reduce the pain of the neurotic patient to the ordinary misery of everyday life. NLP therapy helps clients in great psychological pain or dealing with the aftermath of trauma, as well as those who need to solve again the perennial problems of life: how to relate; how to be happy; without necessarily being very dissatisfied with their lot.

Clients come to the therapist with problems. We often think in terms of 'solving' those problems, but it seems to me that these problems can be dealt with in other ways. The way the therapist thinks about a problem will determine how they approach it and, as Richard says in this book, not all NLP techniques work with everyone, but I think it is true to say that all NLP techniques will work with someone. Part of the magic is knowing what will work with each of us. This book is particularly good at making clear the theoretical and presuppositional basis of NLP change.

Problems can be 'solved'. Problems can also be 'dis-solved'. Perhaps when a problem is dissolved it falls apart into its elements and disappears like sugar into water. Some problems might be 'absolved'. This would mean that you discover it is not your problem after all, but someone else's. What a relief! And of course a problem can be resolved. This book tells you how to do all of these.

As well as being well written and well structured the book offers a historical perspective on NLP and therapy, an element that is very necessary, but often lacking. NLP does not exist in a vacuum, it has roots and connections to other forms of therapy and this book is extremely good at making these clear, giving a sense of what NLP does, what it does not do and how it links with other approaches.

The book is also well documented with research (and not only NLP research), which grounds the ideas and methods.

Finally, as Richard says, all change in the final analysis is self-change, and the therapist needs to have faith in the clients' resources. It was wonderful to see the word 'love' come into a book on therapy as it does here. As this book says, there is a sense that love is necessary for healing. Rapport in its best sense is not an empty attempt to be like the client or even to understand the client. It is about caring. Clients are not a race apart. Neither are NLP therapists, they are not magicians and need not pretend to be. They are real people working with love from a grounded methodology to help the client mobilise their powers to heal. This takes work. Reading this book is a fine start.

Joseph O'Connor, NLP Master Trainer and Author
May 2002

Chapter 1

How You'll be Able to Use This Book

The Need for Effective New Models

This book is written for all those who are passionately interested in finding verifiable ways to assist human beings, as they create a life worth living. While the RESOLVE model is useful in any situation where people want to make major changes, this book emerged out of the work I did in 1998 and 1999 in the city of Sarajevo. At that time, my late partner Margot Hamblett and I were invited to teach our model of therapy to groups of psychiatrists and aid workers, who were working with Bosnian and Kosovar survivors of perhaps the worst trauma that human beings can face.

We were accustomed to teaching counsellors, health professionals and others in the comfort of a custom-designed training venue. We were used to having several weeks gradually to introduce our ways of thinking and our new techniques, from the field of NLP (or Neuro-Linguistic Programming). In Sarajevo, we worked in a hospital meeting room with shell damage still evident around the walls. We had two days, and a group of people who needed immediate and practical help. The psychiatrists themselves had lived through the terror of the war, and wanted the skills to deal with their own distress as much as with their clients. We did not speak Bosnian, and we had no personal experience of the war. We needed to be able to demonstrate that the techniques we taught were:

- Backed up by research supporting their rationale and their clinical effectiveness
- Able to be learned quickly and applied with success in real-life conditions
- Integrated into a compassionate therapeutic relationship

- Compatible with therapists' current therapeutic modalities, which ranged from psychoanalysis to cognitive behavioural therapy

After only two days' training, over three-quarters of those professionals who trained with us in Sarajevo said they now planned to use the methods we taught. For example, Dr Cerny Kulenovic described the model as "Definitely useful. We used it on ourselves and we treated our colleagues too. We got the predicted effects ... We were well informed and gained very good results in the second day. A new treatment which was economical, short and successful." Dr Mehmedika Suljic Enka agreed: "This training gives more practice in dealing with survivors of traumatic experiences or clients with phobias. Used with my own similar problem, it helped to relieve my fear, and I realised how I can help other people. I have improved my knowledge in psychiatry."

But that was not the most important feedback we got. The most powerful experience we had in Sarajevo involved ordinary people whom we had the privilege of taking through the RESOLVE model of therapy. Let's give you one example. A woman whom we will call Fatima began her session with Margot quite tearful, announcing in English, "I hate the war; and I hate talking about it!" She explained that she had had nightmares every night since the war, when many of her friends and family had been killed in front of her. Sounds were powerful triggers for her traumatic memories, and the sound of explosions sent her into sheer panic. The previous week someone had organised a fireworks display in Sarajevo. Rationally, she knew she was safe, but her panic put her right back in the war situation. She ran into a nearby house and hid in their basement until the display was over. Such experiences were deeply humiliating to her, and felt quite uncontrollable. After attempting unsuccessfully to explain the background of our method to her (her knowledge of English was limited), Margot simply took her straight through the model you'll learn in this book, in this case specifically directed at healing her post-traumatic stress response. At the end of the session, Margot asked her to think of the fireworks and find out how it felt now. She laughed. Next, she invited Fatima to remember some of the worst times from the war, and check how those memories were. She gazed ahead with a shocked expression. "So how is it?" Margot asked. "Well," she said, with a smile, "I'm seeing the pictures, and it's as if they're just over there, and I'm here." The entire process had taken twenty minutes. On our return visit in 1999 Fatima reported that she had had no further panic attacks or nightmares, and had actually forgotten how seriously they once disabled her. She was delighted with the change in her life.

Like the psychiatrists in Sarajevo, you probably want to know how this is possible. But, much more, you'll want to know how you can get these results yourself. Consider one of our trainees, a New Zealand counsellor named Jeff, who was previously trained in Gestalt and Client-Centred therapeutic modalities. It was a step away from the mainstream for Jeff to choose to study NLP, the modality that is central to the RESOLVE model. After using the RESOLVE process for some time, he agreed: "As a psychotherapist, my obligation is to help clients change in the ways they request. I know of no other psychotherapeutic tools more likely to accomplish this ... Professionally, my work has just taken off. What a gift it is to be able to remove a person's phobia, relieve a past trauma, halt an eating disorder, end a sense of abandonment, enhance self-esteem, instil a sense of purpose in someone's life – and much more. The possibilities seem endless the better I get at using these understandings of how human beings function."

NLP and the Context of Psychotherapy

Neuro-Linguistic Programming itself is a discipline studying how people achieve success in fields as diverse as sport, education, management and healthcare. Its original developers proposed in 1980 that NLP would provide the user with "a set of tools that will enable him or her to analyze and incorporate or modify any sequence of behavior that they may observe in another human being". (Dilts et al., 1980, p. 3.) This set of tools involve an analysis of a human being's internal and external communications (linguistics) and their effects (programming) on the functioning of the brain (neurology). Centrally, NLP analyses the structure and sequence of the person's internal experiences: their internal images, sounds, self-talk, feelings, tastes and smells. The tools used in NLP are more fully described in Chapter 2. The use of these tools to analyse how someone achieves success is called in NLP "modelling".

Within that wider field, NLP-based "psychotherapy" is first and foremost the study of how highly successful change agents assist others to change. NLP was not originally created with the intention of developing a new "school" of therapy, so much as with the intention of understanding the patterns behind the work of highly successful psychotherapists. Psychotherapists studied in this way by NLP developers include:

- Dr Virginia Satir (Grinder and Bandler, 1975; Andreas, 1991)
- Dr Milton Erickson (Bandler and Grinder, 1975)
- Dr Fritz Perls (Grinder and Bandler, 1976, pp. 62–96)
- Dr Sigmund Freud (Dilts, 1995, pp. 1–296)
- Dr Carl Jung (James and Woodsmall, 1988, pp. 91–109)
- Dr Carl Rogers (Bolstad, 1995, pp. 24–33)

These psychotherapists were often themselves very surprised with the results of NLP-based explorations of their work. Virginia Satir says:

> I do something, I feel it, I see it, my gut responds to it – that is a subjective experience. When I do it with someone else, their eyes, ears, body sense these things. What Richard Bandler and John Grinder have done is to watch the process of change over a time and to distil from it the patterns of the how process ... The knowledge of the process is now considerably advanced by Richard Bandler and John Grinder, who can talk in a way that can be concretised and measured about the ingredients of the what that goes into making the how possible." [Grinder and Bandler, 1975, pp. vii–viii.]

Milton Erickson MD said of NLP that "it is a much better explanation of how I work than I, myself, can give. I know what I do, but to explain how I do it is much too difficult for me." (Bandler and Grinder, 1975, p. viii.)

Other psychotherapists, while not "modelled" by the NLP co-developers, have eagerly incorporated the insights of NLP into their own work. Dorothy Jongeward PhD, author of numerous books on Transactional Analysis, including *Born to Win*, says of the NLP text *Influencing with Integrity*, "It could well make the difference between success and failure in your personal and career relationships." (Back cover, Laborde, 1987.) Hugh Prather, author of

Notes to Myself and other books, says of the NLP book *Heart of the Mind* that it "contains a wealth of understanding that can help people become more fully human. It also contains the insight and basic honesty that ensures this knowledge is used wisely and compassionately." (Back cover, Andreas and Andreas, 1989.)

Some psychotherapists have tended to see NLP as having an affinity with cognitive behavioural modalities. For example, in his review of the development of cognitive behavioural therapy (CBT), Albert Ellis (1989, p. 12) says that between 1975 and 1979 there was a sudden explosion in CBT and RET [Rational Emotive Therapy] literature. He adds, "So many significant texts on RET and CBT were … published that it is difficult to list even the most outstanding ones. Some of the influential ones included those by Bandler and Grinder."

On the other hand, practitioners of more psychodynamic approaches have considered NLP an important psychodynamic method. Dale Buchanan is director of the Psychodrama Section at Saint Elizabeth Hospital, Washington, and author of numerous articles in the *Journal of Group Psychotherapy, Psychodrama and Sociometry*. He has written an article with Donna Little studying the similarities between NLP and psychodrama. They note, "Bandler and Grinder have refined the therapeutic process. Needless to say they have miraculously packaged a process of immense value to all therapists." (1983, 36, p. 114.)

How Well Does NLP Work?

The need for research that provides information useful to psychotherapists was emphasised in the earliest NLP writings (e.g. Bandler and Grinder, 1979, p. 6). However, it was twenty years before the field of NLP itself began to respond effectively to this need. Because much of NLP is a metadiscipline (a way of analysing and describing other disciplines), research conducted in these other disciplines will often validate NLP hypotheses. For example, while NLP has modelled (from Milton Erickson's work) the hypnotic technique of communicating using unconscious hand signals, there is no separate research verifying this procedure and using NLP terminology. However, in the field of hypnotherapy, the technique has already been well studied (see Cheek, 1981). In this work I will consider research both from within the NLP field and from other fields when selecting therapeutic strategies.

There have been several studies of NLP use in psychotherapy published over the last ten years. For example, a study of NLP use in psychotherapy was organised by Martina Genser-Medlitsch and Peter Schütz in Vienna, Austria, in 1996. The test sample of 55 therapy clients and the control group of 60 clients on a waiting list were matched by pattern of symptoms, age, family circumstances, education level, therapy experience etc. The test group were seen by members of a group of 37 NLP master practitioners (22 men and 15 women) who used a full range of NLP techniques as described in this book (in particular in Chapter 3). Clients were assessed with a number of questionnaires before therapy, after therapy, and at six-month follow-up. The assessments checked occurrence of individual discomforts, clinical psychological symptoms, coping strategies used for stress management, locus of control (whether the people felt in control of their lives), and subjective evaluation of the therapy by the client and the therapist. Diagnoses ranged from schizo-affective and other psychotic disorders, through alcohol dependence, endogenous depressions, psychosomatic disorders and other issues to post-traumatic stress disorders (PTSD). These disorders were more severe initially in the test group than in the control group on all scales, and their use of psychiatric drugs was higher. On average, treatments lasted twelve sessions over a period averaging twenty weeks.

After treatment 1.9 per cent of clients who had had NLP therapy felt no different, 38.9 per cent felt better and 59.3 per cent felt considerably better. None of those treated felt worse. In the control group, meanwhile, 47.5 per cent felt no different, 29.5 per cent felt better and 6.6 per cent felt considerably better; 9.8 per cent of the controls felt worse and 4.9 per cent felt considerably worse. At six-month follow-up, 52 per cent of clients who had had therapy felt considerably better, 28 per cent felt better, 12 per cent felt there was no change, and 8 per cent felt worse. Meanwhile, the therapists rated 49 per cent of their treatments as having met objectives well, 47 per cent as having somewhat met objectives, and 4 per cent as of little or no success. The NLP practitioners then evaluated themselves with tougher criteria than their clients, well over half of whom reported feeling considerably better as a direct result of their NLP sessions.

After therapy, the clients who received NLP scored higher in their perception of themselves as in control of their lives (with a difference at 10 per cent significance level), reduced their use of drugs, used more successful coping methods to respond to stressful situations and reduced symptoms such as anxiety, aggression, paranoid thinking, social insecurity, compulsive behaviours and depression. The research showed that a small number of positive changes also occurred in the control group and could not be accounted for by the therapy, including some of the reduction in psychosomatic symptoms, social isolation and some paranoid thinking. Altogether, positive changes in 25 of 33 symptom areas (76 per cent) occurred as a result of the therapy, positive changes in three areas occurred in both groups, and no significant changes occurred in five areas.

Among the group who received therapy, there were some interesting differences. On 63.15 per cent of the symptom scales, changes were more pronounced in those under 36 years than those over 35 years old. On 40 per cent of the symptom dimensions, men improved more than women (especially in the areas of feeling more in control of life, and reducing paranoid thoughts, aggression, depression and anxiety). Clients receiving a longer duration of therapy (more than ten sessions) had more gains (especially in relief from compulsive and psychotic behaviours) at the end of therapy, but also accounted for more of the loss of success at the six-month follow-up.

A further summary of these results is available on the Internet at www.nlp.at/at/oetz. While such results are encouraging, the fact that NLP is successful in a general sense is not enough to have drawn so much attention to it. What is most often commented on by other practitioners is the *speed* at which NLP achieves many of its specific results. This is important because it enables a psychotherapist to incorporate brief NLP interventions into the context of their own modality.

One example of such brief interventions is the one-session NLP "trauma process" for treating PTSD and simple phobias (Bolstad and Hamblett, 2000, pp. 5–22) used by us in Bosnia-Herzegovina. Dr David Muss did a pilot study on this method, with seventy members of the British West Midlands Police Force, all of whom had witnessed major disasters such as the Lockerbie air crash. Of these, nineteen qualified as having PTSD. The time between trauma and treatment varied from six weeks to ten years. All participants reported that after an average of three sessions they were completely free of intrusive memories and other PTSD symptoms. For most, one session was enough to solve the problem. Follow-up ranged from three months to two years, and all gains were sustained over that time (Muss, 1991). This kind of success is almost unprecedented in the field of psychotherapy. Even more important, it can be achieved by anyone with a basic understanding of NLP, and does not depend on the magical talents of a rare "expert".

In Chapter 3, I will review ten basic types of NLP intervention. The trauma cure is just one example of one of these intervention types. In that chapter, I will mention some of the research about each method of intervention, and give an example of its use. I will also relate the method to techniques used in a number of other psychotherapeutic schools. This will give readers familiar with those schools more sense of how one can more fully incorporate NLP techniques into what one already does well.

The RESOLVE Model

The fourth chapter of this book is structured around the RESOLVE model, a model for understanding the steps behind the successful use of NLP-based changework. The NLP trainer Steve Andreas says (1999), "I think that someone who uses the NLP methods exceptionally well has several ways of gathering all the different skills and techniques under a single overarching framework of understanding." In meeting this aim, the RESOLVE model has a similar function to Carkhuff and Egan's "Developmental Models of Helping" (Carkhuff, 1973; Egan, 1975). Most models of psychotherapy propose some structuring of the session, or of the process of psychotherapy. In NLP terms, there are several key elements of this process that enable NLP "tools", such as the trauma process, to work effectively.

The co-developers of NLP (especially Richard Bandler and Dr John Grinder) did not initially teach a framework for understanding the vast array of new patterns they revealed and developed. Dr Tad James was one of the first NLP trainers to do so. His General Model of Therapy (James, 1995) evolved out of his own modelling of Richard Bandler's client work. My colleague Bryan Royds grouped all the NLP interventions we had studied, based on this model. Margot Hamblett and I expanded this grouping and formalised it into the RESOLVE model, which is now taught in a number of NLP training programmes round the world.

RESOLVE is an acronym for a series of steps used in NLP-based change work. As a preview, these steps are summarised here.

Resourceful state for the practitioner: NLP-based changework is centred on a person-to-person interaction between the NLP practitioner and the client. The practitioner's ability to be confident, to be clear about their role, and to embody the basic assumptions of NLP is considered a key to their enabling the client to do so. Because the role of the NLP practitioner has certain unique requirements, I consider it misleading to refer to this role with the previous term "psychotherapist". Increasingly, in this book, I will use the terms "practitioner", "change agent" and "consultant" rather than "counsellor" or "psychotherapist". This is a similar shift in terminology to that made by Robert Carkhuff (1973), who coined the term "helper". Both Carkhuff and I are searching for terms that are more comprehensive and shift away from the medical or healing metaphor towards a model in which the practitioner assists the client to change and extend their choices.

Establish rapport: The NLP change process involves inviting the client to alter their way of responding to their life situation. This will not be successful until a sense of shared understanding, an attunement of practitioner and client, occurs. In NLP this state is known as rapport.

Specify outcome: NLP is an outcome-oriented system. Changework is focused on enabling the client to make the changes they have chosen, and the clarification of these goals is seen as an intrinsically useful process, which ensures that the client is not merely "wheelspinning".

Open up the client's model of the world: By model of the world, we mean the set of internal thoughts, beliefs, images and feelings that a person uses as a model or "map" for understanding the outside world and getting from A to B in it. Just as not all maps are updated and accurate, not all models of the world are equally useful. A person's model of the world may, for example, contain the belief that "people can't change the way they feel". This belief may have been formed at a time when the person was very young, and may not have been updated after the discovery that (for example) some of the foods you avoided as a child are now your favourites. If someone is depressed, this old belief may seriously limit their sense of being able to change. Unless such a belief is effectively loosened, it may obstruct the process of change.

Leading: Leading is an NLP term for any intervention whereby the practitioner assists the client to change their internal experience so that they reach their outcome. The formal "techniques" of NLP, such as the one-session trauma cure (mentioned above), involve leading. Such NLP change techniques often involve apparently simple visualisations, guided relaxation processes or changes in the type of thinking the person does in response to a challenge. However, the term "NLP techniques" also encompasses making physiological (body-management) changes and practising new behaviours in daily life.

Verify change: Just as beliefs can limit a client's willingness to enter into the change process, so they can at times prevent the person from noticing that they have changed, and fully enjoying the change. A lion that has been kept in a small cage for years learns to pace up and down the length of that cage. If it is released into a larger cage, it will tend to pace up and down the same limited area, not noticing that it could move further. In the same way, a client who has had panic attacks in public may be reluctant to go out until they have not only stopped having those attacks, but have also reassured themselves that the attacks will not happen again. In NLP we invite clients to test their success carefully, to prove to themselves that change has actually happened.

Ecological exit process: Ecology is the study of consequences; the study of what else will change if we change one thing. When we help a client to give up an addiction to alcohol, for instance, we also need to consider what other consequences this change will have. In such a case, the person may want to develop new friendships, new skills for meeting people, new ways of resolving conflicts and so on. These changes to deal with the consequences are a key to ensuring that the central change will work for the person.

For a person new to NLP, it is tempting to think of "leading" as the *real* NLP change process. In fact, each step of the RESOLVE model is equally significant in the achievement of change. The steps overlap and reinforce each other, forming a system that increases the chances of success dramatically.

Choosing How You Use This Book

There are three main groups of people who will benefit from this book. First, trained NLP practitioners will find that it gives a system for making sense of the vast choices available to them. I hope they will also value the background research and the links I make between NLP models and other ways of thinking about change. As NLP trainers and coaches, Margot Hamblett and I evolved this model in direct response to the questions and challenges raised by our trainees as they sought to apply NLP in real-life situations with real clients.

Second, I have written this book so that psychotherapists trained in other models can have access to more than just the "pyrotechnics" of NLP. I am a member of the New Zealand Association of Psychotherapists, and have a doctorate in clinical hypnotherapy. My initial psychotherapy training focused on Gestalt therapy and Robert Carkhuff's "Helping" model. When I came across NLP in 1981, I was completely sceptical about its claims of one-session "cures", and disparaging of its lack of focus on catharsis. My own method of dealing with systems I do not believe in is to learn enough about them to refute confidently their basic assumptions. In the case of NLP, I found that the more I read, the more I began to agree with the NLP model. Finally, in 1990, I completed international certification as an NLP practitioner, and began incorporating NLP techniques into my work as a psychotherapist. The first book written by Margot and me (*Communicating Caring*, 1992) presented a general developmental model of helping, incorporating NLP concepts along with Gestalt, Transactional Analysis and Client-Centred models. NLP enhanced my ability to use my previous psychotherapeutic style, and offered me new choices for specific interventions. NLP will also confirm what you are already doing well, and give you new ways to understand and emphasise it.

Third, this book will also be of use to those new to the field of personal change. If you are looking for a structured, research-based model for helping yourself and others to change, you have found it. If you are searching for a way to make almost magical shifts in your experience, quickly and comfortably, NLP can show you how to go about it. I say that because I know how much my own personal and professional life has changed since learning NLP. NLP, remember, is not just a way of helping other people to fix themselves. It is the study of success. The first step in helping someone else with NLP tools is to help yourself, using the same tools. Your success becomes a "model" for their success.

That said, you'll notice already that this book is punctuated with references, and structured as a text. There are other books, which offer a more fluent self-help introduction to NLP (e.g. Andreas and Faulkner, 1996). Of course, if you like to know the research behind what you are doing, or you'd like to learn how to help others while you help yourself, then this book will give you those extra pieces.

In any case, it is contrary to the attitude of NLP to assert that any book, or any model, has the absolute "truth". The most fundamental assumption of NLP is that no particular model of the world, no particular "map", is *real.* Some maps are more useful than others, but even the best map misses out some things and oversimplifies the real-life territory it portrays. My hope is that you will remember that as you read on here. Take what is useful to you, and leave the rest. Use the book as a reference, as a catalyst to stimulate your own thinking, and as a starting place rather than an end. NLP is only a set of tools. It is *life* that is sacred, not our theories *about* life. If you find some new ways to live your life more fully through reading this, then you made a good choice. I am passionate about NLP, because I have seen it used to change lives. But, as I frequently say to clients, NLP by itself doesn't really "work": *you* work! NLP is just a way of understanding *how* you work. Let's begin by learning this way of understanding how you work.

Chapter 2

A User's Manual
for the Brain

The Use of Neurology

Increasingly, those of us working with human beings have come to terms with the fact that we are communicating with and through the human nervous system. Of course, what happens between human beings is not able to be *reduced* to neurology, any more than the beauty of a Rembrandt painting can be *reduced* to the chemistry of oil paints. However, if we want to paint like Rembrandt, a knowledge of that chemistry can be crucial. If we want to understand human communication, a knowledge of how the brain functions (neurology) will be similarly crucial. This is the starting point of the discipline called Neuro-Linguistic Programming.

It was also the starting point for most of Western psychotherapy. Sigmund Freud's declared aim was "to furnish a psychology that shall be a natural science: that is to represent psychical processes as quantitatively determined states of specifiable material particles, thus making these processes perspicuous and free from contradiction." (Freud, 1966.)

Everything we experience of the world comes to us through the neurological channels of our sensory systems. The greatest spiritual transcendence and the most tender interpersonal moments are "experienced" (transformed into internal experiences) as images (visual), sounds (auditory), body sensations (kinaesthetic), tastes (gustatory), smells (olfactory) and learned symbols such as these words (digital). Those experiences, furthermore, can be "re-membered" (put together again) by use of the same sensory information. Let's take a simple example:

Think of a fresh lemon. Imagine one in front of you now, and feel what it feels like as you pick it up. Take a knife and cut a slice off the lemon, and hear the slight sound as the juice squirts out. Smell the lemon as you lift the slice to your mouth and take a bite of the slice. Experience the sharp taste of the fruit.

If you actually imagined doing that, your mouth is now salivating. Why? Because your brain followed your instructions and thought about, saw, heard, felt, smelled and tasted the lemon. By recalling sensory information, you re-created the entire experience of the lemon, so that your body responded to the lemon you created. Your brain treated the imaginary lemon as if it were real, and prepared saliva to digest it. Seeing, hearing, feeling, smelling and tasting are the natural "languages" of your brain. Each of them has a specialised area of the brain, which processes that sense. Another NLP term for these senses is "modalities". When you use these modalities, you access the same neurological circuits as you use to experience a real lemon. As a result, your brain treats what you're thinking about as "real".

Understanding this process immediately illuminates the way in which a number of psychotherapeutic problems occur. The person with post-traumatic stress disorder uses the same process to re-create vivid and terrifying flashbacks to a traumatic event. And knowing how these brain circuits allow them to do that also shows us a number of ways to solve the problem.

Perception is Not a Direct Process

Perception is a complex process by which we interact with the information delivered from our senses. The biochemist Graham Cairns Smith points out that there are areas of the neural cortex (outer brain) that specialise in information from each of the senses (he lists the modalities as olfactory, gustatory, somatosensory, auditory and visual). However, there is no direct connection between the sense organ (the retina of the eyes, for example) and the specialised brain area that handles that sense. The cortex is the outer area of the brain, and each sense has an area of cortex specialised for it. The visual cortex, for example, is at the back of the brain. A great deal of redesigning has to happen at other places, before the raw sensory data gets to areas of the cortex where we can "perceive" it.

Figure A: Specialised areas of the cortex

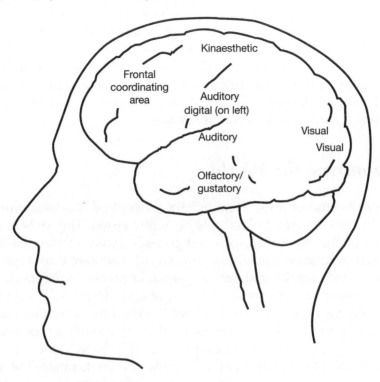

Consider the case of vision, for example. Impulses from the retina of the eye go first to the lateral geniculate body (see diagram below), where they interact with data from a number of other brain systems. The results are then sent on to the visual cortex, where "seeing" is organised. Only 20 per cent of the flow of information into the lateral geniculate body comes from the eyes. Most of the data that will be organised as seeing comes from areas such as the hypothalamus, a mid-brain centre, which has a key role in the creation of emotion (Maturana and Varela, 1992, p. 162). What we "see" is as much a result of the emotional state we are in as of what is in front of our eyes. In NLP terminology, this understanding is encapsulated in the statement "the map is not the territory". The map your brain makes of the world is never the same as the real world.

Because the brain is a system with feedback loops, this process goes both ways. What we see is affected by our emotions, and it also shapes those emotions. Depression, anxiety, confusion and anger are all related to certain "maps" of the world; certain types of perceptual distortion. So are joy, excitement, understanding and love. For example, the person who is depressed often actually takes their visual memories of the day's experiences and darkens them, creating a gloomy world. Notice what that does. Take a memory of a recent experience you enjoyed, and imagine seeing it dull and grey. Usually, this doesn't feel as good, so make sure you change it back to full colour afterwards!

Colouring the World

To get a sense of how "creative" the perception of sensory information is, consider the example of colour vision. Tiny cells in the retina of the eye, called rods and cones, actually receive the first visual information from the outside world. There are three types of "cone", each sensitive to light at particular places on the spectrum (the rainbow of colours we can see, ranging from violet through blue, green, yellow and orange to red). When a cone receives light from a part of the spectrum it is sensitive to, it sends a message to the brain. The cone does not know exactly which "colour" it just saw: it knows only whether the light was within its range. The first type of cone picks up light at wavelengths from violet to blue green, and is most sensitive to light that is violet. The second type picks up light from violet to yellow, and is most sensitive at green. The third type picks up light from violet to red, and is most sensitive to yellow. The most overlap in the sensitivity of these three types of cone happens in the middle colours (green and yellow) and as a result these colours appear "brighter" than red and blue, when independent tests verify that they are not (Gordon, 1978, p. 228).

If the brain gets information from only three overlapping types of cone, how does the brain tell which colour was "actually there"? The answer is that it makes an estimate. In a specific "colour" area of the visual cortex, the brain compares the results from several cones next to each other, taking a sample of the three different kinds, in order to guess which colour was actually present (Cairns-Smith, pp. 163–4). The colour scheme that we "see" is a very complex guess. In fact, you've probably noticed that colours seem to change when placed next to other colours. A blue that looks quite "pleasant" next to a green may look "too strong" when seen next to a red, or vice versa. Placing a dark border around a colour makes it seem less "saturated" or pure (Gordon, 1978, p. 228). Furthermore, what colours we see will also be affected by our emotional state. In everyday speech, we talk about "having a blue day" and about "seeing the world through rose-tinted glasses". Emotional information altering the perception of colour is actually fed into the visual system at the lateral geniculate body, as mentioned above.

The area of the visual cortex that makes final colour decisions is very precisely located. If this area of the brain is damaged in a stroke, then the person will suddenly see everything in black and white (acquired cerebral achromatopsia). At times a person will find that damage results in one side of their vision being coloured and one side being "black and white" (Sacks, 1995, p. 152). This phenomenon was first reported in 1888, but between 1899 and 1974 there was no discussion of it in the medical literature. The medical researcher Oliver Sacks suggests that this resulted from a cultural discomfort with facts that showed how "manufactured" our vision is.

Figure B: The neurology of vision

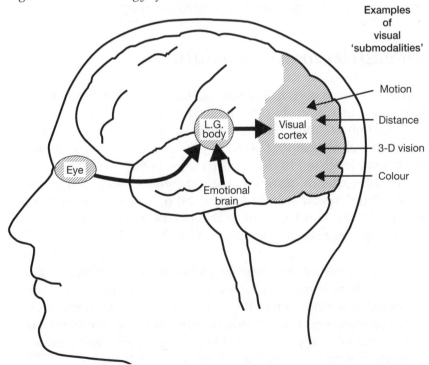

In 1957, Edwin Land, inventor of the Polaroid instant camera, produced a startling demonstration of the way our brain "makes up" colour schemes. He took a photo of a still life, using a yellow light filter. He then made a black-and-white transparency of this image. When he shone a yellow light through this transparency, viewers saw an image of the still life, showing only those areas that had emitted yellow light. Next he took a photo of the same still life, using an orange filter. Again he made a black-and-white transparency, and shone orange light through it. This time, viewers saw all the areas that had emitted orange light. Finally, Land turned on both transparencies at once, shining both yellow and orange light on to the screen. Viewers expected to see a picture in orange and yellow. But what they actually saw was full colour: reds, blues, greens, purples – every colour that was there in the original! The difference between the yellow and orange images had been enough to enable the viewers' brains to calculate what colours might have been there in the "original scene". The full-colour experience was an illusion; but it is the same illusion that our brain performs at every moment (Sacks, 1995, p. 156). That is to say, the colours you are seeing right now are not the colours out here in the world: they are the colours your brain makes up.

Modalities and Submodalities

Inside the visual cortex, there are several areas that process "qualities" such as colour. In NLP, these qualities are known as visual "submodalities" (because they are produced in small subsections of the visual modality). Colour is one of the first fourteen visual submodalities listed by Richard Bandler (1985, p. 24). The others are distance, depth, duration, clarity, contrast, scope, movement, speed, hue, transparency, aspect ratio, orientation and foreground/background. Colour is also one of a list described by the psychology pioneer William James as early as 1890:

> The first group of the rather long series of queries related to the illumination, definition and coloring of the mental image, and were framed thus: Before addressing yourself to any of the questions on the opposite page, think of some definite object – suppose it is your breakfast table as you sat down to it this morning – and consider carefully the picture that rises before your mind's eye.

1. *Illumination* – Is the image dim or fairly clear? Is its brightness comparable to that of the actual scene?

2. *Definition* – Are all the objects pretty well defined at the same time, or is the place of sharpest definition at any one moment more contracted than it is in a real scene?

3. *Coloring* – Are the colors of the china, of the toast, bread-crust, mustard, meat, parsley, or whatever may have been on the table, quite distinct and natural?" [James, 1950, Vol. 2, p. 51.]

Since 1950, another such list has been constructed by research on the physiology of vision. Within the visual cortex, certain areas of cells are specialised to respond to specific visual structures. The function of such cells can be found in two ways. First, in a rather inhumane way, their function can be identified by connecting an electrode to the cells in a monkey's brain and finding out which visual objects result in those cells being activated. Second, the cells' function can be identified by studying people who have accidentally suffered damage to them. When a group of such cells are damaged, a very specific visual problem results.

For example, there are cells that respond only to the submodality of motion. These cells were found in the prestriate visual cortex of monkeys' brains in the early 1970s. When the monkey watched a moving object, the motion cells were activated as soon as movement began. In 1983, the first clinical cases were found of people with these specific cells damaged, resulting in central motion blindness (akinetopsia). A person with akinetopsia can see a car while it is still, but, once the car moves, they see it disappear and reappear somewhere else. They see life as a series of still photos (Sacks, 1995, p. 181).

Neurologically speaking, size, motion and colour are specialised functions, deserving of the name "submodalities". Many other such functions have been neurologically identified, including brightness, orientation (the tilt of the picture), and binocular disparity (depth and distance).

The first research on the neurological basis of visual submodalities was done by David Hubel and Torsten Wiesel in the 1950s and

1960s (Kalat, 1988, pp. 191–4). They showed that even these core submodality distinctions are a learned result of interaction with the environment. We are not born able to discriminate colour, for example. If we lived in a world with no blues, it is possible that the ability to "see" blue would not develop. If this seems unbelievable, consider the following experiment on the submodality of orientation, done by Colin Blakemore and Grant Cooper (1970).

Newborn cats were brought up in an environment where they could see only horizontal lines. The area of the cortex that discriminates vertical lines simply did not develop in these cats, as demonstrated by checking with electrodes, and by the cats' tendency to walk straight into chair legs. Similarly, cats raised where they could see only vertical lines were unable to see horizontal objects, and would walk straight into a horizontal bar. These inabilities were still present months later, suggesting that a critical phase for the development of those particular areas of the brain may have passed.

Higher Levels of Analysis

The story of seeing is not yet complete with submodalities, however. From the visual cortex, messages go on to areas where even more complex meta-analysis occurs, in the temporal cortex and parietal cortex.

In the temporal cortex there are clusters of cells that respond only to images of a face, and other cells that respond only to images of a hand. In fact, there seem to be cells here that store 3-D images of these and other common shapes, so that those shapes can be "recognised" from any angle. Damage to these areas does not cause "blindness", but it does cause an inability to recognise the objects presented (Kalat, 1988, pp. 196–7). There is a specific area that puts names to faces, and damage here means that, while a photo of the person's partner may look familiar, the person is unable to name them. There is also an area of the temporal cortex that creates a sense of "familiarity" or "strangeness". When a person is looking at a picture, and has the "familiarity" area stimulated, they will report that they have suddenly "understood" or reinterpreted the experience. When they have the "strangeness" area stimulated, they report that something puzzling has occurred to them about the image. If you then explain to them "rationally" that the object is no more or less familiar than it was, they will argue for their new way of experiencing it. They will tell you that it *really* has changed! It feels changed! It looks different.

The analysis done in the parietal cortex is even more curious. This area seems to decide whether what is seen is worth paying conscious attention to. For example, there are cells here that assess whether an apparent movement in the visual image is a result of the eyes themselves moving, or a result of the object moving. If it decides that the "movement" was just a result of your eyes moving, it ignores the movement (like the electronic image stabiliser on a video camera). Occasionally, this malfunctions: most people have had the experience of scanning their eyes quickly across a still scene and then wondering whether something moved or whether it was just their own eye scanning.

Interestingly, if one of these meta-analysis areas is stimulated electronically, the person will report that there have been changes in their basic submodalities. Researchers have found that if they stimulate the "familiarity" area, not only do people report that they get the feeling of familiarity, but they also see objects coming nearer or receding and other changes in the basic-level submodalities (Cairns-Smith, p. 168).

This relationship between submodalities and the "feeling" of an experience is the basis of some important NLP processes, called submodality shifts. If we ask someone deliberately to alter the submodalities of something they are thinking about, for example by moving the imagined picture away from them and brightening it up, they may suddenly get the "feeling" that their response to that thing has changed. And in fact, it will have changed. Remember the lemon I had you imagine at the start of this chapter. As you smell the juiciness of it, imagine it bigger and brighter and the smell getting stronger. Changing these submodalities changes your response right down to the body level.

Remembered and Constructed Images Use the Same Pathways as Current Images

So far, we have talked about research on how people "see" what is actually in front of their eyes. We have shown that raw data from the eyes is relayed through the lateral geniculate body (where it is combined with information from other brain centres, including emotional centres), and through the occipital visual cortex (where the submodalities are created in specific areas). From here, messages go on to the temporal and parietal lobes, where more complex analysis is done. One more key point explains how this comes to be so significant for personal change and psychotherapy.

Edoardo Bisiach (1978) is an Italian researcher who studied people with specific localised damage to a specific area of the posterior parietal cortex associated with "paying attention visually". When this area of the cortex is damaged on one side, a very interesting result occurs. The person will fail to pay attention to objects seen on the affected side of their visual field. This becomes obvious if you ask them to describe all the objects in the room they are sitting in. If the affected side is the left, for example, when they look across the room, they will describe to you all objects on the right of the room, but ignore everything on the left. They will be able to confirm that those objects are there on the left, if asked about them, but will otherwise not report them (Kalat, 1988, p. 197; Miller, 1995, pp. 33–4). Bisiach quickly discovered that this damage affected more than the person's current perception. For example, he asked one patient to imagine the view of the Piazza del Duomo in Milan, a sight this man had seen every day for some years before his illness. Bisiach had him imagine standing on the cathedral steps and got him to describe everything that could be seen looking down from there. The man described only one half of what could be seen, while insisting that his recollection was complete. Bisiach then had him imagine the view from the opposite side of the piazza. He then fluently reported the other half of the details.

The man's image of this remembered scene clearly used the same neural pathways as were used when he looked out at Dr Bisiach sitting across the room. Because those pathways were damaged, his remembered images were altered in the same way as any current image. In the same way, the depressed person can be asked to remember an enjoyable event from a time before she or he was depressed. However, the visual memory of the events is run through the current state of the person's brain, and is distorted just as their current experience is distorted.

The successful artist Jonathon I suffered damage to his colour-processing areas at age 65. After this a field of flowers appeared to him as "an unappealing assortment of greys". Worse, however, was his discovery that, when he imagined or remembered flowers, these images were also only grey (Hoffman, 1998, p. 108). If we change the functioning of the system for processing visual information, both current and remembered images will change.

Cross-referencing of Modalities

Submodalities occur neurologically in every sense. For example, different kinaesthetic receptors and different brain processing occur for pain, temperature, pressure, balance, vibration, movement of the skin and movement of the skin hairs (Kalat, 1988, pp. 154–7).

Even in what NLP has called the auditory-digital sense modality (language), there are structures similar to submodalities. For example, the class of linguistic structures called presuppositions, conjunctions, helper verbs, quantifiers and tense and number endings (words such as "and", "but", "if", "not", "being") are stored separately from nouns, which are stored separately from verbs. Broca's aphasia (Kalat, 1988, p. 134) is a condition where specific brain damage results in an ability to talk, but without the ability to use the first class of words (presuppositions etc.). The person with this damage will be able to read "Two bee oar knot two bee" but unable to read the identical sounding "To be or not to be". If the person speaks sign language, their ability to make hand signs for these words will be similarly impaired.

I have talked as if each modality could be considered on its own, separate from the other senses. The opposite is true. Changes in the visual submodalities are inseparable from changes in other modalities, and vice versa.

23

When we change a person's experience in a visual submodality, submodalities in all the other senses are also changed. Office workers in a room repainted blue will complain of the cold, even though the thermostat has not been touched. When the room is repainted yellow, they will believe it has warmed up, and will not complain even when the thermostat is actually set lower! (Podolsky, 1938.) A very thorough review of such interrelationships was made by the NLP developer David Gordon (1978, pp. 213–61). These cross-modality responses are neurologically based, and not simply a result of conscious belief patterns. Sounds of about 80 decibels produce a 37 per cent decrease in stomach contractions, without any belief that this will happen – a response similar to the result of "fear", and likely to be perceived as such, as the writers of scores for thriller movies know (Smith and Laird, 1930). These cross-modality changes generally occur out of conscious awareness and control, just as submodality shifts within a modality do.

Sensory Accessing and Representational Cues

As a person goes through their daily activities, information is processed in all the sensory modalities, continuously. However, the person's conscious attention tends to be on one modality at a time. It is clear that some people have a strong preference for "thinking" (to use the term generically) in one sensory modality or another.

As early as 1890, the founder of psychology, William James, defined four key types of "imagination" based on this fact. He says:

> In some individuals the habitual "thought stuff", if one may so call it, is visual; in others it is auditory, articulatory [to use an NLP term, auditory-digital], or motor [kinaesthetic, in NLP terms]; in most, perhaps, it is evenly mixed. The auditory type … appears to be rarer than the visual. Persons of this type imagine what they think of in the language of sound. In order to remember a lesson they impress upon their mind, not the look of the page, but the sound of the words … The motor type remains – perhaps the most interesting of all, and certainly the one of which least is known. Persons who belong to this type make use, in memory, reasoning,

and all their intellectual operations, of images derived from movement ... There are persons who remember a drawing better when they have followed its outlines with their finger. [James, 1950, Vol. 2, pp. 58–61.]

Research identifying the neurological bases for these different types of "thought" began to emerge in the mid-twentieth century. Much of it was based on the discovery that damage to specific areas of the brain caused specific sensory problems. A. Luria identified the separate areas associated with vision, hearing, sensory-motor activity and speech (the last of these isolated on the dominant hemisphere of the brain) as early as 1966.

By the time NLP emerged in the 1960s, then, researchers already understood that each sensory system had a specialised brain area, and that people had preferences for using particular sensory systems. In their original 1980 presentation of NLP, Dilts, Grinder, Bandler and DeLozier (1980, p. 17) point out that all human experience can be coded as a combination of internal and external vision, audition, kinaesthesia and olfaction/gustation. The combination of these senses at any time (VAKO/G) is called by them a 4-tuple. Kinaesthetic external is referred to as tactile (somatosensory touch sensations) and kinaesthetic internal as visceral (emotional and prioceptive).

The developers of NLP noticed that we also process information in words and that words too have a specific brain system specialised to process them, as if they were a sensory system. They described this verbal type of information as "auditory-digital", distinguishing it from the auditory input we get, for example, in listening to music or to the sound of the wind. In thinking in words (talking to ourselves) we pay attention specifically to the "meaning" coded into each specific word, rather than to the music of our voice.

> The digital portions of our communications belong to a class of experience that we refer to as "secondary experience". Secondary experience is composed of the representations that we use to *code* our primary experience – *secondary* experience (such as words and symbols) are only meaningful in terms of the *primary* sensory representations that they anchor for us. [Dilts et al., 1980, p. 75.]

When we talk to you in words about "music", for example, what we say has meaning only depending on your ability to be triggered by the word *music* into seeing, hearing or feeling actual sensory representations of an experience of music.

Words (auditory-digital) are therefore a metasensory system. Apart from words, there are other digital metarepresentation systems. One is the visual "digital system" used by many scientists, by composers such as Mozart and by computer programmers. This system too has a specific area of the brain that manages it. (Bolstad and Hamblett, "Visual Digital", 1999.) In visual digital thinking, visual images or symbols take the place of words. Hence, Einstein says (quoted in Dilts, 1994–95, Vol. II, pp. 48–9):

> The words or the language, as they are written or spoken, do not seem to play any role in my mechanism of thought. The psychical entities which seem to serve as elements in thought are certain signs and more or less clear images which can be "voluntarily" reproduced and combined. Digital senses do not just meta-comment on "stable" primary representations of course. They actually alter those representations. By learning the word "foot" and the word "leg", you actually perceive those areas of your body as visually and kinesthetically distinct units, for example. This distinction does not occur in the New Zealand Maori language, where the leg from the thigh down plus the foot is called the *wae-wae*, and is considered one unit.

Robert Dilts (1983, Section 3, pp. 1–29) showed that different brain-wave (EEG) patterns were associated with visual, auditory, tactile and visceral thought. The developers of NLP claimed to have identified a number of more easily observed cues that let us know which sensory system a person is using (or "accessing") at any given time. Among these cues are a series of largely unconscious eye movements, which people exhibit while thinking (1980, p. 81). These "eye-movement accessing cues" have become the most widely discussed of all the NLP discoveries. Outside of NLP, evidence that eye movements were correlated with the use of different areas of the brain emerged in the 1960s (among the earliest being the study by M. Day, 1964). William James referred to the fact that people's eyes move up and back as they visualise. At one stage he quotes (Vol. 2, p. 50) Fechner's *Psychophysique*, 1860, Chapter XLIV: "In imagining, the attention feels as if drawn backwards towards the brain."

The standard NLP diagram of accessing cues (below) shows that visual thinking draws the eyes up, auditory to the sides and kinaesthetic down. Note that auditory-digital is placed down on the left side (suggesting that all the accessing cues on that side may correspond to the dominant hemisphere, where verbal abilities are known to be processed). In left-handed subjects, this eye pattern is reversed about 50 per cent of the time.

Eye movements are clues as to the area in their brain from which a person is getting (accessing) information. A second aspect of thinking is which sensory modality they then "process" or "re-present" that information in. Accessing and representing (or re-presenting the experience to oneself) are not always done in the same sensory system. A person may look at a beautiful painting (visual accessing) and think about how it feels to them (kinaesthetic representation). The person's re-presenting of their experience in a particular language can be identified by the words (predicates) they use to describe their subject. For example, someone might say, "I see what you mean" (visual), "I've tuned in to you" (auditorial) or "Now I grasp that" (kinaesthetic). The person who looks at the beautiful painting and represents it to themselves kinaesthetically might well say, "That painting feels so warm. The colours just flow across it." They experience the painting, in this case, as temperature and movement.

Figure C: The NLP eye accessing cues for a "normally organised" right-handed person

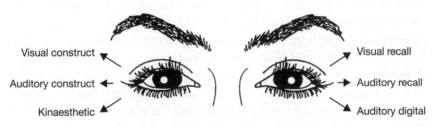

27

Research on the Eye-Movement Phenomenon

Everything in the brain and nervous system works both ways. If place "A" affects place "B", then place "B" affects place "A". We saw previously that, if changing submodalities affects whether you feel familiar looking at a picture, then changing the feeling of familiarity will also change the submodalities of your image.

In the same way, if thinking visually causes your eyes to be drawn up more, then placing the eyes up more will help you to visualise. Specifically, looking up to the left (for most people) will help them recall images they have seen before. Dr F. Loiselle at the University of Moncton in New Brunswick, Canada (1985), tested this. He selected 44 average spellers, as determined by their pretest on memorising nonsense words. Instructions in the experiment, where the 44 were required to memorise another set of nonsense words, were given on a computer screen. The 44 were divided into four subgroups for the experiment:

- **Group One** were told to visualise each word in the test, while looking up to the left.
- **Group Two** were told to visualise each word while looking down to the right.
- **Group Three** were told to visualise each word (no reference to eye position).
- **Group Four** were simply told to study the word in order to learn it.

The results on testing immediately after were that Group One (who did actually look up and left more than the others, but took the same amount of time) increased their success in spelling by 25 per cent; Group Two worsened their spelling by 15 per cent; Group Three increased their success by 10 per cent; and Group Four scored the same as previously. This strongly suggests that looking up and left (visual recall in NLP terms) enhances the recall of words for spelling, and is twice as effective as simply teaching students to picture the words. Furthermore, looking down right (kinaesthetic in NLP terms) damages the ability to visualise the words. Interestingly, in a final test some time later (testing retention), the scores of Group One remained constant, while the scores of the control group, Group Four, plummeted a further 15 per cent, a drop that was consistent with standard learning studies. The resultant difference in memory of the words for these two groups was 61 per cent.

Thomas Malloy at the University of Utah Department of Psychology completed a study with three groups of spellers, again pretested to find average spellers. One group were taught the NLP "spelling strategy" of looking up and to the left into "visual recall"; one group were taught a strategy of sounding out by phonetics and auditory rules; and one were given no new information. In this study the tests involved actual words. Again, the visual-recall spellers improved 25 per cent, and had near 100 per cent retention one week later. The group taught the auditory strategies improved 15 per cent, but this score dropped 5 per cent in the following week. The control group showed no improvement.

These studies support the NLP spelling strategy specifically, and the NLP notion of eye accessing cues in general (reported more fully in Dilts and Epstein, 1995). There are many other uses to which we can put this knowledge. Counsellors are frequently aiming to have their clients access a particular area of the brain. For example, a counsellor may ask, "How does it *feel* when you imagine doing that?" Such an instruction will clearly be more effective if the person is asked to look down right before answering. The English phrase "it's *downright* obvious" may have its origins in this kinaesthetic feeling of certainty.

The claim that which sensory system you talk in makes a difference to your results with specific clients was tested by Michael Yapko. He worked with thirty graduate students in counselling, and had them listen to three separate taped trance inductions. Each induction used language from one of the main three sensory systems (visual, auditory and kinaesthetic). Subjects were assessed before to identify their preference for words from these sensory systems. After each induction, their depth of trance was measured by electromyograph and by asking them how relaxed they felt. On both measures, subjects achieved greater relaxation when their preferred sensory system was used (Yapko, 1981).

Strategies

To achieve any result, such as relaxation, each of us has a preferred sequence of sensory "representations" which we go through. For some people, imagining a beautiful scene is part of their most effective relaxation strategy. For others, the strategy that works best is to listen to soothing music, and for others it is simply to pay attention to their breathing, slowing down, as the feeling of comfort increases.

The concept of strategies was defined in the book *Neuro-Linguistic Programming Volume 1* (Dilts et al., 1980, p. 17). Here the developers of NLP say:

> The basic elements from which the patterns of human behavior are formed are the perceptual systems through which the members of the species operate on their environment: *vision* (sight), *audition* (hearing), *kinesthesis* (body sensations) and *olfaction/gustation* (smell/taste) ... We postulate that all of our ongoing experience can usefully be coded as consisting of some combination of these sensory classes.

Thus, human experience is described in NLP as an ongoing sequence of internal representations in the sensory systems.

These senses were written in NLP notation as V (visual), A (auditory), K (kinaesthetic), O (olfactory) and G (gustatory). To be more precise, the visual sense included *visual recall*, where I remember an image as I have seen it before through my eyes (V^r); *visual construct*, where I make up an image I've never seen before (V^c); and *visual external*, where I look out at something in the real world (V^e). So, if I look up and see a blue sky, and then remember being at the beach, and then feel good, the notation would go: $V^e \rightarrow V^r \rightarrow K$. Notice that, at each step, I did have all my senses functioning (I could still feel my body while I looked up), but my *attention* shifted from sense to sense in a sequence. The digital senses (thinking in symbols such as words) have also been incorporated into this NLP strategy notation, so that we can describe one of the common strategies people use to create a state of depression as $K^i \rightarrow A_d \rightarrow K^i \rightarrow A_d$ ... (Feel some uncomfortable body sensations; tell themselves they should feel better; check how they feel now, having told themselves off; tell themselves off for feeling that way, and repeat ad nauseam!)

The TOTE Model

The developers of NLP used the TOTE model to explain further how we sequence sensory representations. The "TOTE" was developed by the neurology researchers George Miller, Eugene Galanter and Karl Pribram (1960), as a model to explain how complex behaviour occurred. Ivan Pavlov's original studies had shown that simple behaviours can be produced by the stimulus–response cycle. When Pavlov's dogs heard the tuning fork ring (a stimulus; or in NLP terms an "anchor"), they salivated (response). But there is more to dog behaviour than stimulus–response.

For example, if a dog sees an intruder at the gate of its section (stimulus/anchor), it may bark (response). However, it doesn't go on barking for ever. It actually checks to see if the intruder has run away. If the intruder has run away, the dog stops performing the barking operation and goes back to its kennel. If the intruder is still there, the dog may continue with that strategy, or move on to another response, such as biting the intruder. Miller, Gallanter and Pribram felt that this type of sequencing was inadequately explained in Pavlov's simple stimulus–response model. In Miller and Pribram's model, the first stimulus (seeing the intruder) is the *trigger* (the first T in the "TOTE"; Pavlov called this the "stimulus", and in NLP we also call this an "anchor") for the dog's "scaring-intruders-away" strategy. The barking itself is the *operation* (O). Checking to see if the intruder is gone yet is the *test* (second T). Going back to the kennel is the *exit* from the strategy (E). This might be written as $V^e{\rightarrow}K^e{\rightarrow}V^e/V^c{\rightarrow} K^e$. Notice that the checking stage (test) is done by comparing the result of the operation (what the dog can see after barking) with the result that was desired (what the dog imagines seeing – a person running away). In the notation, comparison is written using the slash symbol "/".

Let's take another example. When I hear some music on the radio that I really like (trigger or anchor), I reach over and turn up the radio (operation). Once it sounds as loud as I enjoy it sounding (test), I sit back and listen. The strategy, including the end piece where I listen (another whole strategy really), is $A^e{\rightarrow}K^e{\rightarrow}A^e/A^r{\rightarrow} K^e{\rightarrow}A^e$.

To revisit the strategy for depression mentioned above, we can now diagram it as $K^i \to A_d \to K^i/K^c \to A_d$. The first K^i is the *trigger, stimulus* or *anchor* which starts the strategy. The person feels a slightly uncomfortable feeling in their body. The next step, the A_d, is where they talk to themselves and tell themselves off for feeling that way. Next, they compare the feeling they get internally now (after telling themselves off) with the feeling they got before. (K^i/K^c). Noticing that it feels worse, they tell themselves off some more (the final exit A_d). The feeling of depression can be thought of as the result of repeatedly running this strategy, called "ruminating" by researchers into the problem (Seligman, 1997, pp. 82–3).

Once we understand that every result a person achieves is a result of a strategy that begins with some trigger and leads them to act and test that action, then we have a number of new choices for changing the way they run their strategy and the results they get. We will discuss these later in the book.

Meta-Levels in Strategies

Miller, Gallanter and Pribram (1960) had recognised that the simple stimulus–response model of Pavlov could not account for the complexity of brain activity. Of course, neither can their more complex TOTE model. Any map is an inadequate description of the real territory. The TOTE model suggests that each action we take is a result of an orderly sequence A-B-C-D. In fact, as we go to run such a "strategy", we also respond to that strategy with other strategies; to use another NLP term, we go "meta" (above or beyond) our original strategy.

The developers of NLP noted that::

> A meta response is defined as a response about the step before it, rather than a continuation or reversal of the representation. These responses are more abstracted and disassociated from the representations preceding them. Getting feelings about the image (feeling that something may have been left out of the picture, for instance) … would constitute a meta response in our example. [Dilts et al., 1980, p. 90.]

Michael Hall has pointed out that such responses could be more usefully diagrammed using a second dimension (Hall, 1995, p. 57), for example:

$$K^i$$
$$\downarrow$$
$$V^e \rightarrow V^c \rightarrow V^c$$

This emphasises that the TOTE model is only a model. Real neurological processes are more network-like (O'Connor and Van der Horst, 1994). Connections are being continuously made across levels, adding "meaning" to experiences. The advantage of the TOTE model is merely that it enables us to discuss the thought process in such a way as to make sense of it and enable someone to change it.

States and Strategies

The NLP term "state" is defined by O'Connor and Seymour (1990, p. 232) as, "How you feel, your mood. The sum total of all neurological and physical processes within an individual at any moment in time. The state we are in affects our capabilities and interpretation of experience." Many new NLP practitioners assume that an emotional state is a purely kinaesthetic experience. A simple experiment demonstrates why this is not true. We can inject people with noradrenaline (norepinephrine in the USA) and their kinaesthetic sensations will become aroused (their heart will beat faster etc.). However, the emotional state they enter will vary depending on a number of other factors in their environment. They may, for example, become "angry", "frightened" or "euphoric". It depends on their other primary representations and on their metarepresentations – what they tell themselves is happening, for example (Schachter and Singer, 1962). The same kinaesthetics do not always result in the same state!

Robert Dilts suggests that a person's state is a result of the *interplay* between the primary accessing, secondary representational systems and other brain systems (1983, Section 1, pp. 60–9, Section 2, pp. 39–52, Section 3, pp. 12 and 49–51). Older theories assumed that this interplay must occur in a particular place in the brain – a sort of control centre for "states". It was clear by the time of Dilts's writing that this was not true. A state (such as a certain quality of happiness, curiosity or anxiety) is generated throughout the entire brain, and even removal of large areas of the brain will not stop the state being able to be regenerated. The state does involve a chemical basis (neurochemicals such as noradrenaline, mentioned above) and this specific chemical mix exists throughout the brain (and body) as we experience a particular state.

Ian Marshall (1989) provides an update of this idea based on the quantum physics of what are called "Bose–Einstein condensates". The simplest way to understand this idea is to think of an ordinary electric light, which can light up your room, and a laser, which with the same amount of electricity can beam to the moon or burn through solid objects. The difference is that the individual light waves coming off a normal light are organised, in a laser, into a coherent beam. They all move at the same wavelength in the same direction. It seems that states in the brain are a result of a similar process: protein molecules all across the brain vibrate at the same speed and in the same way. This forms what is called a Bose–Einstein condensate (a whole area of tissue that behaves according to quantum principles; see Bolstad, 1996). This vibration results in a coherent state emerging out of the thousands of different impulses processed by the brain at any given time. Instead of being simultaneously aware that your knee needs scratching, the sun is a little bright, the word your friend just said is the same one your mother used to say, the air smells of cinnamon etc. (like the electric light scattering everywhere), you become aware of a "state". This "state" sort of summarises everything ready for one basic decision, instead of thousands.

States, as Dilts originally hypothesised, are still best considered as "meta" to the representational systems. They are vast, brain-wide commentaries on the entire set of representations and physiological responses present. Our states meta-comment on *and* alter the representations (from the primary senses as well as from the digital senses) "below them". For example, when a person is angry, they may actually be physically unable to hear their partner or spouse telling them how much they love them. The interference from the state reduces the volume of the auditory external input. This often results in a completely different strategy being run! Put another way, the "state" determines which strategies we find easy to run and which we are unable to run well.

States that Regulate States

The psychotherapist Virginia Satir noted that times when a person feels sadness, frustration, fear and loneliness are fairly predictable consequences of being human. In most cases, what creates serious problems is not so much the fact that people enter such states. What creates disturbance is how people feel *about* feeling these states. Satir says, "In other words, low self-worth has to do with what the individual communicates to himself about such feelings and the need to conceal rather than acknowledge them." (Satir and Baldwin, 1983, p. 195.) The person with high self-esteem may feel sad when someone dies, but they also feel acceptance and even esteem for their sadness. The person with low self-esteem may feel afraid or ashamed of their sadness.

Such "states about states" are generated by accessing one neural network (e.g. the network generating the state of acceptance) and "applying it" to the functioning of another neural network (e.g. the network generating the state of sadness). The result is a neural network that involves the interaction of two previous networks. Dr Michael Hall calls the resulting combinations "Meta-states" (Hall, 1995). Our ability to generate Meta-states gives richness to our emotional life. Feeling hurt when someone doesn't want to be with me is a primary-level state that most people will experience at some time. If I feel angry about feeling hurt, then I create a Meta-state (which we might call "aggrieved"). If I feel sad about feeling hurt, a completely different Meta-state occurs (perhaps what we might call "self-pity"). If I feel compassionate about my hurt, the Meta-state of "self-nurturing" may occur. Although in each case my initial emotional response is the same, the Meta-state dramatically alters and determines the results for my life.

How Emotional States Affect the Brain

To understand the effect of emotional states in the brain, it will be useful for us to clarify exactly what happens when a strategy is run in the brain. Strategies are learned behaviours, triggered by some specific sensory representation (a stimulus). What does "learned" mean? The human brain itself is made up of about one hundred billion nerve cells or neurons. These cells organise themselves into networks to manage specific tasks. When any experience occurs in our life, new neural networks are laid down to record that event and its meaning. To create these networks, the neurons grow an array of new dendrites (connections to other neurons). Each neuron has up to 20,000 dendrites, connecting it simultaneously into perhaps hundreds of different neural networks.

Steven Rose (1992) gives an example from his research with new-hatched chicks. After eating silver beads with a bitter coating, the chicks learn to avoid such beads. One peck is enough to cause the learning. Rose demonstrated that the chicks' brain cells change instantly, growing 60 per cent more dendrites in the next fifteen minutes. These new connections occur in very specific areas – what we might call the "bitter-bead neural networks". These neural networks now store an important new strategy. The strategy is triggered each time the chick sees an object the right shape and size to peck at. This is a visual strategy of course. The trigger (seeing a small round object) is visual external (V^e) and the operation (checking the colour) is also visual external (V^e). The chick then compares the colour of the object it has found with the colour of the horrible bitter beads from its visual recall (V^e/V^r) and based on that test either pecks the object or moves away from it (K^e). We would diagram this strategy: $V^e{\rightarrow}V^e{\rightarrow}V^e/V^r{\rightarrow}K^e$.

Obviously, the more strategies we learn, the more neural networks will be set up in the brain. The California researcher Dr Marion Diamond (1988) and her Illinois colleague Dr William Greenough (1992) have demonstrated that rats in "enriched" environments grow 25 per cent more dendrite connections than usual, as they lay down hundreds of new strategies. Autopsy studies on humans confirm the process. Graduate students have 40 per cent more dendrite connections than high school dropouts, and those students who challenged themselves more had even higher scores (Jacobs et al., 1993).

How do messages get from one neuron to another in the brain? The transmission of impulses between neurons and dendrites occurs via hundreds of precise chemicals called "information substances"; substances such as dopamine, noradrenaline (norepinephrine) and acetylcholine. These chemical float from one cell to another, transmitting messages across the "synapse" or gap between them. Without these chemicals, the strategy stored in the neural network cannot run. These chemicals are also the basis for what we are calling an emotional *state*, and they infuse not just the nervous system but the entire body, altering every body system. A considerable amount of research suggests that strong emotional states are useful to learning new strategies. J. O'Keefe and L. Nadel found (Jensen, 1995, p. 38) that emotions enhance the brain's ability to make cognitive maps of (understand and organise) new information. Dr James McGaugh, psychobiologist at the Irvine campus of the University of California, notes that even injecting rats with a blend of emotion-related hormones such as enkephalin and adrenaline means that the rats remember longer and better (Jensen, 1995, pp. 33–4). He says, "We think these chemicals are memory fixatives … They signal the brain, 'This is important, keep this!' … emotions can and do enhance retention."

Neural Networks Are State-Dependent

However, there is another important effect of the emotional state on the strategies we run. The particular mixture of chemicals present when a neural network is laid down must be re-created for the neural network to be fully reactivated and for the strategy it holds to run as it originally did. If someone is angry, for example, when a particular new event happens, they have higher noradrenaline levels. Future events that result in higher noradrenaline levels will reactivate this neural network and the strategy they used then. As a result, the new event will be connected by dendrites to the previous one, and there will even be a tendency to confuse the new event with the previous one. If my childhood nanny yelled at me and told me that I was stupid, I may have entered a state of fear, and stored that memory in a very important neural network. When someone else yells at me as an adult, if I access the same state of fear, I may feel as if I were re-experiencing the original event, and may even hear a voice telling me I'm stupid.

This is called "state-dependent memory and learning" or SDML. Our memories and learnings, our strategies, are *dependent* on the state they are created in.

> Neuronal networks may be defined in terms of the activation of specifically localised areas of neurons by information substances that reach them via diffusion through the extracellular fluid ... In the simplest case, a 15-square mm neuronal network could be turned on or off by the presence or absence of a specific information substance. That is, *the activity of this neuronal network would be "state-dependent" on the presence or absence of that information substance.* [Rossi and Cheek, 1988, p. 57.]

Actually, all learning is state-dependent, and examples of this phenomenon have been understood for a long time. When someone is drunk, their body is flooded with alcohol and its by-products. All experiences encoded at that time are encoded in a very different state from normal. If the difference is severe enough, they may not be able to access those memories at all – until they get drunk again!

At times, the neural networks laid down in one experience or set of experiences can be quite "cut off" (owing to their different neurochemical basis) from the rest of the person's brain. New brain-scanning techniques begin to give us more realistic images of how this actually looks. Psychiatrist Don Condie and neurobiologist Guochuan Tsai used an fMRI (functional magnetic resonance imaging) scanner to study the brain patterns of a woman with "multiple personality disorder". In this disorder, the woman switched regularly between her normal personality and an alter ego called "Guardian". The two personalities had separate memory systems and quite different strategies. The fMRI brain scan showed that each of these two personalities used different neural networks (different areas of the brain lit up when each personality emerged). If the woman only pretended to be a separate person, her brain continued to use her usual neural networks, but, as soon as the "Guardian" actually took over her consciousness, it activated precise, different areas of the hippocampus and surrounding temporal cortex (brain areas associated with memory and emotion) (Adler, 1999, pp. 29–30).

Freud based much of his approach to therapy on the idea of "repression" and an internal struggle for control of memory and thinking strategies. This explanation of the existence of "unconscious" memories and motivations ("complexes") can now be expanded by the state-dependent memory hypothesis. No internal struggle is needed to account for any of the previously described phenomena. The "complex" (in Freudian terms) can be considered as simply a series of strategies being run from a neural network that is not activated by the person's usual chemical states. Rossi and Cheek note:

> This leads to the provocative insight that *the entire history of depth psychology and psychoanalysis now can be understood as a prolonged clinical investigation of how dissociated or state-dependent memories remain active at unconscious levels, giving rise to the "complexes" ... that are the source of psychological and psychosomatic problems.* [Rossi and Cheek, 1988, p. 57.]

Dr Lewis Baxter (1994) showed that clients with obsessive compulsive disorder (OCD) have raised activity in certain specific neural networks in the caudate nucleus of the brain. He could identify these networks on PET (positron emission tomography) scans, and show how, once the OCD was treated, these networks ceased to be active. Research on post-traumatic stress disorder has also shown the state-dependent nature of its symptoms (Van der Kolk et al., 1996, pp. 291–2). Sudden re-experiencing of a traumatic event (called a flashback) is one of the key problems in PTSD. Medications that stimulate body arousal (such as lactate, a byproduct of physiological stress) will produce flashbacks in people with PTSD, but not in people without the problem (Rainey et al., 1987; Southwick et al., 1993). Other laboratory studies show that sensory stimuli that recreate some aspect of the original trauma (such as a sudden noise) will also cause full flashbacks in people with PTSD (Van der Kolk, 1994). This phenomenon is Pavlov's "classical conditioning", also known in NLP as "anchoring". State-dependent learning is the biological process behind classical conditioning. The results of such classical conditioning can be bizarre. Mice that have been given electric shocks while in a small box will actually voluntarily return to that box when they experience a subsequent physical stress (Mitchell et al., 1985). This is not a very nice experiment, but it does shed light on some of the more puzzling behaviours that humans with PTSD engage in.

People come to psychotherapists and counsellors to solve a variety of problems. Most of these are due to strategies run by state-dependent neural networks that are quite dramatically separated from the rest of the person's brain. This means that the person has all the skills they need to solve their own problem, but those skills are kept in neural networks that are not able to connect with the networks from which their problems are run. The task of NLP change agents is often to transfer skills from functional networks (networks that do things the person is pleased with) to less functional networks (networks that do things they are not happy about).

The Brain and State-Dependent Strategies: A Summary

A number of the factors I have discussed in this chapter create choices for an NLP practitioner wanting to help a client transfer functional skills to the neural networks where they are needed. To summarise what we have said about the brain with this in mind:

- The brain responds to visual, auditory, kinaesthetic, olfactory-gustatory and auditory-digital (verbal) cues. Remember the lemon!
- Each of these modalities is run by a particular area of the cortex (outer brain).
- The sensory organs are only indirectly connected to the areas of the cortex that analyse their data. On the way, the deeper areas of the brain where emotion and memories are stored influence the results of perception.
- Within each modality (sensory system) in the cortex, there are specific smaller areas that adjust the qualities of that sensory experience (the "submodalities"). These include such qualities as colour and distance, visually. When these submodalities change, the person's "feeling state" about the experience will change.
- Memories and imagined experiences are run through the same sensory areas of the brain as new experiences. The submodalities

of our memories and our imaginings are altered by our emotional state as we think of those memories or imagine those possibilities.

- All the outcomes people generate in their brains are the result of a series of internal sensory "representations". In NLP such a series is called a strategy.

- As people run through a strategy, and access information from the different modalities, there are a number of ways we can observe their thinking in these modalities. By watching their eye movements, we can see which area of the brain they are drawing information from. By listening to their words, we can hear which sensory system they are using to re-present the information to themselves.

- Strategies can be thought of as having a *trigger* that starts them (also called an "anchor" in NLP); an *operation* whereby the person acts and collects information in some sense; a *test* whereby the person checks whether the results they got are the results they wanted; and an *exit* whereby they act based on this test. This sequence is known by the acronym TOTE.

- In real life, strategies are not simple sequential operations. The brain is able to meta-respond to a strategy.

- Each strategy is run by a neural network (a set of neurons connected by dendrites and supported by a chemical mix of neurotransmitters).

- This chemical mix, which supports a specific neural network, is a key ingredient of what we call an "emotional state", which is a brain-wide experience.

- When a neural network is dependent on a state that is very different from those usually occurring, then the person's usual coping skills may not be available while that state is active.

- Helping someone change involves helping them access or trigger useful neural networks (running useful strategies) at the times they need them (often times when, in the past, they were triggered into using unresourceful strategies).

In the next chapter we look at the specific change processes that NLP has developed to help people use the resources they have to solve the problems they have been running in their brains.

Chapter 3

Choices for Change

A Range of NLP Intervention Choices

The cases of post-traumatic stress disorder I worked with in Bosnia-Herzegovina provide a good example of the problems created by state-dependent strategies. In persons with PTSD, memories of a traumatic event such as a motor-vehicle accident are reactivated by any future events that involve motor vehicles or any events that generate high levels of adrenaline in the body. The person has of course had many other mildly disturbing experiences that they have coped with effectively in their life before (by "reframing" the meaning of the event, and by distancing themselves as they review the event, for example). But, in the case of their memory of the motor-vehicle accident, they find themselves unable to use these healthy resources. This is because, as soon as they begin to re-experience the traumatic event, they are operating from a neural network that has inadequate connection to their "healthy" state. When reliving the accident, they are unable to remember their usual skills. They can run only the strategies that are associated with the neural networks laid down at the time of the crash.

Using NLP-based techniques, we have several choices for getting the resources from where they reside in the person's other neural networks, and shifting them into the neural network where the accident has been coded. The following categorisation of these methods is not intended to be comprehensive. NLP is a vast and constantly evolving field, and these are merely some of the models in use within that field. Furthermore, the techniques to be explained in this section are not simply tools that can be taken out and "used on" human beings. These techniques work when offered within the context of the RESOLVE model, to be explored in the next chapter.

I will group the NLP interventions in ten categories:

1) **Anchoring** (in the PTSD example, having the person remember a time they felt relaxed, get back that feeling, and associate that relaxation with the situation they want to heal)
2) **Installing** a new strategy (teaching the person a new sequence of responses to go through each time they experience discomfort related to the PTSD)
3) **Changing** submodalities (having the person alter the qualities of the memory they have trouble with: for example, by distancing themselves from it visually)
4) **Trancework** (relaxing the person and asking their unconscious mind to deal with the PTSD issue more resourcefully)
5) **Parts integration** (connecting the part of them that is trying to protect them from further danger by flashbacks with the part of them that wants to relax)
6) **Time-line changes** (going back to the time in their memory storage where they first experienced the problem and changing the way they recall that memory)
7) **Linguistic reframing** (changing their understanding of the meaning of the events they went through, so those events no longer trigger panic)
8) **Changing interpersonal dynamics** (teaching them interpersonal skills to get support and meet their needs in other ways in their daily life)
9) **Changing physiological contexts** (changing the body posture they use to recall the events: for example, having them recall the events while doing rapid side-to-side eye movements or while doing some enjoyable and challenging physical activity)
10) **Tasking** (giving the client a task to complete in their own time, in order to produce one of the above results)

In each case, I will give a case study of the use of the process, and make some links between the NLP model and other psychotherapeutic models for using this type of technique. Most therapeutic modalities have some variant of all ten techniques. NLP, remember, is not so much a new model of therapy as a "meta-model" of how therapy in general works.

Astute readers will certainly be able to recognise the ways they already use these techniques, and even learn to use these specific

NLP processes more easily after reading these case studies. However, it is not my intention here to teach these processes, which can all be learned on an NLP practitioner-training course. My aim is to ensure that you can understand what is meant when I refer to these processes later on in the book. In each case I will give examples of the use of the process in other models of psychotherapy. Once again, this is not intended to be an exhaustive acknowledgment, but merely enough indication for therapists trained in other systems to begin to see the "NLP" in what they already do.

You will also, I'm sure, recognise that these are not ten *separate* techniques in terms of the changes that they produce. These are ten roads leading to the same changes; I could even say these are ten different perspectives on that one change.

Anchoring

In the 1890s a Russian scientist named Ivan Pavlov (1849–1936) was studying digestion in dogs. He noticed that the dogs began salivating *before* they were given meat – as soon as they saw their feeder or even as soon as they heard the person's footsteps. Pavlov found that, if he sounded a tuning fork immediately before feeding the dogs each time, after a few meals he could simply sound the tuning fork and the dogs would salivate. They would salivate even though there was no meat available, because salivating was "anchored" in their minds to the experience of hearing the tuning fork (Pavlov, 1927).

The dogs didn't *plan* to salivate. This unconscious response was, in an equally unconscious way, associated with or *anchored* to the sound of the tuning fork. All of us have had similar experiences. Hearing a song on the radio that you haven't heard for many years can *anchor* you back to the memories of that time when you heard it years ago. You begin to *feel* the feelings you had back then. The whole state you were in at the time is re-created by the anchor of that music. All the strategies used at that time are reactivated by the anchor (for example, perhaps the ability to perform a dance you haven't done since hearing that music last time). Anchoring can happen in any sense. A specific sound (auditory), sight (visual), taste (gustatory), smell (olfactory), or touch (kinaesthetic) can anchor the entire state originally associated with it. The process of anchoring was "rediscovered" by Richard Bandler and John Grinder (1979, pp. 79–136). It can be used to take any emotional state that a person has experienced at some time in their life, and "connect" it to situations they would like to experience that state in. In a controlled research study published in Germany (Reckert, 1994), Horst Reckert describes how in one session he was able to remove students' test anxiety using this simple technique, described below. In another study, John Craldell discusses the use of anchoring to access a "self-caring state" useful for adult children of alcoholics (Craldell, 1989); and in a third study Mary Thalgott discusses the use of anchors to support children with learning disabilities (Thalgott, 1986). For an anchor to work, four things have to happen.

1) **State**: When the anchor (say the tuning fork) first occurs, the person must be in the state you'd like to be able to reproduce later. If Pavlov had first rung the tuning fork in a situation where the dogs weren't very hungry, it wouldn't be associated with a strong enough state. When he rang it later, hoping to re-anchor salivation, the effect wouldn't be so strong then either. He needed to use the anchor when the dogs were *really* hungry.

2) **Precise timing**: Similarly, Pavlov had first to ring the tuning fork exactly when the dogs salivated, not five minutes before or after.

3) **Uniqueness**: The anchor has to be unique. If Pavlov's dogs heard tuning forks at other times during the day, he'd need to find a more unique sound to use as an anchor.

4) **Repeatability**: If you want to use an anchor later, you have to be able to repeat it. Imagine that Pavlov had a huge gong which he sounded. It's unique, but, when he wanted to show off the dogs' new trick at the Russian Academy of Sciences, he'd have to carry in the gong as well.

Anchoring: case study

Because anchoring is always happening, and is not a conscious process, most people have picked up a few anchors they could do without. In my work as a counsellor I've assisted many people to change such experiences using an NLP process called collapsing anchors. Here's one example:

Tony asked if I could assist him to be in a better state during math-ematics tests. He said he got incredibly anxious about maths: it was associated with a lot of bad memories – times he'd failed at maths as a kid. It puzzled him, because he knew that there were some subjects, such as biology, where he could feel completely at ease. He knew he was smart enough to learn maths, but something about it "triggered" him off. For Tony, maths – even just seeing maths problems written down – *anchored* him into a state where he felt hopeless. All his resources, his confidence and intelligence, weren't available once he saw a maths test.

I explained to Tony that I'd use anchoring, by pressing on the back of his knuckles, to solve this problem. One knuckle would become an anchor for "being in a maths test" and another knuckle would be an anchor for confidence and relaxation. Once I'd set up these two anchors, by pressing them both at once I would cause the two states to reconnect in his brain. In that way the resources of confi-dence and relaxation would be *automatically and unconsciously* asso-ciated with maths. Tony was sceptical but ready to try anything.

I started off by anchoring resources. I asked Tony to remember a time he had felt *really* relaxed, maybe on holiday. I had him step into his body at that time and experience what it felt like, see what he saw, listen to the sounds there, and listen to anything he might say to himself. I watched him carefully as he re-experienced this time. As he got back into the *state* of relaxation fully (rather than just "thinking" about it) there were changes in his voice, posture, breathing, skin tone and so on.

I needed to see and hear these changes to know that Tony was fully in the *state* I wanted. As he remembered especially the things he saw, I pressed one of his knuckles. As he remembered the things he heard, I pressed it again. As he remembered the feeling in his body, I pressed once more. He didn't have any internal self-talk at the time. I had now anchored a relaxed state with a unique pressure on his knuckle. I asked him to stand up and stretch, to "clear the screen". Next I went through the same procedure with a time Tony had felt incredibly confident. Again I watched for the nonverbal shifts that told me he was in a confident state before anchoring on the *same* knuckle. I had now "stacked" this knuckle "anchor" with two resourceful states.

After clearing the screen again, I asked Tony to remember being in a maths test. His whole body immediately tensed up and his voice got shaky. I anchored this state on a *different* knuckle, and told him to clear the screen. Now one knuckle was linked to his resources, and one to the problem situation. I simply pressed down on both knuckles at once and waited for the change. Tony's eyes flickered and I began to see his body relax. I held the resource anchor down a few seconds longer.

Then I asked Tony, "Now, try to think of that maths test."

Tony frowned. "It's funny," he said, "I'm finding it hard to even remember what it looked like. But it feels totally different."

"Try to get back the feeling you used to have," I suggested.

"No, I can't do it," he said after a pause.

"You used to be good at that," I reminded him.

"That's right, but now it just feels relaxed."

I asked Tony to think ahead to his maths test, and asked what happened when he thought of that. "Well" – he smiled – "I can imagine it being OK. But I don't know. I'll tell you on Monday."

However, he saw me the next day with some dramatic news. "Last night," he bubbled over, "I went to study for the maths test. And I thought, This'll be a drag, because I've always found maths hard. But somehow it was completely easy. In fact I enjoyed it so much I studied everything for that test and went on to study for the next one as well."

I nodded. "So I guess now you're convinced that Friday's test will go OK."

"Well, I'll wait and see."

Not a man who's easily convinced. The Monday after the test he was finally willing to accept it. He announced with pride, "For the first time in my life, I felt totally relaxed in a test."

To me as the person who assisted Tony, what's most exciting is that he overcame his "problem" with his own resources. His brain already knew how to be relaxed and confident. It just needed the neurological connection from this state to the maths test situation. Even though collapsing anchors is one of the simplest NLP techniques, my colleagues and I have successfully used it with phobias, obsessional disorders, learning disorders, insomnia, depression and many other situations where a person's resources need reconnecting to new areas of their life.

Anchoring in other models of psychotherapy

Anchoring, being a direct expression of state-dependent learning, is the basis of most of what happens in psychotherapy. In psychoanalysis, for example, both transference and countertransference are anchored responses. The therapeutic relationship re-creates stimuli (anchors) that were present in the client's early significant relationships, accessing those neural networks and enabling the therapist to explore and modify what happens there (Kernberg, 1986, p. 163). Reparenting in the cathexis school of transactional analysis is another explicit use of an anchored experience from childhood (Stewart and Joines, 1987, p. 276). In fact, the reparenting process is the collapsing of the positive anchor of therapist support with the anchor from a previous problem state. In Reichian-style body therapy, the therapist uses kinaesthetic and auditory-digital anchors to access powerful states that are expressed in catharsis. For example, a client may be instructed to reach their arms out forward and plead "Mamma!" using this action as an anchor for a powerful childhood state (Lowen and Lowen, 1977, p. 107). In Jungian analytic psychology, the power of symbols to evoke (i.e. anchor) entire emotional responses is described as the power of their numinosity or "spell" (Jung, 1976, p. 83).

Once states have been accessed, many therapies *anchor* these states to specific places in the therapy room. For example, in psychodrama or Gestalt therapy, a client may be asked to sit in a particular chair and re-experience a strong feeling of confidence from a previous experience. The state of confidence will be anchored to sitting in this chair, and, if the therapist wishes the person to re-access it, they can have the client sit back in that chair. "Setting out the scene" for an enactment is a process of setting up "spatial" anchors ready to use (Kipper, 1986, pp. 98–100). On the other hand, the hypnotherapist Milton Erickson (1902–80) describes his recognition that a client has anchored their reluctance to talk in a particular chair. By having them sit in another chair, he has them leave their reluctance in the previous chair (Erickson, 1981, pp. 8–9).

Attention from the therapist is itself an anchor. If a therapist nods and smiles each time the person talks about their childhood, the person will soon tend to talk about their childhood whenever the therapist nods and smiles. In this sense, a therapist cannot ever be entirely "nondirective" (Ivey et al., 1996, p. 361). Of course, in behavioural therapies the Pavlovian stimulus–response model enables the explicit use of such anchors to condition-chosen responses. Systematic desensitisation is a good example of the use of a relaxation anchor to resolve anxiety (Wolpe, 1958). Mary Anne Layden and colleagues give many examples of the use of anchoring with patients diagnosed with borderline personality disorder. They have clients do their cognitive restructuring while "utilising a non-verbal stimulus that represents comfort for the patient" (Layden et al., 1993, p. 94). Examples they give include one person who felt safe as a child when his nanny washed and powdered him. He washed himself using the same brand of hair shampoo and the same talcum powder before doing his cognitive-therapy sessions. Another person was instructed to remember times when her mother held her and affirmed her as a child. The woman was told to wrap her own arms around herself and say to herself the positive things she recalled her mother saying. This enabled her more readily to reframe the meaning of a problematic memory.

The psychosynthesis developer Roberto Assagioli (1888–1975) describes another dramatic use of collapsing anchors decades before the development of NLP. In the first session of this technique, he has the client talk about their problem, while he plays a piece of music. The next session, he has them talk about the *solution* to their problem, while he plays a second piece of music. In the third session, he has them listen to a piece of music that combines both the previous sections (Assagioli, 1976, pp. 262–4).

Installing a New Strategy

In NLP terms, every result that a person generates can be thought of as the result of a strategy – an order and sequence of internal representations (Dilts, Grinder, Bandler and DeLozier, 1980). Each strategy has a trigger – some stimulus that lets them know its time to start the process. The person then takes action that changes things enough so that they can assess whether or not they have reached their goal with the strategy. This sequence (trigger-operation-test-exit) explains how complex behaviours are organised from within the person, rather than merely as a stimulus–response knee-jerk reaction.

Of course, every "problem" a person is able to repeat in their life (such as depression, anxiety or addiction) will also have a strategy. In the case of such problems, the person is frequently running a strategy that was developed at a time in their life when they were not able to use other, resourceful states and strategies. One of my choices in NLP terms is actually to rehearse the person through a more useful strategy in the context where they have previously been running a "problem-generating" strategy. People usually need to be rehearsed through a strategy only a few times before it is "installed" and runs unconsciously.

Consider learning a strategy such as cooking a meal from a new recipe. The first time you do it, you may need to go rather cautiously. But, after perhaps three or four times, you begin to do it almost automatically, and feel more confident about it. After perhaps a dozen times, the new strategy may run so unconsciously that you cannot even consciously remember it: you just know that, in the situation, it will "come to" you. That means that the strategy has been "anchored" to the situation you want to use it in. Often, phone numbers are remembered this way. You may not remember a person's phone number until you have the phone in your hand ready to dial it. At that point, the strategy runs automatically.

Strategies can also be rehearsed by imagining oneself doing them. Samuels and Samuels (1975) conducted a famous experiment where they had groups of high school basketball players practise free throws for twenty days. One group practised physically each day, and one group merely practised on Day One and Day Twenty.

A third group practised physically on Day One and Day Twenty, and spent the rest of the days simply visualising themselves throwing perfect goals. At the end, the improvement of this third group (23 per cent) was essentially the same as that of the first group (24 per cent). Rehearsing the strategy in their imagination installed it as effectively as doing it physically. Therapeutically, strategies can be rehearsed directly, or by visualisation, including even the visualisation that occurs when people hear a *story* about someone running a new and successful strategy.

The most obvious research on NLP-based strategy installation is the study mentioned earlier of installing the visual-recall spelling strategy (Dilts and Epstein, 1995). In this study, students were rehearsed through the new strategy by learning it from a computer screen. Thomas Malloy at the University of Utah has demonstrated the success of installing both the spelling strategy (Malloy, 1989) and a strategy for problem solving (Malloy et al., 1987). In this latter study, three groups of school students were given a range of cognitive problems to solve. One group were exposed to examples of the problems before, and another group had an NLP-based problem-solving strategy installation. The third group were a control. The group who had the NLP strategy installation not only did better on the task, but also scored higher on a post-test Piagetian multiplicative classification task (indicating that broad-based cognitive advances had been made as a result of the change). In the following example, I demonstrate how to use this process to achieve a simple therapeutic change:

Installing a new strategy: case study

Jane came to see me because, she was "sick and tired of being poor". When she was young, her parents explained to her that it wasn't really very important for a girl to get money, because her husband would usually help out. Anyway, they said, "Rich people are usually selfish and stuck up." Jane was too young to realise that she deserved happiness just as much as anyone else, so she believed them. *Now*, as an adult, she knew rationally that she wanted to change, but somehow she never got round to doing the things that would help her earn more money. This was obviously the result of a well-established strategy and I was curious to know how she did it. I asked her what happened when she thought about earning money.

Jane said that she always started thinking about it by noticing how poor she was. She made pictures in her head of how bad her life was, and how hard things were. Then she would yell at herself internally, in a harsh voice – things like, "You have to get out of this", "You should be able to cope". Sometimes she'd try to imagine herself getting a job where she could earn more money, but the pictures she saw were rather dull-looking – of her stuck halfway through some hard work. It hurt to look at those, especially when she saw hundreds and hundreds of them – one picture for every day she'd have to cope with. In the end she just became overwhelmed and avoided the issue. No wonder this didn't work. How did we change it?

Previously, Jane made two kinds of internal representation. First, she thought about what she wanted to avoid (being poor). That might be an OK way to notice what's wrong, but, the more Jane's brain thought about being poor, the less time it had to work out how to create the life she wanted. Jane was going through life like a driver looking in the rear-view mirror. She knew exactly what she was trying to get away from, but she never gave her car good instructions about where to go. Needless to say, she had her share of crashes.

Second, if Jane ever thought about earning money, she saw herself stuck halfway through unpleasant tasks. Imagine if someone looking forward to their holiday saw themselves stuck trying to pack their bags. Or if someone excited about a party they were going to, kept making dull, still pictures of ironing their shirt. That's *not* the way your brain gets excited.

I had Jane make a picture of herself living the life she wanted: a movie, big and bright, with her favourite inspirational music in the background (the theme from a film she loved). Then I had her talk to herself about that, but not the way she used to talk to herself. Instead of harsh "shoulds" and "musts", she chose to talk to herself in a more enticing, excited voice. "Wouldn't it be *great* to do that?" "I'd really *like* to have that." "*That's* the life I want." Then she could see a movie of herself taking the very next step to get herself into a job, and see that movie merge into the picture of her living the life of her dreams. She could look at that movie and check how *that* felt! Just that one little change *showed* her that she was on her way. We rehearsed her through this new strategy a few times and she noticed that it was now running by itself. *That* felt exciting.

But then, it *would* feel exciting. It happened to be the exact same way Jane got herself excited about building a relationship, something she already did well. That's where I found the design for this "new" strategy. Her successful motivation strategy would be written in NLP notation as $V^c \rightarrow A_d \rightarrow V^c \rightarrow V^c / V^c \rightarrow K$.

- See the goal (big, bright images)? Talk about wanting it (slower, quieter, "enticing" voice) →
- See the next step leading to the goal (big, bright, moving images) →
- Compare the pictures and see if that looked more like what she wanted →
- Feel excited if it did.

In fact, it felt exciting just to hear about Jane's successful change. Over the next few weeks, she found herself thinking about success more and more. Right now she has a job: not just any job, but a job working with children (something she'd always wanted) where she gets holidays to do the things she now allows herself to dream of. In her spare time, she uses NLP to help other people discover the secret of *their* own success.

A problem-solving strategy can be installed far more casually, of course, by rehearsing the person through it in a metaphor. Joseph O'Connor gives a fascinating example (O'Connor and Seymour, 1994, p. 184).

I went to the newsagent's the other day and found a very traumatised elderly lady telling the shopkeeper how she had just been mugged. The story went on and got worse. Awaiting my moment, I interrupted and recounted the tale of my friend who was beaten up in her home and could not seem to get the incident out of her head. Then, a few weeks later, when she realised what she was doing, she said, "Being beaten up is bad enough, but I'll be damned if I'll give them the satisfaction of ruining my life" and she decided to push the whole incident so far away that it was as though she had forgotten all about it … "Can I have a *Guardian* please?" The old lady paused, her eyes focused off into the distance, and then her state changed and she calmly walked out of the shop. The unexpected thing was that as I left with my paper, the person behind me smiled and said two words: "Nice work."

Installing a strategy in other models of psychotherapy

The structure of therapy itself is a strategy, and, from the beginning of psychotherapy, practitioners have been rehearsing their clients through problem-solving strategies as diverse as free association, catharsis and intermittent positive reinforcement. In psychoanalysis, a therapeutic alliance is formed between the therapist's "work ego" and a section of the client's ego, which observes with the therapist and assists her/his problem-solving. This observing ego identifies with the analyst and learns the *strategy* of analysis, explains Dr Stanley Olinick (Olinick, 1980, pp. 53–61).

In some therapies, such as transactional analysis, this learning is even more explicit, with the client being taught the therapist's model in some detail and being encouraged to analyse their own transactions using it (Stewart and Joines, 1987, p. 8). Often, the strategies being taught come from a specific sensory system that is highly valued by the therapeutic model. Alexander Lowen, a body therapist, says, "All sensing starts with a sensing of the self, that is, of one's own body ... One of the main purposes of these bioenergetic exercises is to help you sense or get in touch with your body." (Lowen and Lowen, 1977, p. 46.)

By contrast, the Rational Emotive therapist Albert Ellis complains that in such books "Psychotherapy tended to become highly confused with physiotherapy" (Ellis, 1972, p. 7). Ellis reveals (at the same time as rehearsing clients through) the core strategy of the Rational Emotive Therapy (RET) model, where some stimulus (visual, auditory or kinaesthetic) leads the person to talk to themselves (auditory-digital). The result of this A_d operation and test is the kinaesthetic feeling they get at the end. Rational Emotive Therapy teaches a number of auditory-digital strategies for solving problems. Indeed, it is with cognitive psychology in general that strategy installation comes into its own, under names such as Cognitive Restructuring (Beck and Emery, 1985, pp. 190–209) and Behavioural Rehearsal (Beck and Emery, 1985, pp. 271–272).

The notion of strategies is easily recognisable within other models explaining how action occurs. In psychodrama, a role is said to have five components. These equate to some extent with the TOTE: so that Context = the Trigger; Behaviour = the Operation; Belief = the Test; and Feeling and Consequences = the Exit (Williams, 1989, p. 58).

Even within a Client-Centred framework, therapists teach strategies. In the famous filmed session where Dr Carl Rogers (1902–87) works with a client named Gloria, a breakthrough clearly comes after Rogers teaches her a strategy for solving her problems. Gloria has repeatedly asked Rogers to give her a solution. He says instead, "One thing I might ask: 'What is it you wish I would say to you?' " Gloria replies, "I want you to say to me: 'Go ahead and be honest.' " This becomes her solution, and she herself uses the strategy of asking "What do I want Dr Rogers to say?" again later in the interview to clarify what she herself will do.

Changing Submodalities

Direct instructions to someone to "feel happy" do not usually elicit the desired change. However, in our experience in NLP, people can be easily taught to change the submodalities of their experiences at will. The results are almost as miraculous as if they were told to "be happy". Clients are able to take memories of experiences where they would like to be happy, and "brighten up" the images, or "step back from" the images to get some distance. Clients who find that they cannot simply stop their own internal critical voice are able nonetheless to change that voice so that it sounds like a cartoon character and to turn the volume down so that it whispers. Clients who have a headache are usually able to shift it two centimetres to the left and change the shape of it. Such submodality shifts have dramatic implications. Remember that people in a yellow room will feel warmer than in a blue room, even if the temperature in the yellow room is set lower (Podolsky, 1938). Changing the qualities of our internal experiences changes their meaning.

We can simply instruct the person to change such submodalities, but a number of NLP processes do this with a little more "flair", by generating a whole new strategy, which "locks in place" the desired submodalities. Two examples of such processes are the "Swish" and the "NLP phobia/trauma process" (Bandler, 1985). The Swish is a technique with a wide range of applications. It has been used successfully to resolve compulsive behaviours such as nail biting (Wilhelm, 1991) and explosive violence (Masters et al., 1991), as well as to deal with anxiety conditions (Andreas and Andreas, 1992). It involves having the person rehearse through a "visualisation" in which the submodalities of the problem situation are "reduced" in intensity, while the submodalities of an imagined resourceful self-image are enhanced.

The NLP fast phobia/trauma process is the most well researched of all NLP techniques. I will discuss it in depth because of its importance in the process of therapy. It was developed in the early 1970s in a rather interesting way. The NLP trainer Richard Bandler simply put advertisements in the paper asking for people who had once had phobias, and then "got over them". He studied the way these individuals recalled the subject of their phobia, and compared this to the way people still suffering from phobias recalled the focus of their panic. The difference was absolutely consistent. In every case, those people had shifted from remembering using visual recall to remembering using visual construct. When they remembered the phobic situation, they saw themselves as if from outside, rather than from inside the experience. It quickly became evident to the NLP developers that the same change process would work for the phobia-like results of post-traumatic stress disorder (found in survivors of war and other disasters). A phobia is a response to a traumatic experience (either real *or* imagined). Whether the person is reacting to an imagined event with a spider, or to an actual sexual assault, it's the way the person stores their memory that generates the various symptoms of PTSD.

Many research studies have confirmed the success of Bandler's method. I will mention just a few examples here. The psychologist Dr Marla Beth Liberman (1984) of Saint Louis University studied twelve subjects with specific phobias, using a control group who imaged pleasant scenes. Subjects in the NLP-treated group showed reduction in global fears and specific fear responses, as well as reducing a wide range of problem symptoms. A test of hypnotic susceptibility showed that this success was unrelated to hypnotic ability.

In 1988 the University of Miami Phobia and Anxiety Disorders Clinic confirmed the value of the fully developed technique (used this time in combination with Ericksonian hypnotherapy). Thirty-one clients were studied, with specific phobias, social phobias or agoraphobia. All of them completed the Beck Depression Inventory and the Mark Phobia Questionnaire before and after an average two or three sessions. Clients showed marked improvement on inventories for both phobia and depression symptoms (Einspruch and Forman, 1988).

In his book *The Trauma Trap*, Dr David Muss MD documents his extensive use of the NLP trauma process with victims of PTSD. A policeman involved in the 1989 Hillsborough soccer tragedy in northern England – when 96 football supporters were crushed in a rush to get into the stadium – describes how his flashbacks (sudden horrific memories of the trauma), insomnia and alcohol abuse disappeared after two sessions. A patient (Barbara Drake) tells how one session with Dr Muss completely resolved flashbacks and other symptoms resulting from a sexual-abuse experience. These and the other stories documented by Muss parallel our own experiences as trainers and master practitioners of NLP. Muss says, "I know that it has worked for every patient I have dealt with so far, without exception." (Muss, *The Trauma Trap*, 1991, p. 10). Muss did a pilot study with seventy members of the West Midlands Police Force, who had witnessed major disasters such as the Lockerbie air crash in Scotland in 1988. Of these, nineteen qualified as having PTSD. The time between trauma and treatment varied from six weeks to ten years. All participants reported that after an average of three sessions they were completely free of intrusive memories and other PTSD symptoms. Follow-up ranged from three months to two years, and all gains were sustained over that time.

The phobia/trauma cure changes several submodalities in the traumatic memory. These include distance (or changing position from "associated" into the body to "dissociated) and colour. Following is a list of some of the more common submodalities that an NLP practitioner might change in order to alter the client's experience of a memory:

Visual submodalities

Number:	Is there one or more image?
Simultaneous/sequential:	If more, do you see them all at once?
Location:	Where do you see the image in space?
Distance:	How far away is it?
Size:	Are things life-size, larger or smaller?
Border:	Is the image all around or in a set place?
Border type:	If in a set place, does the border fade out or have an edge?
Colour:	Is it colour or black and white?
Colour type:	If colour, is the colour vivid or pale?
Brightness:	How bright or dark is it?
Focus:	How focused is it?
Focus variation:	Is one part (e.g. the centre) more in focus?
Movement:	Is it a movie or a still?
Associated:	Do you see it through your own eyes, or are you looking at yourself?
3-D:	Is it three-dimensional or flat like a photo?

Auditory external submodalities

Number:	Is there one sound or more?
Location:	Where do the sounds come from?
Volume:	How loud are they?
Tempo:	Are the sounds fast or slow?
Rhythm:	Do the sounds have a rhythm or are they steady?
Pitch:	Are the sounds mainly high or low in pitch?
Clarity:	How clear are they?

Auditory-digital (internal self-talk) submodalities

Number:	Is there one internal voice or more (self-talk)?
Location:	Where is the voice coming from?
Volume:	How loud is it?
Tempo:	Is it fast or slow?

Rhythm:	Does it have a rhythm?
Pitch:	Is it high or low in pitch?
Clarity:	How clear is the voice?

Kinaesthetic submodalities

Location:	Where in your body do you feel it?
Movement:	Is the feeling moving or still?
Rhythm of movement:	If moving, is there a rhythm to the movement?
Intensity:	How strong is the movement?
Temperature:	Does it feel warm or cool?
Moisture:	Is it wet or dry feeling?
Texture:	Does it feel soft/hard/rough/smooth etc.?

Gustatory/olfactory submodalities

Smell:	Is there a smell associated with it?
Intensity of smell:	How intense is it?
Location of smell:	Where does it come from?
Taste:	Is there a taste associated with it?
Intensity of taste:	How intense is it?
Location of taste:	Where do you taste it?

Changing submodalities: case study

In an article introducing NLP, Steve and Connirae Andreas present a transcript of their work with a woman named Kate, who suffered anxiety after seeing a fatal accident (Andreas and Andreas, 1992, pp. 24–8). Kate said she kept "zooming in on" the image of the dead man's face through the day. This visual submodality pattern (zooming in) would provide the focus for Connirae's intervention. First, she assisted Kate to design a picture of a "Kate who could deal with that kind of situation really well ... She has the resources to deal with it effectively ... You can know that by the expression on her face, the way she moves, breathes and gestures, the sound of her voice, etc." Steve and Connirae explain:

"Connirae knew what made Kate panic: the memory of zooming in on the man's face. She had also helped Kate create an image of her capable self ... The next step is to connect these two images in her mind, so that every time Kate thinks of the man's face, it will automatically transform into the image of seeing herself with the resources to deal with this kind of situation ... NLP teaches many ways to connect images in our minds and each of us is unique in what works best for us. Connirae already knew that 'zooming in' had an impact on Kate, so she decided to use that to connect the two images. She first tested her guess, to find out if Kate felt more attracted to the capable Kate of the future if she brought the image closer and zoomed in on it. When she tried this she smiled and said 'Yes.' Then she asked her to clear her visual screen in preparation for linking the two images. 'Now see the unconscious man up close and zoomed in. As soon as you can see that, also see a very small image of the capable Kate, way out on the horizon ... Now let the image of the capable Kate zoom in close very rapidly at the same time as the image of the man in the accident quickly "unzooms" and moves off so far away you can't see it any more.' "

Kate expressed doubt that she was "really seeing" these images, and Connirae reassured her that she needed only to "pretend" to see them. She continued, "Now blank your internal screen and do the same thing five more times." After running this process, called a "Swish", Connirae tested to check how Kate felt. She felt much better thinking about the accident, and was able to drive home past the scene of the accident without the usual panic that she had been suffering. At a follow-up seven years later, Kate reported that she had never again had the problem. The Swish process changes the submodalities on the original event, in this case by shifting the remembered images far away. It also uses the same submodality in reverse to bring in a metaphorical "resourceful" person.

A similar submodality shift is involved in the NLP phobia/trauma process. In the following example, Margot Hamblett described her use of the NLP trauma-cure process with a client. Notice how the process teaches this woman's brain to shift her *perspective* on the traumatic event. The new perspective is called, in NLP jargon, "dissociated", meaning safely distanced from the event. Hamblett explains:

"Jane is a mother of three primary school age children. Four years ago her younger son, then aged 2 years, had a very painful and gruesome accident while playing at home. Since that day, although her son was totally recovered, Jane had suffered typical symptoms of PTSD.

"When she tried to describe what happened to her son she immediately started crying, and getting very distressed. I reassured her it was OK to tell me later. She told me she was constantly anxious about her family, especially her children, but also her husband. She was continuously imagining awful things happening to them, was constantly watchful, needing to know their every move. She could only relax if the children were still and quiet so she was tending to stop them or yell at them if they did any normally boisterous activities. A child's yell in play caused her to panic. If her children had minor childhood accidents, cuts and scrapes, she was immobilised with panic and could not help them. She was planning her life now so there would always be a backup adult there.

"Jane very much wanted to relax with her kids, enjoy and encourage their adventurousness, take them skiing, and also let them have some space to themselves. I asked her to imagine she was sitting comfortably at home, sitting where she would usually sit to watch a video on TV. 'Make that TV screen one of those really small ones, almost like a toy one. Now, on that small screen over there, imagine you can see a still picture of yourself, just like you are now, and make it black and white. Is that easy ?'

" 'Yes.'

" 'Great. Now imagine you were standing right outside the house some distance away. Looking through the window. You can see that you sitting inside on the couch, looking at the screen ... As you stand outside the house, notice that you have in your hand the remote control, and you are going to just watch her inside on the couch, as you show her some special videos. Is she comfortable out there ? Can you see the back of her head? ... Great ... Now have her look at a still black and white picture of herself in a safe time just before the accident happened, while she's relaxed and happy at home there ... And now put up a picture for her, of herself in a safe time *after* the accident time, when she *knows* it was all over now.

She might feel relieved to know its over now. OK? ... Now play through for her the video of what happened, from the first safe picture to the end safe picture. Play it quite quickly, and *you just watch her*, as she watches and learns what she needs to know to let it all go.'

"Jane looked a little bit tense at times as she did this, but she remained fairly comfortable, and completed this step.

" 'How was that?'

" 'Not too bad. Easier than I thought.'

" 'Great. Now, I'd like you to imagine you could float right over into that end safe picture, as if you're right inside that experience, seeing through your own eyes, hearing through your own ears ... Turn up the colour. Now come backwards inside that experience very quickly, like a video on rewind, to the first safe picture. Take one to two seconds. Zip! Then be standing, looking in the window again. How was that?'

" 'Fine.' She nodded. I guided her through this last step again, then asked her to repeat it by herself very quickly, a few more times, until the picture began to disappear or disintegrate, 'so you can't do it any more.'

"After a few moments, she nodded, 'Okay.'

" 'Great. Well, that's pretty much it really.' She laughed in disbelief.

" 'Well, let's see. Try and remember the accident now, and find out how it's different now.'

" 'It's just gone back into the past,' she said, with a shrug. 'I know it happened, but it's just over there.'

" 'Can you get back the feelings you used to have? Really try and see if you can, or not.'

"She laughed and said, 'I've never felt so relaxed.' I asked her to imagine a kid yelling and shouting outside in play. She shrugged again and said, 'It's just normal. Just a kid playing.' As we tested and confirmed the changes she had made, Jane found she could easily and comfortably imagine tending effectively to her kids after minor cuts and scrapes, and enjoying their more adventurous sports and games. She was really excited about looking forward to a *relaxing* weekend with the family. She even practised how she might explain to her kids how very different she was around them now, because she was sure they would wonder what on earth had happened!

" 'So what did happen to your little boy?' I asked. This time she told me the story, quite calmly. When she finished she said she felt a bit sad, telling it, and that was OK. She was amazed to be able to talk about it now and feel so calm and relaxed."

Submodality shifts in other models of psychotherapy

Submodalities are central among the brain functions that enable the various ego defence mechanisms discussed in the psychoanalytic literature. For example, *substitution* is the defence mechanism by which a desired object is replaced by another "similar" object. Thus, Freud might say, "A young woman who is very much attracted to her tall, blond, blue-eyed brother may become quickly and much involved with boyfriends who are tall, blond, and blue eyed." (Solomon and Patch, 1974, p. 503.) It is by classifying such young men in the same submodalities (colour, size etc.) as her brother that the woman achieves this result. *Identification* is another defence mechanism easily recognised as a submodality shift. In identification, the person sees through the eyes and experiences from the body position of the person they have identified with. This is the opposite of the shift produced by the phobia/trauma cure. When a psychoanalyst unpacks a defence mechanism, they are making a submodality shift.

In active therapies such as psychodrama and Gestalt therapy, visual/kinaesthetic submodalities may be utilised and altered by using the actual movement of the client. Fritz Perls (1893–1970) describes altering a small body movement made by the client (representing a strategy that has been contained within reduced submodalities). "The patient will be asked to exaggerate the movement repeatedly, usually making the inner meaning more apparent." (Levitsky and Perls, 1982, p. 152.) The field of sociometry, in psychodrama, involves the elicitation and alteration of submodalities such as distance, height and size, using actors to represent the elements of the internal experience being studied. Clients will be asked to position the auxiliary actors and themselves in ways that clearly reveal their internal submodality positions (Starr, 1977, pp. 75–87).

In cognitive psychology, we find a range of proposals for submodality shifts in the other sensory systems. For example, Beck and Emery recommend teaching clients to alter disturbing visual images. They suggest defocusing areas of the picture, putting the image on a TV screen and adjusting the brightness or even changing the channel, and exaggerating the image (Beck and Emery, 1985, pp. 222–4).

Carl Rogers (1902–87) noted that in his Client-Centred Therapy certain characteristic changes in perception occurred in clients (in Shostrom, 1965). For example, before his work with a client called Gloria in 1965, he says, "From being rather remote from her experiencing, remote from what's going on within her, it's possible that she'll move towards more immediacy of experiencing … from construing life in somewhat rigid, black and white patterns, she may move towards more tentative ways of construing her experience and of seeing the meanings in it." These are submodality shifts, and they are supported by Rogers's phrasing of his restatements to Gloria. In her very first statement, Gloria demonstrates her "black and white" way of talking and her focus on the past events. Of her daughter, she states, "I lied to her; and ever since that it keeps coming up to my mind, 'cause I feel so guilty lying to her; 'cause I never lie, and I want her to trust me." Rogers replies, suggesting that she is focused on how she feels "now" in her present relationship, and that she is tentative (using the words "kind of"). He says, "And it's this concern about her, and the fact that you really aren't; that this *open relationship* that *has* existed between you, *now* you feel is kind of damaged." She agrees, "Yes", accepting the subtle submodality shifts that are implied in his restatement.

Trancework

The model of "trancework" used in NLP is developed from Richard Bandler and John Grinder's study with Dr Milton Erickson (1902–80; see Bandler and Grinder, 1975). Erickson initially held that,

> What hypnosis actually is can be explained as yet only in descriptive terms. Thus it may be defined as an artificially induced state of suggestibility resembling sleep wherein there appears to be a normal, time-limited and stimulus-limited dissociation of the "conscious" from the "subconscious" elements of the psyche. This dissociation is manifested by a quiescence of the "consciousness" simulating normal sleep and a delegation of the subjective control of the individual functions, ordinarily conscious, to the subconscious. [Erickson, 1980, Vol. III, p. 611.]

A large body of research verifies the healing power of communication with the "unconscious mind" in this state of hypnosis or trance. Studies show that hypnosis can override what would have been considered "incurable congenital conditions". For example, the *British Medical Journal* in 1952 published a study of a sixteen-year-old boy with congenital ichthyosis erythroderma, whose skin was covered in a horny layer, which wept fluid at the joints. In a week following hypnosis, small areas of the body were clear of this problem, and the results spread to the rest of the body over the second week (Crasilneck and Hall, 1985, p. 376).

Ernest Rossi developed a model of hypnosis based on state-dependent neural networks. He says, "All methods of mind–body healing and therapeutic hypnosis operate by accessing and reframing the state-dependent memory and learning systems that encode symptoms and problems." (Rossi and Cheek, 1988, p. 111.) Thus, the areas of the mind previously known as the "subconscious" or "unconscious" are now recognised by Rossi as being simply neural networks that are dissociated from usual awareness, owing to the very different state in which they were encoded. Communication with such neural networks can be done by re-establishing the state in which they are encoded (i.e. by creating an altered or "trance" state). Rossi points out that such neural networks are often poorly connected to the cortex and to the auditory-digital (verbal) areas of the brain. He suggests that it is easier to communicate with them by having them signal using finger movements or some similar body movement. These are called "ideomotor" signals in the literature, because the ideas of the neural network are transferred directly into motor responses without "conscious thought".

Ernest Rossi's co-writer, David Cheek, has done a great deal of research on the ideomotor phenomenon. He showed, for example, that he was able to evoke hand movements for "yes" and "no" in response to his questions to a thousand hospital patients under full general anaesthetic (Cheek, 1981). Milton Erickson first learned to create "ideomotor signals" from Leslie Le Cron in the 1920s. He used a number of different methods such as hand movements, finger jerks, head nods and the movement of a pendulum suspended from the fingers (Erickson, 1981, pp. 111–80). Erickson's method of inviting ideomotor signals, like his method of trance induction, was unique to each specific client he worked with. He described his conversation with them as a "utilisation" process. The specific language patterns used by him, to facilitate trance, were analysed by Bandler and Grinder (1975) and called the "Milton model". Much of his language was based on presuppositions. For example, Erickson might say to a client, "Are you in a deeper trance now than the trance you are in as you fall asleep, or is this a lighter trance for now?" In answering the question, either "yes" or "no", the client must presuppose that she or he is already in a trance.

Trancework: case study

Craig could only just walk into my office when he came for his session of NLP-based hypnotherapy. Three years before, he had injured his back and ended up spending twelve months lying in bed, unable to get up safely. Gradually, he rehabilitated himself, and changed careers from a job involving heavy manual labour to work as a counsellor and trainer. As he built up confidence, he began going to the gym, and felt his old strength returning. Then, on a fateful day three months before his visit to me, he pushed himself too far. He collapsed at the gym, again unable to move and in severe pain. Over these three months, his condition had not improved much, and he was afraid that he was facing another year lying down recovering.

I began by asking him what he thought, as a counsellor, was happening with his back. He replied, "I think my unconscious mind is punishing me for pushing myself too hard. And maybe telling me I have to stay with the new job I have, and not go back to manual work."

"Wow," I replied in astonishment, "I would have thought that your unconscious mind is lovingly protecting you from injury. It sends you pain messages to warn you when you nearly injure something, and it makes the muscles go limp so you can't do any more harm. I think before we start it would be good to get a sense of how helpful it has been, and thank it for that. I want your unconscious mind to know that I understand that it has a positive intention in what it is doing. And of course, there may be ways that it can be even more helpful if it knows for sure it has your cooperation. Does that make sense?"

Craig agreed. Interestingly, it was easy then to invite him to relax and go into a deep trance state. I spoke increasingly slowly and reminded Craig of experiences he'd had before, when he had relaxed fully. I pointed out that his unconscious mind knew how to relax him so that he could sleep every night, because this was certainly not something he did consciously by direct control. I lifted up his arm and suggested that it would float there in front of him, while his unconscious mind held it in place, tightening the muscles on both sides so as to produce an "arm catalepsy". The response was dramatic. Craig realised with shock that he could not move his hand at all. "That's a sign of how easily your unconscious mind can change your body when you allow it to help," I pointed out.

Next, I asked Craig's unconscious mind to jerk up one of the fingers on that hand as a signal for "yes" and his index finger jolted upward, while the other fingers remained perfectly still – quite a feat consciously, but easy for the unconscious mind. I thanked the unconscious and asked it to move another finger for "no". This time his little finger responded with an upward and sideways movement. He looked on with puzzled amusement. I asked his unconscious mind, "Remembering how you healed Craig's back last time this happened, do you understand what you need to do to make him able to walk and move safely and comfortably again now?" The yes finger moved up.

"And is it OK for you to do that, provided that you have Craig's assurance that he is committed to his current career and will take the exercising at the gym gently within the limits you have set?" Again the yes finger moved up. "Great," I said. "So I'd like you to start doing that right now. Have you begun making those changes already?"

Another yes movement led to my final check. "And will you be complete with that healing in a week's time?" The yes finger moved again. I thanked Craig's unconscious mind, suggested it wake him up again now, and told it to give free movement back to his arm and hand. He relaxed it in his lap with some relief, and arched his back to check how that felt. "It's already feeling much better," he noted. In fact, he walked comfortably out of the office, and within three days he was able to carry on with his normal life activities. A year later, he had had no further trouble.

Trancework in other models of psychotherapy

Historically, there are as many explanations of what "trance" or "hypnosis" is as there are hypnotists. The French healer Franz Anton Mesmer (1734–1815) believed that the phenomenon was due to "animal magnetism", an electrical energy that "inducted" clients into a state of magnetic rapport with the healer. In 1784, a scientific commission declared that they could find no evidence of electromagnetism in Mesmer's charismatic healings, and that his results were due to "the imagination". It was a Swiss "magnetiser" trained by Mesmer, La Fontaine, who in 1841 at Manchester, England, introduced Dr James Braid to the process. Braid (1795–1860) coined the term "hypnosis" to describe the phenomenon (from the Greek *hypnos* meaning sleep).

Across Europe, others studied Braid's work and broke away from Mesmer's model to explain hypnosis in their own way. In France, Dr August Liébeault (1823–1904) and Professor Hippolyte Bernheim (1837–1919) proposed that ordinary "suggestion" was the explanation for the effects that were being attributed to some special hypnotic state. Bernheim's book *De La Suggestion*, published in 1884, argued that "trance" was just a name for normal phenomena. Meanwhile, at the University of Salpêtrière, Dr Jean-

Martin Charcot took the opposing view that hypnosis was an artificially induced neurosis.

Two younger neurologists studied with both Charcot and Bernheim, and published an integrative theory of hypnosis called *Studies on Hysteria* in 1895. They were Joseph Breuer (1842–1925) and Sigmund Freud (1856–1939). The next year, Freud coined the term "psychoanalysis" for the theory and "free association" for the modus operandi that he evolved from his original hypnotherapeutic method. He continued to describe the state that is evoked by this method in hypnotic terms. He says, for example that free association will "dissociate the patient's attention from his conscious searching and reflecting" (in Rossi, 1996, p. 186). He advises the psychoanalyst to remain in a trance state, saying:

> Experience soon showed that the attitude which the analytic physician could most advantageously adopt was to surrender himself to his own unconscious mental activity in a state of evenly suspended attention, to avoid so far as possible reflection and the construction of conscious expectations, not to try to fix anything that he heard particularly in his memory, and by these means to catch the drift of the patient's unconscious with his own unconscious. [Freud, 1923, p. 239.]

The entire history of Western psychotherapy is interwoven with the evolution of new hypnotherapeutic methods. Carl Jung (1875–1961), also an accomplished hypnotherapist, developed a method for inducing a hypnotic state called "active imagination", in which the person had a dialogue with a significant image from a dream or fantasy (see Rossi, 1996, p. 187). Such imaginative tasks, paralleling later Gestalt dialogue (Levitsky and Perls, 1982, p. 149) and Reichian acting out of infantile longings (Lowen and Lowen, 1977, p. 107), are tasks that require the person to demonstrate "hypnotic phenomena" such as regression and hallucination. Ernest Rossi points out that these methods are "mild rituals of induction that evoke a special state of therapeutic communication and expectation" (Rossi, 1996, p. 190).

Jacob Moreno (1892–1974) wrote on the application of hypnosis within psychodrama (Moreno, 1950). His own work is full of standard hypnotherapeutic methodology. For example, in directing a psychodrama at the First International Conference of Psychodrama in Paris, he guides the protagonist into a dream by having her lying down, placing his hand on her forehead and telling her repeatedly, "Fall asleep, deep asleep, deep asleep, deeper and deeper and deeper, and try to fall asleep ..." This, of course, is a standard hypnotic induction. In introducing the film of this session, Moreno also describes the psychodrama audience as "... all involved, they're almost like hypnotised by the procedure ..." (Moreno, 1964). Moreno conceptualises hypnosis as role training while in a relaxed state (Moreno, 1977, p. 160).

Carl Rogers (1902–87) studied hypnosis while working as a clinical psychologist at the Rochester Society for the Prevention of Cruelty to Children in the 1930s (in Suhd, 1995, p. 11). Like Freud, he rejected hypnosis per se because of concern about the risk of symptom replacement (worrying that hypnosis would be resisted by the person's unconscious mind). But in a famous film from the early 1960s, Rogers explains that, following his filmed counselling session,

> as is characteristic of me, there are not more than one or two statements or incidents which I recall from the interview. I simply know that I was very much present in the relationship, that I lived it in the moment of its occurrence; and I realise that after a time I may begin to remember it too; but at the present time I really have a very non-specific memory of the whole interview. [In Shostrom, 1965.]

This is the same state of therapeutic trance that Freud recommends and Rogers's description matches our experience in NLP-based trancework.

Behavioural psychology is often contrasted with "dynamic" psychotherapy such as hypnosis. In fact, though, there is a longstanding association of hypnosis and behaviour therapy. Ivan Pavlov studied hypnotic states in both dogs and people, and proposed that they were a result of a localised cortical inhibition, similar to but smaller than that occurring in sleep (in Crasilneck and Hall, 1985, pp. 26–7). The American behaviourist Clark Hull (from whom Milton Erickson learned hypnotherapy) wrote *Hypnosis and Suggestibility* in 1933, refuting Pavlov's model and arguing that there was no special brain state needed to account for the suggestion-based responses of "trance".

Cognitive behavioural therapy has been more reluctant to accept hypnosis officially as a method, although Beck and Emery (1985, p. 249) agree that hypnotic relaxation is a useful choice for reducing anxiety. But, once again, many of the techniques of cognitive therapy are actually hypnotic. The Ericksonian therapist Michael Yapko analysed the transcript of a session by the cognitive therapist Aaron Beck in these terms, finding all the major hypnotherapeutic techniques. He identified Beck's use of indirect suggestion and presuppositions, and of guided visualisation of the type used in hypnotic inductions. He noted that Beck described the client's success as being proved by the fact that she was able to rehearse (hypnotically) her desired activity and "imagine the various steps without any interfering cognitions" (Yapko, 1992, pp. 61–74).

Parts Integration

In describing trance, above, Milton Erickson makes the distinction between the "conscious mind" and the "unconscious mind". This recognition of two separate "subpersonalities" within the brain is one specific example of a wider model, describing what are called in NLP "parts". For our purposes, the word "part" refers to any state-dependent neural network with enough functional autonomy to run its strategies without control by the rest of the brain. The "conscious mind" is, in this sense, as much a part as the unconscious.

The first model of parts work used in NLP was called six-step reframing. Bandler and Grinder explain its rationale in an early demonstration by saying:

> This only makes sense if you have a belief system that says "Look. If he had conscious control over this behavior it would have changed already." So some part of him which is *not* conscious is running this pattern of behavior … I also make the assumption that the part of you that makes you X – even though you don't like that consciously – is doing something on your behalf, something that benefits you in some way. [Bandler and Grinder, 1979, pp. 139–40.]

Six-step reframing involves communicating with the part and asking the person's unconscious mind to think up some equally effective and more acceptable ways to meet the positive outcome of that part. This method has been shown to be as effective as relaxation training at curing psychosomatic physical symptoms (such as headaches; see Bacon, 1983). Six-step reframing, unlike relaxation, does not need to be consciously applied in an ongoing way to keep the problem solved. The method has also been successfully used with addictive and compulsive behaviour patterns such as bulimia (Glöser, 1991) and alcoholism (Sterman, 1990).

The parts-integration model demonstrated below is a development of six-step reframing. It is discussed by Robert Dilts in the book *Beliefs* (Dilts, Hallbom and Smith, 1990, pp. 101–26, p. 165), where Dilts gives a transcript of its successful use to treat an allergy to cats, tested in the training room immediately after.

Parts integration: case study

Pam came to see me wanting to improve her relationship with her two primary-school-age kids. She found herself yelling at these children most of the time she was with them, and she knew it was an ineffective method of getting their cooperation. She said, "I don't know what makes me do it, but at the time I feel so angry!" She felt bad about the lack of closeness between them. I suggested to Pam that perhaps there was a "part" of her that had a "reason" to keep yelling at her kids. I asked her if she'd like to find out that reason. She was curious.

I asked her, "Which hand would the part of you that causes the yelling stand on, if it was to stand on the palm of your hand?"

"The right hand." She held out her right hand, palm up, and I held out my left hand mirroring hers.

"If that part was standing on that hand right now, what would it look like?" Pam laughed, looking intently at her hand.

"It's me with a ferocious look on my face."

"And what would it feel like? Does that hand feel heavy or light, warm or cool?"

"It's heavy and quite hot."

"Great. And if you were to ask it what it's purpose in yelling is, what would it say and what sort of voice does it have?" Pam looked to the side, a little tearfully.

"To make them feel sorry for what they're done to me; to make them realise," she said in a shaky voice.

"I'd like to thank that part for talking to us," I said, more to the hand than to Pam, "and ask it: if it makes them sorry and makes them realise, if it totally achieved that, what would that do for you that's *even more* important?" Seeing her puzzlement, I repeated the question for Pam's conscious mind. She listened inside.

"Then I'd feel respected and valued."

"Excellent. And if you felt respected and valued, what's even more important than that? What would that do for you?"

"I guess I'd know that I was doing well as a parent."

"And what's the part's intention for doing that? What would knowing *that* do for you that's even *more* important?"

"A sense of inner confidence."

She smiled, feeling some of that confidence. "So this part wants inner confidence," I summarised.

"Yes," she agreed. "It seems so, but it's got a weird way of doing it!"

Next I asked Pam, "Now, there's a part of you that has been most opposed to this part that causes the yelling, and, if it was to stand on your left hand, where would it stand – the part that wants to stop yelling?"

She held her other hand up and I mirrored, holding up my right hand. Her hands were now both palm up, about 50 centimetres (20 inches) away from each other.

"The part that wants to stop the yelling is in the *centre* of my left hand," Pam explained, and in answer to my questions she added, "It's me sitting down looking peaceful ... My hand feels cool and light, and it says it wants for me to be loving and accepting of the kids."

"So, if this part gets to be loving and accepting, what even more important thing does that do for you?"

"I'd be close to my family."

"And what that would do for you is ...?"

"Wow." Pam was staring at a space between her hands. "If I was close to my family I'd have that feeling of inner confidence."

I nodded. "So do these two parts notice that they have the same highest intention?"

"Mm-hmm."

"And does this part [gesturing to her right hand] notice that this part [left hand] has resources that can help it achieve its intention?" She nodded. "Well, does this part [left hand] realise that this part [right hand] has resources that could help it achieve its intention?" She moved back a little.

"Sort of ... It does now."

There were tears in her eyes again. "So," I checked, "these parts have the same highest intention, and do they understand now that they were once part of a greater whole ... and it's OK for them to become one now?"

As she looked up and agreed "Yes", her hands began to float slowly, gently, towards each other. I followed by moving my hands together.

"Richard, I'm not moving my hands. How are they doing that?" Pam queried, watching in astonishment.

"Your unconscious," I explained, "is moving. The hands know where to go."

Once Pam's hands had floated together I had her feel that they now had the *same* weight and temperature. She could see the new, integrated her, with all the resources each of the old parts had had, speaking with one voice. I invited her to feel where in her body her hands felt drawn to, and move her hands together to that place to "bring that new wholeness back inside your body and let it spread through your entire body".

As I watched, continuing to mirror Pam's actions, I could see a *dramatic* change in her appearance. Her skin glowed, her face was very flushed and her breathing was full and deep. Her posture was more upright. When she spoke, her voice had a resonance to it.

"That is *amazing*," she concluded.

"It was powerful," I agreed. "You'd been waiting a long time to heal that."

When I spoke to Pam a few weeks later, the yelling was a thing of the past. She was discovering new ways to give a voice to her new confidence, not just with her children but in all areas of her life.

Parts integration in other models of psychotherapy

Each model of psychotherapy has had to account for the activity of state-dependent neural networks, and evolve some model of such "parts" of the mind. In each case, the structures are defined differently, and the precision of these definitions is often of importance to the development of techniques within that therapy. In respect of this, I will attempt to acknowledge carefully some of these distinctions here, while drawing attention to the universality of parts work in the field.

The notion of parts has its psychotherapeutic origins in the dynamic model of psychoanalysis. There, the core parts of the psyche spoken of are the id (which Freud says is based on "untamed passions"), the ego (the area based on "reason and circumspection") and the superego (which upholds socially required, moral "norms of behaviour"). Freud suggested that the psychoanalyst is allied with the ego to defend it from anxiety and extend its "territory". He says his aim is "to strengthen the ego, to make it more independent of the super-ego, to widen its field of vision, and so to extend its organisation that it can take over new portions of the id. Where id was, there shall ego be." (Freud, 1933.)

Freud emphasises that his treatment is not aimed at "cutting out" something, though. He says, "Nor does the treatment consist in extirpating something – psychotherapy is not able to do this for the present – but in causing the resistance to melt and in thus enabling the circulation to make its way into a region that has hitherto been cut off." (Freud and Breuer, 1974, p. 377.) This is a clear description of parts work.

Modern object-relations-based psychoanalysis has paid more attention to certain splits within the ego itself – particularly splits that occur pathologically if too severe a challenge confronts the ego early in life. A healthy mature ego, says Otto Kernberg, can repress undesired material out of conscious awareness, without needing to split it off completely. He says, "Splitting consists in dissociating or actively maintaining apart identification systems with opposite valences (conflicting identification systems) without regard to access to consciousness or to perceptual or motor control." (Kernberg, 1976, p. 44.) The result is severe personality disorders and what NLP calls "sequential incongruity" – doing and desiring one thing at one time, and the opposite at another time. Healing is a process of "learning of 'managerial skills' in order to understand one's self, one's boundaries, one's internal needs, one's environment and one's life tasks". (Kernberg, 1976, p. 265.) This managerial or coordinating function of the healthy ego is what NLP refers to as parts work.

By contrast, the focus of transactional analysis (TA) has been on healthy functional divisions within the ego. It defines three core ego states called the Parent (using strategies copied from parents/caregivers), Adult (using strategies developed in adult life and as here-and-now responses) and Child (using strategies learned as a child), and some subdivisions of these. Each ego state is "a consistent pattern of feeling and experience directly related to a corresponding persistent pattern of behaviour" (Stewart and Joines, 1987, p. 15). In other words, each ego state is a state-dependent set of strategies. The aim of TA work with these ego states is often to prevent one state "contaminating" another or "excluding" another from expression. Again, the aim is the development of a situation where each state has access to expression in ways that are useful to the entire person, and this is what we are doing in parts work in NLP. In the re-decision approach to TA, the focus is on impasses (unresolved conflicts between ego states). The Gestalt two-chair approach is used to resolve these parts conflicts (Stewart and Joines, 1987, p. 275).

In these formulations we have been discussing, the assumption is made that the main "parts" to be found in a human being are largely similar from one person to another. With the theory of archetypes common to the collective unconscious of humanity, Carl Jung takes this a step further. He describes an archetype as "an inherited mode of psychic functioning ... In other words it is a 'pattern of behaviour'." (Quoted in Whitmont, 1991, p. 104.)

He describes in this way such elements as the anima (inner feminine principle in a male) and animus (inner masculine principle in a woman), the persona (our adaptation to social expectations) and the self (a suprapersonal summation of one's life and its meaning). Archetypes are the central elements of complexes. Jung explains that each complex "appears as an autonomous formation intruding on consciousness ... While complexes owe their relative autonomy to their emotional nature, their expression is always dependent on a network of associations, grouped round a centre charged with affect." (In Whitmont, 1991, pp. 63–4.) Once again, we have here a definition of state-dependent strategies. Unlike Freud, however, Jung did not see it as the ego's task to replace such other complexes. He says:

> Conscious and unconscious do not make a whole when one of them is suppressed and injured by the other ... Both are aspects of life ... It is the old game of hammer and anvil; between them the patient iron is forged into an indestructible whole, an "individual".
> [In Whitmont, 1991, p. 18.]

The work of Roberto Assagioli describes parts work in a very similar frame to that used by NLP. The aim, in both cases, is the integration of separate parts into one unitary whole (a process called by Assagioli "psychosynthesis"). Assagioli describes his aim as "co-ordination and subordination of the various psychological energies and functions, the creation of a firm organisation of the personality" (Assagioli, 1976, p. 29). In psychosynthesis, as in NLP, this process is recognised as ultimately leading to transcendent states of pure awareness, joy, peace and love, and as extending beyond the "individual human being" as normally understood in the West (Assagioli, 1976, p. 5).

The metaphor Jacob Moreno uses for parts is drawn from the theatre. By "role", he refers to "the functioning form the individual assumes in the specific moment he reacts to the specific situation in which other persons or objects are involved" (Moreno, 1977, p. iv). Moreno points out that the role, with its strategies, its emotional state etc., evolves directly from the individual's interaction with the world, even before the person has a unifying sense of "self".

> Role playing is prior to the emergence of the self. Roles do not emerge from the self, but the self may emerge from roles ... It is possible, as we see with infants and psychotics, for the individual to operate with several alter egos. [Moreno, 1977, p. 153.]

Part of the task of therapy, then, is to help individuals to reduce role conflict, to harmonise the functioning of roles and to allow the smooth transition from role to role as required by the situation. The ability to produce roles that respond adequately and effectively to unprecedented situations (spontaneity) is a highly valued aim of Moreno's work (Moreno, 1977, pp. 85–9), and parallels the aim of parts work in NLP.

Alexander Lowen describes the healthy individual after body-oriented psychotherapy in physiological terms:

> He is aware of his contact with the ground and feels more rooted. He says he feels connected with his body, his sexuality and the ground. To be so connected is not an ideal of health; in my opinion it is the minimum of health. [Lowen, 1972, pp. 61–62.]

What stops this connectedness, Lowen argues, is patterns of chronic muscular tension, which prevent contact between the various layers of body tissue. Each layer, he suggests, holds a state and the strategies that express it. Body tension is the key way people inhibit the activation of what are literally important "parts" of their experience. "In effect, the area of the body that would be involved in the expression of the impulse is deadened, relatively speaking, by the chronic muscular tension that develops as consequence of the continual holding pattern." (Lowen, 1972, p. 81.) By enabling full-flowing breathing and movement, the body therapist creates access between the various "parts" of the person.

Arthur Janov evolved a model of Primal Therapy, which is closely based on brain research. He says that the aim of his cathartic therapy is to release pain impulses that have been locked in lower brain circuits. Once the original events are re-experienced consciously, connection between these memories and the conscious mind has a profound healing effect. He says:

> Unconsciousness represents a breakdown in the integrative capacities of the brain as it mediates bodily processes. It occurs when the system is overloaded so that impulses (resulting from action potentials mediated by synapses) which normally have specific innervations with the cerebral cortex to make us conscious, overwhelm the integrative faculties and become shunted into alternate cerebral pathways rendering us, in that sense, unconscious. [Janov, 1977, pp. 4–5.]

> It is consciousness which finally conceptualises and interprets these deep pains and makes sense of them. [p. 35.]

The concept of parts as used in NLP was present directly in the work of both Fritz Perls and Virginia Satir. Perls explains:

> If some of our thoughts, feelings, are unacceptable to us, we want to disown them. *Me* wanting to kill you? So we disown the killing thought and say, "That's not me – that's a *compulsion*," or we remove the killing, or we repress and become blind to that. There are many of these kinds of ways to remain intact, but always only at the cost of disowning many, many valuable parts of ourselves ...

You do not allow yourself – or you are not allowed – to be totally yourself. [Perls, 1969, p. 11.]

So what we are trying to do in therapy is step-by-step to *re-own* the disowned parts of the personality until the person becomes strong enough to facilitate his own growth … [p. 38.]

Satir's way of dealing with this was through a psychodramatic method she called the "Parts Party". She explains:

We all have a number of different parts, each with expectations of fulfillment. These parts often find it difficult to get along with each other and may have inhibitory influences on one another … The process of the parts party offers a person an opportunity to observe these parts and to learn how they can function more harmoniously when they co-operate rather than compete. [Satir and Baldwin, 1983, p. 258.]

Carl Rogers is far more cautious about suggesting that there may be organised "structures" within the human psyche, but he makes it clear that he is working with what NLP would call parts, when he says:

From a descriptive clinical point of view … we may say that successful therapy seems to entail the bringing into awareness, in an adequately differentiated and accurately symbolised way, those experiences and feelings which are currently in contradiction to the client's concept of self. [Rogers, 1973, pp. 148–9.]

A central result of therapy, Rogers notes, is "increased unification and integration of the personality" (Rogers, 1973, p. 178).

Behavioural psychotherapy began by carefully avoiding any speculation about the inner "structuring" of the mind. In the 1980s, cognitive behaviouralists evolved the concept of *schemas* to account for many of the phenomena that we are discussing here. A schema is defined in two ways:

On the one hand, the term *schema* has been used to refer to a hypothesised *structure* of cognition, such as a mental filter or template that guides the processing of information … More regularly, however, we use the construct of *schema* in reference to the *content of fundamental, core beliefs*: the basic rules that an individual uses to organise his or her perceptions of the world, self and future, and to adapt to life's challenges. [Layden et al., 1993, p. 7.]

Such schemas can be restructured (creating a whole new way of responding), modified (altered so that there are times the schema need not apply, for example) or reinterpreted (reframed as having a positive meaning rather than a limiting one) – all methods that clearly relate to NLP parts work (Layden et al., 1993, pp. 11–12).

Time-line Changes

What we call "memory" actually describes a collection of different brain functions. There is a difference neurologically between procedural memory (e.g. how to ride a bike), which is stored in the lower brain and the deeper caudate nucleus, and semantic memory (facts and information about the world, categorised like an encyclopaedia), which is stored in the upper areas (cortex) of the brain. These in turn are different from what neurologists call episodic memories – the movie-like memories of events we have lived through, which are encoded by the hippocampus and stored throughout the cortex (Carter, 1998, p. 267). As mentioned earlier, some of these episodic memories are associated with traumatic distress, and thus stored in neural networks that may be poorly connected with the rest of the brain.

The brain remembers the sequence of these and other "episodes", using what NLP has termed a "time line". A time line is a spatial metaphor in which events are thought of as occurring along a line that stretches out in one direction to the past, and in another direction to the future. Examples of this way of mentally organising events are referred to in everyday speech: for example, when we say "I'm going to put that whole experience *behind* me now" or "I'm looking *forward* to seeing you again."

This set of submodality distinctions for time was first described by Connirae and Steve Andreas (1987, pp. 1–24). Since then, a number of other NLP practitioners have developed ways to work with the brain's coding of memory. These include "re-imprinting" and "changing personal history" (Dilts, Hallbom and Smith, 1990) and "Time Line Therapy" (James and Woodsmall, 1988). Like parts integration, these techniques seem to have a significant effect on physical health conditions. They tend to involve viewing the original traumatic events from a new time perspective, and while accessing emotional resources from other areas of the person's life.

A one-year research study (May 1993–May 1994) into the treatment of asthmatics, using Time Line Therapy, was done in Denmark. Results were presented at a number of European conferences, including the Danish Society of Allergology Conference (August 1994) and the European Respiratory Society Conference (Nice, France, October 1994). The study was run by Jorgen Lund, a general medical practitioner, and the NLP master practitioner Hanne Lund, from Herning, Denmark. Patients were selected from eight general practices. Thirty were included in the NLP intervention group, and sixteen in the control group. All received basic medical care, including being supplied with medication. Most had never heard of NLP before, and many were completely unbelieving in it, or terrified of it. Their motivation to do NLP was generally low. The intervention group had an initial day introduction to NLP and Time Line Therapy, and then 3–36 hours (average 13) of NLP intervention. The NLP focus was not mainly on the asthma: it was on how the people lived their daily lives. The results affected both the people's general lives and their asthma. Patients tended to describe their change subjectively as enabling them to be "more open", get "colossal strength and self-confidence", "a new life" etc.

The lung capacity of adult asthmatics tends to decrease by 50ml a year average. This occurred in the control group. Meanwhile, the NLP group increased their lung capacity by an average of 200ml (like reversing four years of damage in a year!). Daily variations in peak flow (an indicator of unstable lung function) began at 30 to 40 per cent. In the control group they reduced to 25 per cent but in the NLP group they fell to below 10 per cent . Sleep disorders in the control group began at 70 per cent and dropped to 30 per cent. In the NLP group they began at 50 per cent and dropped to zero. Use of asthma inhalers and acute medication in the NLP group fell to near zero.

Hanne Lund points out that the implications of this project reach far beyond asthma management. She says, "We consider the principles of this integrated work valuable in treatment of patients with any disease, and the next step will be to train medical staff in this model." (Lund, 1995.)

Time Line Therapy: case study

In the following example, Margot Hamblett describes her use of Time Line Therapy.

"When Jenny came to see me she was in pain both physically and emotionally. She said she had always been sick, continually catching the flu, having migraines and so on. She felt depressed about her life. She had a relationship she wasn't happy with, and nothing much that she could look forward to. It was when she was only seven years old that she was first sexually abused, and there had been other experiences from then on into her adult life. Whenever she thought about those incidents, which was frequently, she felt 'sick' inside. This was the issue she wanted to solve first.

"The first thing I did was check where her time line was. Jenny had the past behind her and the future in front. The future was short: she couldn't imagine times a year from now.

"Next I had her ask her unconscious mind *when*, in its way of storing memory, the 'sick' feelings had begun. It was important not to assume that age 7 was the beginning just because that was the age Jenny's conscious mind recalled. The Time Line Therapy process asks, 'What is the root cause of this problem, the first event which, when disconnected, will cause the problem to disappear? If you were to know, was it before, during, or after your birth?' This gave the unconscious mind an easier job. Jenny simply checked each of the three possibilities to find out which *felt* true.

" 'After,' she confirmed.

" 'Great. And if you were to know, what age were you?'

" 'Two years old.'

" 'That's good. I'd like to thank your unconscious mind for co-operating.'

"Having found the time which was the 'root cause' of Jenny's problem, she could now relax and close her eyes. Next, in her imagination, she was to float way up in the air above her body, so that she was far up above her time line. From there, I asked Jenny's unconscious to float her back up above her time line till it was directly up above the event at two years, and told her to 'trust your unconscious knows exactly where to take you'.

"Once she was up above the event I suggested, 'As you look down on that event, you can see what emotions are down there, whether or not you have any conscious memory of that time. And there were some things for you to have learned in this event. So what I'd like you to do is to preserve all the positive learnings, whatever you need to have learned from this event, preserve it in that special place you reserve for all such learnings.'

"Notice that Jenny doesn't need to understand how her unconscious does any of this. She just needs to go ahead and imagine it. Once she had a sense that all the learnings were preserved, I added, 'Now, I'd like you to float back up above your time line even further, so that you're at least fifteen minutes before any of the events leading up to that event, and *way* up above. And from way back and way up there, turn and look across the vast reaches of time towards NOW. And as you look from way back and way up above, all the way to now, the question is, "*Now* where are the emotions that were in that event?" '

"Jenny was astonished. 'I don't know. They're gone.'

"In hundreds of cases, as long as I follow the Time Line Therapy process as taught by Tad James, this has been my experience. From way back and up above the event, in the perspective of all that has happened since, having preserved the learnings, the unconscious simply lets go of the feelings.

" 'Now,' I continued, 'I'd like you to imagine an infinite source of love and healing above your head, and allow that healing to flow down to your heart and out to that earlier you in the memory below. Just continue flowing that healing until the event is completely filled with light, completely healed.'

"She nodded. 'It's done.'

" 'That's good. Now I'd like you to float down *into* that event on the time line, and notice that it feels healed and emotionally balanced. Stay there as long as it takes for you to know for sure that it's okay.' This is an important check. If Jenny had discovered it still felt bad to imagine herself down in the event, she would have been best to go back up before, and clear the emotion more fully. As it was, she smiled.

" 'So what I'd like you to do next is to float way up above there. In a moment you'll float up above, all the way back to up above now. And when you do, notice that all the events below you that had similar feelings to that original event are healed in exactly the same way: the learnings stored, the feelings released as you look from above and before them, the event filled with healing light, in exactly the same way, all the way back to now.'

"After a minute or so, Jenny returned up above now. Before she came back down into now, she happened to look out into the future, and gasped. 'Hey! My future's now extending way out in front of me, and it's full of light,' she announced delighted.

"And that was only the first of many changes. A couple of weeks later Jenny said that she was now waking up in the morning looking forward to each day. She enjoyed her family more and was asking more of her relationship. Her body felt healthy. She had reconnected with old friends, and enrolled in courses to learn new skills. What about the traumatic events that used to haunt her? Now when she thought of them, she explained, it was like 'So what?' "

Time line changes in other models of psychotherapy

In a sense, all psychotherapy has been aimed at recoding the specific memories associated with life problems. In 1895, Sigmund Freud published the "founding document" of Western psychotherapy: *Studies on Hysteria*. In it he announces his discovery that child-hood trauma "causes" psychiatric problems:

> Quite frequently it is some event in childhood that sets up a more or less severe symptom which persists during the years that follow … Not until they have been questioned under hypnosis do these memories emerge with the undiminished vividness of a recent event. [Freud and Breuer, 1974, p. 60.]

Freud notes that the patient's memories are "arranged in linear sequences (like a file of documents, a packet etc.)" (Freud and Breuer, 1974, p. 374). His aim in exploring this file with the patient is not to "change the past" but to change the person's response to it. The person may still regret the past, but they need not be tor-mented by it. They can "succeed in transforming your hysterical misery into common unhappiness" (Freud and Breuer, 1974, p. 393).

Carl Jung sought to emphasise that merely exploring the past was not enough to benefit a person's life:

> The recollection of infantile memories and the reproduction of archetypal ways of psychic behaviour can create a wider horizon and a greater extension of consciousness – on condition that one succeeds in assimilating and integrating in the conscious mind the lost and regained contents. [Jung, 1976, p. 90.]

Jungian analysts will recognise Time Line Therapy as a ritual for such integration – a metaphorical journey analogous to the shamanic inner voyage (Grof, 1998, pp. 164–6).

Transactional analysis (TA) begins with an understanding of the Parent and Child ego states as having been formed in childhood experiences. In the re-decision process, the TA therapist guides the person to

> re-contact the Child feelings he experienced at the time of the early decision, finish the business by expressing those feelings, and change the early decision for a new and more appropriate *redeci-sion*. This may be accomplished through fantasy or dreamwork, or by "early scene work", in which the client tracks back in recollection

to an early traumatic scene and re-experiences it. [Stewart and Joines, 1987, p. 275.]

This process builds on the earlier TA intervention of giving the Child "permission" to enjoy life and make good decisions. It clearly parallels the Time Line Therapy process.

One of the most important principles of Gestalt therapy is its focus on the "now". Does this mean that Time Line events are not dealt with? Not at all. It means that, as in NLP, they are dealt with from a different temporal perspective from usual. Both NLP and Gestalt maintain that the past is not resolved by looking back at it from "now", but by shifting our perspective. Fritz Perls explains:

> It would not be accurate to say that there is no interest in historical material and in the past. This material is dealt with accurately when it is felt to be germane to important themes of the present personality structure. However, the most effective means of integrating past material into the personality is to bring it – as fully as possible – into the present ... to "be there" in fantasy and to enact the drama in present terms. [Levitsky and Perls, 1982, pp. 144–5.]

This way of dealing with the past closely parallels psychodrama, of course, and allows for the introduction of surplus reality (the creation of alternative histories of the event and the exploring of the event from perspectives not available at the time – see Blatner, 1988, pp. 83–5). NLP techniques such as Time Line Therapy and reimprinting use the same principle. In Reichian therapy, the process of dealing with the past is similar, and emphasises both the physiological expression of past events and the need to resolve the conflicts and feelings present there (see Lowen, 1972, p. 44).

In his nondirective approach to psychotherapy, Carl Rogers does not directly ask clients to revisit earlier experiences. He does, however, acknowledge the importance of them for all clients. He says, "The problem appears to be the same in all cases; it is the problem of assimilating denied experience into a reorganised self." (Rogers, 1973, p. 104.) This happens, Rogers notes, largely because the therapist assists the client to review their experiences in a new light – the light of the therapist's own "calm acceptance of them" (Rogers, 1973, p. 194). This gives the experiences a new meaning.

In Milton Erickson's work, we see the notion of redeveloping memories taken to its ultimate conclusion, with the story of the February Man (Erickson and Rossi, 1989). In a series of sessions, Erickson works with Jane, who says she had a childhood without loving parenting, and is afraid that now she herself will be unable to be a good mother. In trance, Erickson "journeys back" to her childhood, visiting her every February to provide loving support and reframes for her childhood experiences. For example, he points out to her that, although stubbing her toe is a painful experience, "Maybe someday you will talk to a little girl about her stubbing her toe. You will really want to know what a stubbed toe felt like. Isn't that right?" (P. 47.) He explains to Ernest Rossi about this process: "You don't really alter the original experience, you alter the perception of it, and that becomes the memory of the perception." (P. 77.) Jane will now remember this moment of childhood "pain" as a moment of learning about how to be a good mother.

Superficially, Ericksonian hypnosis may seem a far cry from cognitive behavioural approaches. In terms of working with the past, though, the "imaginal" techniques of CBT (Layden et al., 1993, pp. 86–92) clearly parallel both Erickson's work in hypnosis, and the visualisation of Time Line Therapy. Mary Anne Layden and colleagues describe such an imaginal process for exploring "critical incidents" in the past and altering the client's self-defeating interpretations of them. After a brief relaxation process (which Erickson or an NLP practitioner would call a trance induction) the cognitive therapist has the person recall the first time when they experienced the feelings that have been a problem to them. As they remember that time, the client is asked to describe it, to find out what they thought they "learned" about life at the time of that experience, and to re-decide what is truly important to learn now from the experience. They are then invited to add to the experience whatever imaginary images will assist them to heal the memory: for example, introducing a support person to comfort them, or imagining themselves using a skill that they have learned since the event to deal with the event more adequately.

Linguistic Reframing

As its name suggests, Neuro-Linguistic Programming began with the linguistic analysis of the communications used by psychotherapists such as Virginia Satir, Milton Erickson and Gregory Bateson. John Grinder and Richard Bandler categorised the patterns in these therapists' work, using recognised linguistic labels. The result has been three main collections of patterns. Once again, my intention is not to teach these patterns here, but to give readers some sense of what I'm referring to by "language patterns". In actual therapy, as we'll discuss later, these patterns need to be used with considerable care, skill and appropriate timing, to be anything more than "moralistic intrusions".

1. The metamodel

This model, based on Virginia Satir's work, generates a series of questions for eliciting clearer, more reality-based descriptions of a client's experience (Grinder and Bandler, 1975). The appropriate question is identified based on the category of statement (the "metamodel pattern") made by the client; for example:

Presupposition. If the client says, "I wonder why I made such a mess of my marriage", I might challenge the presupposition that the person has accepted before asking this question – the presupposition that they did "make a mess" of their marriage. I might say, "How do you know that you made a mess of your marriage?"

Mind-read. If the client says, "I can tell my wife hates me", I might ask, "What do you see or hear that tells you that?"

Lost performative (where a judgment is performed and the judge is not identified). If the client says, "It's wrong to talk back to your boss", I might ask, "According to whom is it wrong?"

Complex Equivalent (where two things are said to be equivalent to each other). If the client says, "I failed the exam, so I guess I'm a hopeless case", I might ask, "How does not passing the exam mean that you as a person are a hopeless case?"

Universal quantifier. If the client says, *"Nothing* I do *ever* works", I might ask, "Nothing? Ever? Has there ever been a single time when you did something and it worked?"

Modal operator of impossibility. If the client says, "I *can't* relax and trust myself when I'm at work", I might ask, "What would happen if you did?" or "What stops you?"

Unspecified verb. If the client says, "My father really *hurts* me", I might ask, "How, specifically, does he hurt you?"

Unspecified noun. If the client says, "People have been telling me I need to listen more", I might ask, "Which people? Who, specifically, told you that?"

Simple deletion. If the client says, "I'm really unhappy", I might ask, "About what?"

Dr Thomas Macroy at Utah State University did a detailed study of 31 families, members of which were asked to rate their level of satisfaction with the family. Next, a family session was held for each family and recorded on audiotape. The audiotapes were analysed for the occurrence of 150 specific metamodel patterns. In those families where people were less satisfied, substantially more metamodel patterns were being used, especially deletions and unspecified nouns. This study supports the notion that challenging metamodel patterns is an important way to enhance the ability to achieve satisfaction socially (Macroy, 1978).

2. The Milton model

This model also begins with the metamodel language categories listed above. Instead of challenging them with a question, though, it utilises them purposefully. Interestingly, Milton Erickson used these categories to create indirect suggestions for successful hypnotherapeutic change. He also used many other identified categories of language such as *pacing* (acknowledging what the client is already experiencing) and *metaphor* (Bandler and Grinder, 1975). Following is an example of this "constructive" use of such patterns to suggest change in an "artfully vague" way. The words in bold would be said with a slightly different voice tonality, to create "embedded suggestions" (another Milton model pattern) in the paragraph, but you probably already realise how easily **you can use this**.

> You're reading this now [pacing], and you might **be very interested** [mind read] to hear a story about the way that Milton Erickson talked [use of metaphor beginning]. And the fact that you've chosen to **enjoy this right now** [presupposition] is a good thing [lost performative], because just reading this kind of example means that **you're learning much** about the way that Milton would talk to people [complex equivalent], and every time [universal quantifier] you reread this, you *can* find that you [modal operator of possibility] **learn more** [unspecified verb] of the kind of things that Milton said [unspecified noun] and no doubt you realise that this is how Milton Erickson assisted people to **make changes** [simple deletion].

While the Milton model is the opposite of the kind of clear communication that makes ongoing cooperation possible, it has a different kind of use. It is the language of influence. Erickson used this language to suggest changes. Donald Moine at the University of Oregon studied 45-minute audiocassette recordings of insurance salespeople. His sample included top producers of sales from their companies, as well as "average" producers. The highly successful salespeople used far more embedded suggestions, complex equivalents, mind-reading, metaphors, pacing and modal operators of possibility. This artfully vague and suggestive language was part of their skill in enabling others to change (Moines, 1981).

3. The sleight-of-mouth patterns

Also called criteria-utilisation patterns, these are a series of ways to "reframe" (using Gregory Bateson's term) a person's experience. They were first codified by Robert Dilts (Dilts, 1999). The sleight-of-mouth patterns include the use of the metamodel and Milton model as well as a number of other patterns that intentionally alter the person's sense of what a specific event "means" (i.e. what the psychological "complex equivalent" of the event is for them). For example, a client may say, "My mother was always depressed, so I guess I'll always be depressed." This is a complex equivalent state-ment, telling us that, currently, the meaning of this person's mother's having been depressed is that *they* will always be depressed ("My mother was always depressed" = "I will always be depressed"). There are a great many things I can do to break this equivalence (i.e. to "deframe" the statement) or to create a new, more useful equivalence (i.e. to "reframe" it). The original sleight-of-mouth framework lists twenty or so patterns. For example:

a) **Use the metamodel questions to deframe**. I could ask, "Was she always depressed? Was there ever a single moment when she wasn't depressed?" or "How, specifically, do you plan to 'always be depressed'?" or "How does her being depressed mean that *you* have to be?"

b) **Use the Milton model to reframe**. I could tell a story (metaphor) about Ted Turner, whose father committed suicide after a lifetime of depression; Ted loved life and went on to turn his father's failing advertising business into the multime-dia giant CNN Time Warner, and to give the largest single donation to charity ever given by one person. As I tell this story, I could include embedded suggestions and a new com-plex equivalent, having Ted say to himself, "Ted, you saw how your father got himself depressed, and so you know more than anyone how to *enjoy life fully*."

c) **Apply the person's way of thinking (and even their wording) to itself**. This might involve saying, "That's always a depress-ing kind of guess to be nurturing, isn't it?"

d) **Identify an issue that's more important**. I might say, "Rather than think about what happened to you or your mother in the past, isn't it more important to think about how you could become a positive role model for your own children?"

e) **Identify the intention behind the person's statement and dis-cuss that instead**. I could point out, "I guess your intention is to protect yourself from being disappointed by trying and fail-ing. I wonder if you've noticed that the only way to really pro-tect yourself from a sense of failure is to know you did your very best to live the kind of life you really want to live."

Is a simple language pattern like a sleight-of-mouth reframe enough to change a severe psychiatric problem? Sometimes it is. Dr Lewis Baxter (1994) showed that clients with obsessive compulsive disorder had raised activity in neural networks inside the caudate nucleus of the brain (demonstrated on PET scans of the brain). Drugs such as Prozac raise serotonin levels and the caudate nucleus activity is thus reduced. Baxter found that when clients repeated a simple reframe to themselves, the PET scan showed the same raising of serotonin levels and the same lowering of activity in the caudate nucleus. Precisely chosen words affect state-dependent neural networks.

Linguistic Reframing: case study

Lucy came to talk to me during morning tea at a training seminar. She explained that she was trying to give up smoking cigarettes and had tried several NLP processes to no avail. Knowing I had only five minutes, I decided to use a sleight-of-mouth pattern. I said to her, "So if you've tried several things and it still hasn't worked, that means there's a part of you that hasn't thought, It's OK to change – right?" She nodded. "And if you were to know, what is that part's intention in having you smoke? What is it trying to do for you by having you continue smoking?"

She thought a moment and replied, "To help me relax."

"OK," I agreed. "So I'd like you to consider this next statement very carefully. Anything less than completely stopping smoking and having healthy lungs is not totally enabling you to relax the way you deserve to."

Lucy looked bewildered. "I know you said some words, and I followed each word, but I couldn't 'hear' the sentence."

"That's right," I explained, "because your brain would need to change in order to fully process that statement. It starts out speaking to the neural network where smoking is generated and expands out to contact your higher intention. It's a kind of linguistic parts integration." I repeated the sentence four times carefully, and Lucy still just "had a feeling that the meaning was important and almost *there*". She asked me to write down the sentence, and I told her to read it over to herself until she understood it. This conscious understanding took some time to emerge.

Lucy reported to me some months later that she had been "unable" to smoke a cigarette since that discussion. The reframe I used is a specific pattern developed by Tad James and called "quantum linguistics" (James, 1996).

Linguistic reframing in other models of psychotherapy

From its beginning, psychotherapy has paid attention to the form of the language used by the therapist. When a psychoanalyst makes a standard interpretation such as, "You want from me what you wanted from your mother" (Olinick, 1980, p. 19), the therapist is offering a new meaning for the behaviour. A behaviour that might previously have been framed as demanding, annoying or sick is now reframed as a strategy that had a usefulness earlier on in the person's history, and is now being misapplied to a new situation. Generally, each therapy has its own models for understanding human events. Each therapist offers reframes that first make sense of the client's dilemmas in these terms and, second, show how the process of therapy can resolve these dilemmas.

In a book edited by Carl Jung (1976, pp. 329–35), the analytical psychologist Jolanda Jacobi reports on a case in which his client dreamed of a young woman – an actress wearing long flowing robes. The client was not himself an actor in the play, but was impressed by this woman's role. Jacobi points out that the woman represents both the client's mother and his own unconscious feminine side. The client, Jacobi suggests, is evading taking an active part in life's drama, as his more emotional, feminine side would have him do. Again, this reframe of the experience transforms a merely puzzling message into an opportunity to learn new strategies and re-own "parts" of experience.

In some psychotherapies, direct interpretations are not offered. In Gestalt therapy, if the therapist identifies another meaning to a situation, she/he might say, "May I feed you a sentence?" and ask the person to make a statement that deepens the meaning they have been attributing to their experience. Fritz Perls agrees that this is an interpretive move (Levitsky and Perls, 1982, p. 153) but emphasises that it is left up to the client to find the new meaning relevant or to reject it. In body therapies, interpretation focuses on the body structure. Alexander Lowen says that a good bioenergetic therapist is one who can "read the body characterologically" (Lowen, 1971, pp. 5–7). Explaining the meaning of the body patterns again both makes some new "sense" of the person's problem and frames it as something that can be changed (by bioenergetic exercises).

While many therapies have explicitly included the reattribution of meaning, or reframing, as a part of their aim, Carl Rogers's stated aim was to stay with the client's own meaning. However, it is important to note that every time a therapist makes an empathic statement to their client, they use their own frames to do so. If a client says, "My mother is always blocking my progress" and the therapist replies, "You feel frustrated by the things she does", this is a radical reframe. The client has claimed that their mother is the active one in this story. The therapist has focused on what the person's own feelings are, as if this were the key issue. As Rogers notes, the fact that the Client-Centred therapist focuses on the client's own emotions, perceptions and evaluations causes the client to shift to this focus (Rogers 1973, p. 135). And that is reframing.

Changing Interpersonal Dynamics

One of the earliest NLP books was *Changing With Families*, written by the NLP co-developers and Virginia Satir (Bandler, Grinder and Satir, 1976). In it, the core elements of an NLP approach to cooperative relationship building are introduced. These include a model for building rapport, a model of personality differences and a model for conflict resolution.

Two types of personality difference are discussed in NLP. One is the difference in the criteria used in a person's prioritising strategies – their "values". Values are usually described in generalised terms, and are criteria by which we make decisions and evaluate our actions. If I value "honesty", for example, I make decisions about what I say and do based on that criterion, and I check whether I'm satisfied with my action, using the same criterion. People tend to have a "hierarchy of values". For example, I may value "honesty", and I may value "not hurting people's feelings". When my friend asks me if I like their new clothes, and I don't, my response will be based on the hierarchy in which I think of these two values (which one is more important). If honesty is higher in my values I'll probably gently tell them the truth; if not hurting people's feelings is a higher value, I may "politely" compliment them.

The second type of personality difference described in NLP is difference in the higher-level strategies that people use to sort their experiences. These are differences in a person's meta-strategies or "Meta-programs". For example, when people study a subject (such as NLP), they may be most interested in the big picture and the general ideas, or most interested in the detailed facts and research data. In NLP we call this Meta-program "chunk size". Your individual preference for "chunking up" to the generalised or "chunking down" to the specifics is a strategy. But it is a strategy that applies in a wide range of situations, and even decides which other strategies you run. Another example of a Meta-program difference that we have already discussed in this book is sensory preference (whether you prefer to process information visually, auditorially or kinaesthetically). This preference decides which other strategies you will select and run. The personality types discovered by Carl Jung (introvert/extravert, thinker/feeler, intuitor/sensor) are treated as Meta-programs in NLP.

Creating cooperative relationships involves helping people understand differences such as those in values and Meta-programs. It involves helping them align with different personalities, and it involves giving them a framework for finding solutions when differences create conflict. As a simple example of aligning Meta-programs, counselling generally involves the counsellor in using reflective listening to build empathy with clients. A study by William Brockman found that this process is greatly enhanced if the counsellor matches the sensory system that their client talks in (e.g. saying, "So, the way you see it ..." if they spoke about their experience visually; saying, "It feels to you like ..." if the person spoke kinaesthetically; saying, "Sounds like your call on this is ..." if the person spoke auditorially). In Brockman's study, counsellors who matched the client's sensory Meta-program were preferred by a ratio of three to one.

Changing the way people relate interpersonally has both immediate effects on the relationship being changed, and flow-on effects on the persons involved and their other relationships.

In research at a New Zealand high school, my partner Margot Hamblett and I taught a 24-hour course in NLP communications skills to ten teachers. The course was based on our book *Transforming Communication* (Bolstad and Hamblett, 1998). We studied seven classes (200 students), three of which had these trained teachers taking more than half their sessions. At six month follow-up, we were able to show marked differences between the classes who had NLP-trained teachers and those who did not (Bolstad and Hamblett, September, 2000). First, students' attitude to school was different. The teachers we trained reported that their biggest problem, low motivation, had simply ceased to be an issue in their classes. Their students agreed: the number who rated themselves as "not at all" wanting to co-operate at school dropped from 6 per cent to 4 per cent in the nontrained teachers' classes, but from 6 per cent to zero in the classes experiencing NLP-trained teachers. The number of students who said that they asked questions in class "whenever they could" dropped in the control group from 12 per cent to 3 per cent – they became less motivated as the year went on. In the group with NLP-trained teachers, it rose slightly to 13 per cent.

But the most interesting information was not about the relationship between the teachers and the students: it was about the relationship among the students themselves. The school had been very concerned about student–student violence (bullying), and instituted its own programme to reduce bullying. We asked students how often they saw a student threaten, hit or injure another student in the last week. The number who said this never happened remained stable at about 40 per cent in the control group, but rose to 64 per cent in the group with NLP-trained teachers. This and other similar results strongly supported our hypothesis that students would model effective communication skills from their teachers. This same NLP-based course is taught to managers at the Bank of New Zealand, to parents, to couples, to health professionals, to Christian ministers and to counsellors. In each case, effects flow on to the "clients" of these groups. Changing the relationships changes the internal psychological world of these clients.

Changing interpersonal dynamics: case study

Sally and Andrew came to see me because of repeated conflicts in their marriage. Looking up at the ceiling, Andrew explained, "One of the things that I see about our relationship is a lack of care about me. Sometimes I come home and the kitchen is a total mess … And the things I've tidied up in the hall have been spread out over the floor. Sometimes she looks like she hasn't even brushed her hair!"

Sally sighed and looked down at the floor. "Well, when you get home you're in such a rush anyway. I feel like we just don't make contact. And I suppose it's true that I shift things around. I put my energy into making sure the house feels comfortable for the kids … and for us, so I guess I'm not so aware of exactly where things are as you are. But I don't feel as if you really want to be there with us anyway."

From the beginning, I could hear that these two people loved each other – but they didn't speak the same language. In NLP terms, Sally was concentrating on kinaesthetic information to check if Andrew loved her; and Andrew was focusing on visual cues to check if Sally loved him. They were tuned in to different channels. Just hearing that explanation was a profound revelation to both of them. My explanation of the sensory systems was, in NLP terms, a "reframe". Each of them had assumed that a conflict meant that the other one was in error. There were tears in both their eyes as they talked together about the fact that they were *different* rather than one person being "right" and one "wrong".

As our discussion continued, I used a variety of NLP language patterns to guide Sally and Andrew to discover their own style of relating, and modify it to create more of the kind of enjoyment they wanted in the relationship. Let me give you another example from later in this same discussion:

Andrew (to Sally): "You just don't want to see it from my side, though; that's what's staring me in the face right now!"

Richard: "So that's the big thing. Can I just check, how, specifically, do you know she doesn't want to see?"

Andrew: "Well, I could see she wasn't listening when I said all that."

Richard: "Oh, so you had the impression she wasn't listening. [To Sally] Were you?"

Sally: "Of course I was. I took in every word. You always throw those kind of insults at me."

Richard: "So as far as you were concerned you were listening. [To Andrew] And as far as you were concerned, she wasn't. What would let you see she actually was listening?"

Andrew: "Well, if she looked in my direction of course."

Richard (to Sally): "Did you know that was what he needed to see to feel listened to?"

Sally: "No."

Richard: "So this may have happened several times, and when he complained you would have felt insulted. Is that right?"

Sally: "Yes. And I suppose that, once I feel that way, I actually do listen less."

Andrew: "Exactly. So how am I supposed to know if you're listening if you don't even look at me?"

Richard: "That's what we're looking for, isn't it? A way you can know that she's really hearing you. And one solution is for her to look at you. Another thing I might add is, do you feel listened to by me?"

Andrew: "Sure."

Richard: "Because I'm aware that one thing I'm doing is checking whether I've understood what you're showing me before I reply each time. Sort of reflecting it to find out if I got the picture. And that gives us both feedback about whether I understand you."

My comments here include using the metamodel (to check what happens specifically, and to challenge mind-reading), and verbal pacing (reflective listening/restating what has been said). I am also explicitly teaching the NLP communication skills. My aim is not merely to solve their current problems, but to equip them both to solve future challenges and create a more cooperative relationship. As I teach, though, I'm using our interaction as a model of what I'm recommending. I'm actually teaching conflict resolution at the same time. In this case, the conflict is about how to talk and listen. We identify a disagreement about this, where the two people have had different ways of reacting. Rather than try to find out who is "right" and who is "wrong", I direct the conversation to generating solutions that will satisfy both their concerns.

Working with couples is immensely enjoyable. Within four hour-long sessions, Andrew and Sally had learned how to use the NLP distinctions to explain their own preferences, and how to use basic communication skills to resolve conflicts in a mutually satisfying way. This relationship, which had seemed so impossible to them both, was actually rich in positive intentions and possibilities.

Changing interpersonal dynamics in other models of psychotherapy

By recognising the transference (the client's interpersonal response to the therapist, based on previous relationships) as its defining content, psychoanalysis confirmed the key role of interpersonal dynamics in the field of human change (Olinick, 1980, p. 198). By the time NLP developed, the importance of interpersonal dynamics in psychotherapy was widely understood. There was even a confusingly shared jargon of interpersonal psychotherapy developing. For example, the word "game" is used in Gestalt therapy to describe any playful structured interactions (Levitsky and Perls, 1982, p. 149), while it is used in TA to describe certain unpleasant Child–Child ego-state transactions with an unexpected switch (Stewart and Joines, 1987, pp. 231–58). The term "game" largely replaced terms such as "transference", to which it clearly has a relationship.

NLP evolved in a context where therapy occurred mainly in groups. Virginia Satir worked using a psychodrama model in family therapy (Satir and Baldwin, 1983); Fritz Perls claimed that individual therapy was obsolete (Perls, 1969, p. 73); and Carl Rogers said that his whole focus in Client-Centred Therapy had shifted to work with large organisations and the encounter group (Rogers, 1974, p. 7). Transactional analysis was by definition the analysis of transactions between people (Stewart and Joines, 1987, pp. 3–4), and Milton Erickson set his clients tasks to interact with other people rather than merely to be introspective (Walters and Havens, 1994, pp. 173–6). Behavioural therapy focused on social reinforcement and modelling (Krumboltz and Thoreson, 1976, pp. 2–24), and Jungian therapy explored the interaction between people of different psychological types and the significance of the shadow for social relationships (Whitmont, 1991, pp. 138–55; p. 168). Wilhelm Reich, who largely initiated the field of body therapy, actually argued that the cause of all neurosis was the sexual suppression required by hierarchical societies and saw himself as a social revolutionary (Reich, 1971). In some way, each form of therapy has found a way of recognising the importance of relationship for healing.

Changing Physiological Contexts

Most NLP change processes require relatively little actual body movement to complete. However, NLP uses psychodramatic techniques to create "spatial anchors" (see Grinder and Bandler, 1976, p. 67), and has always recognised the importance of physiology (body movement and positioning) in determining state of mind and other psychological results (O'Connor and Seymour, 1990, pp. 63–5).

Early on in the development of NLP, John Grinder presented a change process called sometimes "editing" and sometimes "circuit clearing", based on processing a psychological issue while engaging in a physical task that required side-to-side movement; one example described by him was the use of juggling (see DeLozier and Grinder, 1987, pp. 162–3; 247–8; 371–2). Steve and Connirae Andreas taught this process as the NLP finger technique, and then as the Eye Movement Integrator (Andreas, 1992, pp. 9–10). In it, they have the client follow the practitioner's finger as it moves across in front of their eyes, from side to side, up to down and from corner to corner, while they hold in their mind the issue that they want to resolve.

Outside the official field of NLP, Dr Francine Shapiro has developed a variation of the Eye Movement Integrator called EMDR (Eye Movement Desensitisation and Reprocessing). A vast amount of research has supported the use of this method, especially for post-traumatic stress disorder (Shapiro, 1995, pp. 328–41). In these studies, EMDR outperforms training in relaxation, biofeedback, orthodox counselling, systematic desensitisation and other inpatient treatment programmes. Shapiro's way of explaining this success, Accelerated Information Processing, is essentially the same one I presented in the last chapter (Shapiro, 1995, pp. 28–54). She suggests that by holding the "target memory" in awareness, the person activates the neural network where it is stored. The rapid eye movements then activate the person's normal information-processing system and shift information until it makes contact with neural networks where new resources are stored. Shapiro notes that, as with other NLP-like techniques, EMDR leads to changes in beliefs, changes in emotional response and submodality changes in the person's memory of significant events (e.g. seeing their remembered image of an aggressor shrink in size). While Francine Shapiro acknowledges her links to Ericksonian therapy and cognitive behavioural therapy, she does not see her EMDR model as an NLP process.

Dr Roger Callahan is a psychologist trained in NLP, acupuncture and applied kinaesiology. Based on insights from these three fields, he evolved Thought Field Therapy (TFT) (Callahan, 2001), another rapid-healing model based on holding the challenging situation in mind while making a physiological intervention. In the case of TFT, Callahan has the therapist tap with their finger on certain acupuncture points on the head, on the back of the hand and on the chest. At times these tappings are accompanied by eye movements similar to EMDR or the NLP Eye Movement Integrator. Callahan also has clients repeat certain affirmations to themselves while doing the TFT procedure. Algorithms prescribe a specific sequence for each type of emotional problem. Thought Field Therapy is based on an energy model of the human body, much like traditional acupuncture. Studies at Florida State University compared EMDR, TFT and the NLP phobia/trauma cure in treatment of phobias and PTSD. While all three were successful, in this study, TFT produced the fastest and most sustained benefits as measured by the clients' subjective reports (Callahan, 2001, p. 42).

Changing physiological contexts: case study

In a videotaped demonstration at the 1993 Brief Therapy Conference of the Milton Erickson Foundation, Steve Andreas works with J, a Vietnam veteran who has had post-traumatic stress disorder for 24 years. Steve uses his version of the NLP Eye Movement Integrator. At the beginning of the session, he asks J to rate his level of distress as 100 per cent; this includes experiences of his racing heart, tense body feelings and internal images of Vietnam. He can then have him report any changes either down or up in terms of percentages. He explains that the quality of the feeling may change, and the memories that occur to him may also change, through the session.

Steve begins by checking various submodality and strategy distinctions (such as where in J's visual field the image seems most intensely disturbing – which J says is directly in front). Steve then uses a pointer to direct the client's eye movements from side to side a dozen or so times, and then checks the result. Even after the first set of movements, the client reports that the feeling of distress has dropped to 90 per cent and the image is less obvious. Steve moves his pointer in a number of different ways, in straight lines back and forth as well as in circles, checking after each movement type to assess the results.

After ten minutes or so, J finds that he is able to recall the entire war scene that has disturbed him most (previously he was only flashing back to the start of it). At this point he rates his distress at 150 per cent – higher than when he began – and his hands are sweating profusely. After another five minutes, this scene too is manageable, and he rates it at 60 per cent. He is soon reporting that the original mental "scene" has moved several metres further away from him, and he is at 20–30 per cent. Only some of the sounds from the memory still have any potential to be disturbing. Finally, J says, "I have a feeling that I should be nervous ... but *I'm not!*"

Steve asks, "Is there any way that you can get those images back?" J says that, while he can still see some of the images, they do not have any of the feeling they had, and in fact he is able to enjoy the colours of the "tracers" being fired across the scene. After forty minutes, the disturbing experience that has haunted him for a quarter of a century is over. He completes the session by telling his audience the story of the firefight that was previously disturbing him, and reports that he is quite calm as he does so.

Changing physiological contexts in other models of psychotherapy

Although not central to these models, similar physiological processes have been known since the beginning of psychotherapy. In fact, the alternating breathing through left and right nostril, used in yoga (Rossi, 1986, pp. 121–4), is a form of editing similar to juggling or eye-movement integration. Sigmund Freud reports a technique where he applies a pressure to the client's forehead and holds it there while asking the person what comes into their mind (Freud and Breuer, 1974, pp. 354–63). Images, insights and changes often flooded into the person's mind when Freud did this.

Again and again, through the history of therapy, such processes have been stumbled on almost by accident. Alexander Lowen (Lowen and Lowen, 1977, pp. 96–7) describes the eye-movement integration process as a bioenergetic exercise (moving the eyes from side to side, up and down, and in circles) at least a decade before either NLP or EMDR had written it up. Many of the bioenergetic exercises are clearly based on this principle.

Simply changing state by using the body differently is a very powerful intervention in itself. This is particularly so in depression, where body movement has been slowed down. Thayer (1996, p. 191) cites a study where depressed women were given the task of walking briskly fifteen minutes a day. Those who completed the task reported elevation of mood, but only 50 per cent completed the task. Dr Robert Holden (1993) runs the Laughter Clinic at West Birmingham Health Authority in Britain. He quotes William James's insight: "We don't laugh because we are happy. We are happy because we laugh." Holden sites evidence that laughter boosts immunoglobulin levels, restores energy, lowers blood pressure, massages the heart and reduces stress (1993, pp. 33–42). A hundred laughs a day is the equivalent of ten minutes' jogging.

On the other hand, for the anxious person, physiology offers several simple ways to relax. This includes showing them how to stop tightening muscle groups, to pay attention to the out breath rather than the in breath, to breathe through the nondominant nostril (Rossi, 1996, pp. 171–2) and to orient towards enjoyable internal imagery. The aim is to teach the person to go into a trance on their own, using anchors under their control. Ernest Rossi points out (Rossi 1996, pp. 279–313) that clients benefit from doing this several times a day, so as to re-establish a natural ultradian rest cycle. Like Rossi, we have found that many anxious clients will have no further problems if they arrange every ninety minutes to rest for ten minutes lying on their dominant side (thus opening the nondominant nostril).

Tasking

Tasking shifts the focus of change from the psychotherapy session back to the client's daily life. It involves assigning the person a therapeutically useful activity to do in their daily life, between the therapy sessions. This may be as simple as the Formula First Session Task prescribed by Solution Focused therapists, which is: "Between now and the next time we meet, I would like you to observe, so that you can describe to me next time, what happens in your [family, life, marriage, relationship] that you want to continue to have happen." (Miller et al., 1996, pp. 256–8.) This task requires the person to practise a new Meta-program (personality strategy) – sorting their experience to identify what they want more of. Research suggests that clients who receive this task will be far more likely to report that their problem has improved, and to feel positive about the course of therapy.

Milton Erickson achieved much of his clinical success by means of carefully designed tasks. These were of several different kinds, including:

- Tasks that have the client practise a useful new strategy that is obviously useful for their own goal (for example, in a marriage-counselling process, I might ask a man to "tell your wife one thing you genuinely appreciate in her behaviour every day").
- Tasks that have the client use a strategy that deals with the underlying problem that the therapist suspects has prevented their change (for example, in the same situation, if I thought the man did not compliment his partner because of his own low self-esteem, I might ask him to "find one thing each day that you appreciate about yourself and practise giving a compliment by looking at yourself in the mirror and telling yourself how you appreciate that thing").
- Tasks that have the client practise an ambiguous, metaphorical function (for example, in the same situation I might ask the man to "buy a potted plant and each day of the next week turn it so you can enjoy looking at it from a new perspective; then consider what effect your doing this might be having on the growth of the plant, and on its attractiveness").
- Tasks that prescribe the problem (for example, I might ask the man to "avoid making any remarks that might be construed as compliments to your wife, with the exception of one remark a day; choose that remark carefully and make sure you do not say anything about any other behaviours or qualities of your wife's that you notice yourself feeling positive about").

Tasking: case study

The following story is told by Milton Erickson in David Gordon and Maribeth Meyers-Anderson's book *Phoenix* (1981, pp. 44–6). It demonstrates a variety of different types of task.

> Quite a number of years ago I received a telephone call from L.A. A young man who told me, "I'm working on a ship as a seaman and I'm awfully afraid I'm going to go into orbit." I told him I thought it would be inadvisable to continue working on board that ship. So he got a job working in a *mine*. And he found that even if he were a mile deep into the earth, he was still obsessed with the *fear* of going into orbit. And he came to Phoenix to see me. I don't know how he got my name, or why he chose me, but I do know he saw a NUMBER of psychiatrists and they all wanted to give him *shock therapy* – electro-shock therapy – because of his delusion that he was going to go into

orbit. Now I didn't think he should get shock therapy. I had him get a job in a warehouse. And he was afraid he was going into orbit. And that delusion was so persistent that he couldn't count as far as ten without having to stop and reassure himself that he was not YET in orbit. He was entitled to perspire because of the heat but not to perspire THAT much! But he was dreading so much going into orbit. I tried to distract his mind by asking him to count his steps as he walked along the street and to memorize the street names. But that, "I'm going to go into orbit, I'm going to go into orbit", obsessed him ... interfered with him. He couldn't get very much sleep because he was afraid he was going to go into orbit. And finally, I realized I couldn't do anything for him except settle down with him and EXPLAIN to him "Now apparently it is your *destiny to go into orbit*. Now the astronauts go into orbit, and there's always an end to the orbit ... They come back to earth again. And as long as you're going to go into orbit, why not get it OVER with?" So I had him take salt pills and a canteen of water and I had him walk about fourteen hours a day along the tops of MOUNTAINS around here, and he had to come in at 10.30 at night to report that he had not yet gone into orbit. But he slept well, as you would walking around on mountain tops with a canteen of water and walking for about fourteen hours a day. And finally, he began to get just a little bit dubious about going into orbit. Then his sister came to me asking if he could go to California where she lived. She said her husband had a job but that he would not or could not fix up things around the house. And she had a picket fence that needed some painting, a gate that needed to be repaired, some shelves to be built, and so I told the young man that he could go to California because he would be in sight of the mountains and he could take his canteen with him and his salt pills, and if he got a sudden feeling that he was destined to go into orbit he could get up on top of a mountain so he could go easily into orbit. Now a few months later he came back and said, "That was a delusional psychotic idea", and he didn't know what had made him so crazy and he felt I had saved him from hospitalization at the State Hospital. And he decided that since I hadn't charged him for my services, he would give me a portable water bed.

Tasking in other models of psychotherapy

While psychoanalysis began as a strictly session-by-session process, Freud accepted that at times it was useful for clients to study psychoanalytic literature between sessions (Freud, 1982, p. 12). The focus on dream analysis in the work of Freud, Jung and other psychodynamic therapists makes dream experiencing and recording itself an important homework task (Jolande Jacobi, in Jung, 1976, pp. 323–74). Early on, it was models of psychotherapy that supported behavioural rehearsal that adopted tasking most fully (e.g. psychodrama; see Kipper, 1986, p. 106). By the 1950s, doing therapy by providing the client with therapeutic tasks was a well-established practice, and the era of "self-help" therapy had begun. For example, Fritz Perls put out a book of Gestalt exercises for home use (Perls, Hefferline and Goodman, 1951), and Alexander Lowen published a book of bioenergetic exercises to guide oneself through (Lowen and Lowen, 1977). Carl Rogers and his Client-Centered movement began exploring a number of ways to provide empathic communication experiences outside the therapy room, including setting up self-directed groups, friendship support systems and family communication trainings (see Hart and Tomlinson (eds), 1970, pp. 314–425). Homework and tasking are central to the newer cognitive and brief-therapy approaches (Beck and Emery, 1985, p. 189; Miller et al., 1996, p. 256).

Chapter 4
RESOLVE

The RESOLVE Model and the Relationship of Changework

The ten categories of therapeutic intervention discussed in Chapter 3 cover the key NLP "techniques". But NLP as a "psychotherapeutic" modality is much more than this collection of techniques. The NLP trainer Steve Andreas says (1999), "I think that someone who uses the NLP methods exceptionally well has several ways of gathering all the different skills and techniques under a single overarching framework of understanding." In this section I explain the framework that I use. A framework for the process of therapy is recognition that therapy is not a prepackaged product, but a *relationship*, which has a beginning, a middle and an end. Several such frameworks exist in the psychotherapy field.

Sigmund Freud used the metaphor of chess for this relationship sequence (Olinick, 1980, pp. 3–4), and referred to the opening game (where the therapeutic alliance is established), the middle game (where the actual analysis of the transference occurs) and the end game (completing treatment). Edward Whitmont explores Jungian therapy using the metaphor of a quest (Whitmont, 1969, pp. 305–10). He suggests that the stages of this quest are:

- Uncovering feelings in the personal unconscious
- The "long pull", exploring the labyrinth of the unconscious
- An impasse, a turning point where the individual "ego" gives up trying to control the process, and transformation occurs
- The establishment of a new relationship between the ego and the self as a result of this transformation

In psychodrama, a metaphor from the theatre (Blatner, 1988, pp. 42–101) is used to identify the three stages of:

- **Warm-up**, in which the director warms up to their own role, then the group warm up to each other and to the task, then a protagonist/client is selected and warms up to their role and contract with the director
- **Action**, in which the problem is presented, auxiliary actors are engaged, resistances are dealt with, action explores the protagonist's issues, often leading to catharsis, and, finally, surplus reality enables the exploration of other possibilities in the drama
- **Working through/integration**, in which the protagonist explores how they want to act in real life, they and the group share their responses to the psychodrama, and the session is closed by dealing with "re-entry" to real life, checking what support is needed and what unfinished business is left, and saying goodbye

Gestalt writers have used the cycle of Gestalt formation as a model for the process of therapy from the client's perspective (e.g. Clarkson, 1989, pp. 36–40). This cycle moves through:

- **Sensation** (the client feels some discomfort in their life)
- **Awareness** (they begin to pay attention to what is going wrong)
- **Mobilisation** (they arrange psychotherapy and confront the issues)
- **Action** (they build a therapeutic relationship and explore the issues)
- **Contact** (they reach the deeper conflict underlying their problems)
- **Satisfaction** (having resolved this conflict they enjoy integrating the learnings into their life)
- **Withdrawal** (they prepare to leave the counselling relationship)

The notion of beginning with superficial issues and gradually working to deeper ones occurs in a number of such models. Aaron Beck identifies the stages of cognitive behavioural therapy similarly (Beck and Emery, 1985, pp. 178–80):

- **Setting an agenda**: The therapist restates the person's concern until they agree on what needs to change

- **Designing and enacting a treatment plan**: In sequence it (1) provides symptomatic relief, (2) teaches how to identify distorted thought patterns, (3) teaches how to respond to these patterns and (4) identifies and modifies deeper patterns
- **Concluding**: The session concludes with some feedback and the setting of homework assignments to practise the new skills

Robert Carkhuff developed a training-based model of "helping" or psychotherapy (Carkhuff and Berenson, 1977, p. 249). The phases are:

- **Prehelping**: At this stage the helper simply attends and listens to the person's concern
- **Exploring**: The helper "responds" by restating the person's concern to check it is accurately understood
- **Understanding**: The helper then "personalises" their restatements, focusing on what the person wants and how they have been blocking themselves from achieving that; this includes the helper sharing their own responses to the person
- **Acting**: Finally, the helper is involved in "initiating" by guiding the person through setting goals, planning action to reach those goals and acting

There are three insights that all these models share. One is the understanding that what a helper does at the start of the process of change needs to be different from what they do in the middle of the process. The first steps involve building a relationship within which the central steps can occur. Second, all these models share the understanding that, as the middle process of therapy continues, deeper issues are able to be dealt with. There is a building of strength through the process of therapy. Third, the end of the process of therapy needs to be different from the middle. It is focused on the person's new life, with the changes they have made in therapy. The last steps involve completing or finishing the relationship that has been built up.

How People Change on Their Own

Brief Motivational Interviewing is another multistaged model for helping people make life changes. Unlike the models we have considered so far, though, it did not emerge out of studies of psychotherapy, but those of people's own individual response to the need to change (Finney and Moos, 1998, p. 157). James Prochaska, John Norcross and Carlo Diclemente interviewed 200 people who quit smoking on their own, to find out what happened (Prochaska et al., 1994). How did these people change a behaviour that psychotherapists have found so hard to alter? The researchers followed up with studies of people who had given up a number of other self-defeating behaviours, finding the same patterns.

Their results confirm that people are quite good at changing their own behaviour *in certain circumstances*. This is even true where the behaviour is a serious "addiction". Over two-thirds of those addicted people who stop drinking alcohol do so on their own with no help. Ninety-five per cent of the 30 million Americans who have quit smoking in the last decade or so did so without medical or AA-style help (Prochaska et al., 1994, p. 36). These people have better long-term success than those who choose treatment programmes: 81 per cent of those who stop drinking on their own will abstain for the next ten years, compared with only 32 per cent of those who are going to AA (Trimpey, 1996, p. 78; Ragge, 1998, p. 24). What has happened in the lives of successful self-changers? Research on 2,700 British smokers showed that, at the time they stop, they often change their job, alter their relationship or otherwise solve some lifestyle problem. Also, they stop when they "lose faith in what they used to think smoking did for them" while creating "a powerful new set of beliefs that non-smoking is, of itself, a desirable and rewarding state." (Marsh, 1984).

The same seems to hold true for lifestyle-based "addictions". In 1982, Stanley Schachter announced the results of a long-term study into obesity. He set out in the early 1970s with the idea that, while most overweight people can lose weight, few ever keep it off. In two separate community-based studies, what he actually found was that 62 per cent of obese people succeeded in taking off an average of 34.7 pounds and keeping this weight off for an average of 11.2 years. Those who never entered weight-loss programmes showed better long-term weight loss. Incidentally, he stumbled on the truth that many smokers give up smoking on their own. He followed up this variable, too, and again found that those who attended treatment programmes did not do as well as those who gave up on their own (Schachter, 1982, pp. 436–44).

What about so-called "hard" drugs? In a 1982 study of morphine use, fifty surgery patients were given uncontrolled use of morphine for six days. Though they used far more than street addicts, they all decreased the use of the drug and stopped with no problems after their discharge from hospital. Of US soldiers who used heroin in the Vietnam war (and most did) 73 per cent became addicted and displayed withdrawal on return. Authorities were terrified, expecting a huge surge in addiction numbers. In fact, 90 per cent simply stopped once they got back to America. Researchers noted:

> It is commonly believed that after recovery from addiction, one must avoid any further contact with heroin. It is thought that trying heroin, even once, will rapidly lead to re-addiction ... Half the men who have been addicted in Vietnam used heroin on their return, but only one in eight became re-addicted to heroin." [Peele, 1989, pp. 167–8; Trimpey, 1996, p. 78.]

If we look beyond the addictions field we find the same story of successful self-change. For example, 80 per cent of individuals suffering major depression will "spontaneously" cease to be depressed in 4–10 months (Yapko, 1992, p. 16). People normally find their own way out of depression. Michael Yapko points out that this also means that if any type of "assistance" continues for ten months it will seem to have solved the problem of depression in 80 per cent of cases. Genuinely successful strategies for assisting are those that can show benefits in the short term.

The same pattern occurs with psychoses. Recovery rates from schizophrenia vary depending on where people live, but World Health Organisation studies show that in Nigeria, 58 per cent of diagnosed schizophrenics fully recover within two years, and in India 50 per cent recover within two years. In Denmark, only 8 per cent recover within two years, despite having vastly more drug treatment. (Jablensky et al., 1992.) Nonetheless, if we follow up even Western people with "well-diagnosed and severe forms of schizophrenia" we find that within 20–30 years a full 50 per cent will be functioning normally (Kopelowicz and Liberman, 1998, p. 191). Schizophrenia is certainly not usually a lifelong disorder. Most people with schizophrenia will recover fully. Western levels of drug treatment do not enhance their recovery (and may inhibit it). Family and social support, as well as simplicity of lifestyle, are clearly associated with more successful outcomes. With support, a calm lifestyle and helpful feedback, the person diagnosed schizophrenic will learn new skills that fully resolve their "problem".

Motivational Interviewing

To return to the question this research raises, what do successful self-changers do that much of therapy fails to replicate? Prochaska and DiClemente (Prochaska et al., 1994; Miller and Rollnick, 1991, pp. 14–18) found that successful self-changers cycle through a series of six stages. Helping a person in one stage, they say, requires an entirely different approach from helping someone at another. Part of what makes therapy less successful is that everyone is being treated as if they were at the same "stage". The methodology of Motivational Interviewing does not focus on the content of the problem (e.g. by educating an alcoholic about the dangers of drinking), but on the process of becoming motivated to quit. The authors describe "resistance" as a result of applying a change strategy designed for the wrong stage of change (e.g. treating a person in the contemplation stage as if they should be ready for action). The stages can be diagrammed in a cycle as below.

Figure D: The self-change model

116

The self-change model

Summarising, the stages and the effective responses to each stage are:

Pre-contemplation. The person doesn't consider the problem an issue at this stage. Helpers can refuse to collude with the problem, and simply seek permission to give information.

Contemplation. The person see-saws between wanting to change and keeping their old pattern. Helpers can assist the person to explore and clarify their values (what's important to them) and to use decision-making processes.

Commitment. The person says they really want to change. Helpers can assist the person to set goals, and can provide preparatory tasks for the person, to check out their intention to act.

Action. Once the person is ready to act, a helper can elicit and alter their old strategy for creating the problem, and integrate the conflicting neural networks to resolve the problem.

Maintenance. At this stage the person needs to build a new lifestyle by integrating change at the level of their life mission, values and time line. Helpers can also teach interpersonal skills, state-changing skills and other useful new strategies to back up their change.

Recycling. Finally, it is important to have the person think through how they would respond to possible future "lapses" into the old patterns and have them check that they can continue supporting their new choices.

Self-changing and Milton Erickson

The Motivational Interviewing model has emerged out of the study of successful self-change. This parallel with NLP is reflected in the many similarities between the approaches of the two models. Dr Milton Erickson, who was one of the original models studied in the development of NLP, considered psychotherapy to be first and foremost a naturalistic phenomenon. He told an interesting story about how he decided to become a psychotherapist himself (Gordon and Meyers-Anderson, 1981, pp. 167–72).

When Milton was ten years old, and living in a small town in Wisconsin, a notorious criminal named Joe was released into his community after a long jail term. Within four days of Joe's return, three of the town's stores were broken into at night. Everyone in the village was terrified, as Joe had a history of uncontrolled violence, both in and outside of jail. At this time, there was a young unmarried woman named Susie, whose father was a very wealthy farmer near the town. Susie was in town on an errand for her father, when Joe wandered out on to the sidewalk and blocked her path. Joe looked Susie up and down very slowly, and she responded in kind. "Can I take you to the dance next Friday?" Joe asked. Susie, considered the most "choosy" woman in town, thought for a moment, and said, "You can if you're a gentleman." Joe stepped out of her way and she went on down the street.

The next morning, boxes with all the stolen goods were left outside the three stores. Joe walked out to Susie's farm that day and got himself hired as a labourer. He went to the dance with her, that Friday and every Friday for some time. And he behaved in every way like a gentleman. The two of them were married the next year, and Joe began helping manage the farm. When Milton considered what to do with his future at the end of elementary school, it was Joe who encouraged him, as he did many other children, to go on to high school and then to university. By then, Joe was on the school board and was one of the "pillars" of the community.

Milton said of this, "And all the psychotherapy Joe received was 'You can if you're a gentleman.' ... Psychotherapy has to occur within the patient, everything has to be done by the patient, and the patient has to have a motivation." Erickson's interest was in how to create this motivation within the client, and allow them to solve their own problems. From observing Joe, he had a strong belief that even the most "hopeless case" could change if this was achieved.

No sweat: a preview of RESOLVE

To preview the RESOLVE model and demonstrate its links with the Motivational Interviewing pattern, I will consider an example from the work of Milton Erickson (Erickson and Rossi, 1979, pp. 143–234). This two-session therapy (each session lasted two hours) was done with "Miss X", a trained social worker who had a severe anxiety condition. She was an accomplished harpist, and her anxiety caused her to sweat so profusely from the hands that she would drip a puddle of water on the floor within a few minutes. Various doctors had recommended surgery to deal with this. The sweating had prevented her becoming a *professional* harpist, which was her stated goal. Although she did not initially discuss this, she also had great anxiety about enclosed spaces, including the inside of aeroplanes. The two sessions with Erickson completely cured this claustrophobia and the sweating problem, as confirmed in Christmas cards sent to him over the next three years.

Resourceful State. Erickson begins his first session by telling his client, "Now the first step, of course, is to untangle your legs. And untangle your hands. Now, what do you think I should do?" She replies, "Well, to be perfectly honest with you, I guess I probably feel that you ought to hypnotise me. In that if you don't, I might be aware of what you're doing, and that would wreck it." Erickson then explains to her that she dreams with her unconscious mind, but at times she remembers her dreams in the morning. He emphasises, "All right, so that eliminates this question of preventing you from knowing what I'm doing. You can know what I'm doing, but I can also do some things you don't know about." (pp. 147–9.) In this initial "contracting", Erickson has set the terms of his interaction with Miss X. He is confident and lets her know that he expects that she can change herself. He also defines her role and his role. He refuses to buy into the idea of her magically changing while she is "unconscious". Being willing to define the interaction in this way is, as I'll discuss later, part of Erickson's being in a "resourceful state". It is also the appropriate action to take in the "pre-contemplation" stage of self-change. If she accepts his offer to provide a learning situation, then they have moved on to the "contemplation" stage.

Establish rapport. Erickson then chats with Miss X, apparently randomly. He asks her what her favourite piece of music is, and suggests that she can enjoy listening to it in her mind now. He asks, "And how well can you enjoy that piece of music?" She replies, "Immensely." He says, "You're sure of that." And he tells her to continue listening and enjoying (pp. 149–50). At this stage he is "pacing" her internal experience. He continues doing this, inviting her into a trance and gradually showing her that her unconscious mind can run her body – even to the extent where she can find herself consciously unable to stand up (hypnotic paralysis). She also begins to get a sense of how her unconscious mind has opinions and responses that are separate from her conscious ones. In terms of self-changing, this is the "contemplation" stage. While Miss X is definitely intrigued by learning this, she has not committed herself yet to making a significant change.

Specify outcome. Miss X has identified her sweating as the issue to be dealt with (she does not reveal that she has some problem with claustrophobia until the second session). Once he has guided her into a trancelike state of rapport, Erickson mentions this goal again and speculates about whether it is actually a single issue or not. He discusses what it will take to solve this specific issue, and what else it might be related to in Miss X's life. Speaking to Ernest Rossi, who is observing, he says, "And the next question is: she's got a definite and limited problem. And that has interfered with her as a personality very much. Now. is that personal problem a serious emotional problem, or is it a superficial emotional problem. I can think of a serious case of claustrophobia. The solution was somebody walking rapidly across the floor and down the steps, clicking her shoes at each step. When she was a little girl, her mother punished her by putting her in the closet and then walking noisily out of the house and down the steps." (P. 184.) Miss X admits the next day that when Erickson told this story (one of many he told over the session) she was shocked: how did he know that she was claustrophobic? It is important to remember that Erickson may not have known consciously – until that moment. That moment pushes Miss X into the "commitment" phase of self-changing. She actually has committed herself to two goals (to solve the sweating problem and to feel comfortable in confined spaces such as aeroplanes), though only one has been discussed openly.

Open up the client's model of the world. Through most of the first session, Erickson is teaching Miss X how to relax, how to go into a trance and trust that her unconscious mind can take care of her. He begins by having her allow her hand to float up unconsciously. Having shown her that her unconscious mind controls her hands, he then points out that, in the time since she has been in a trance, her hands are hardly sweating at all. He says, "Do you think you could make a puddle now?" She says, "I could give you a little stream." But she is unable to. Erickson comments, "Looks like your poorest performance on record." She agrees. "I can't understand it," she says (pp. 186–7). At this stage, Erickson is simply demonstrating that she can change. He summarises, "And you are really becoming aware of how effectively your unconscious mind can control you." (P. 202.) This sequence acts as a "preparatory task" testing her commitment to change, in terms of the self-change model.

Leading (change process). In the second session, Erickson has Miss X go into a trance again, and tells her a series of stories suggesting that there is some secret that her unconscious mind knows, that will solve this problem for her. At one point, she says of her hand's sweating, "It is as if at any moment this sort of sign emerges that I am not what I seem or something like that." Erickson picks up on this important hint and says, "That you are not what you seem. And what exactly is that big lie? Do you know it? Have you fully admitted it to yourself?" (P. 223.) She says that she will admit it "later" and, when Erickson asks her how much later, she says, "In fifteen minutes." But, before that time is up, she suddenly announces, "I never did want to be a harpist." She says that her dad wanted her to be a concert harpist, but she just wanted to play for herself. Erickson says, "Now why did you have wet hands?" (This is a question that presupposes that the problem is solved.) She replies, "I know why. So I wouldn't have to play." (Pp. 227–8.) A flood of understandings then pour out about her family, including the memory that when she was little her brother locked her in a closet, and that this was the origin of her claustrophobia. This stage represents the actual "change process" or the "action" stage in self-change terms.

Verify change. After this change process is complete, Erickson confirms with Miss X that she has indeed changed. He asks her, "How

121

do you feel about it – in two days' time learning all this about your-self?" (P. 229.) Whatever she answers, she will have confirmed that she has indeed been "learning all this". She is moving into the "maintenance" stage of self-change.

Ecological exit. Ecology is the study of consequences. As Milton Erickson finishes his second session, he wants to check that Miss X can imagine herself living with dry hands and without anxiety in aeroplanes. He is checking if there are any other consequences of this change, and says, "You have had lots of practice having sweat-ing. Now you can have ahead of you a little practice of being dry-handed and hot-handed. Now, is there any more help that you want?" She replies, "No, right now I have a compelling need to run to the airport and catch the first plane out." This confirms again that her anxiety problems are over (p. 229). Knowing that he has led her to rediscover some significant and not entirely pleasant memories, Erickson asks, "Any anger at me for uncomfortness?" She says "No" and arranges to send him a Christmas card to let him know how things go (pp. 230–2). This sequence completes the "maintenance" phase of self-change, and prepares her for "recy-cling" the process as needed.

The RESOLVE Model

1. Resourceful state for the practitioner

Let's review these steps in more detail. First, what do I mean by "Resourceful state"? Like Erickson, the effective NLP practitioner begins the session confident of their ability to utilise the approach of NLP, and clear about their role in relation to the client.

In the 1960s and 1970s, two counselling developers, Robert Carkhuff and Bernard Berenson, published a number of research studies showing that helping interactions tend to influence clients either for better *or* for worse. They identified several measures of successful human functioning, and showed that helpers who func-tion well on these dimensions are able to assist others to function well on these dimensions too. Helpers who function poorly on these dimensions actually influence clients to deteriorate in their functioning (Carkhuff and Berenson, 1977, p. 5, p. 35)! Carkhuff and Berenson likened most psychotherapists to professional life-guards with extensive training in rowing a boat, throwing a ring buoy, and giving artificial respiration, but without the ability to swim. "They cannot save another because, given the same circumstances, they could not save themselves."

Effective NLP practitioners are those who have learned to swim! They have used NLP processes to access resourceful states themselves, so they convey congruently to clients that change is possible. They anchor themselves into positive states of curiosity, fun and creativity when they work with clients. They build rapport without getting caught in the same patterns their clients are accessing. They also have the following understandings and attitudes (see Dilts, 1998, pp. 7–10):

- The map is not the territory. The client's map of how events happen is only a map – and so is the NLP map used by the consultant.   *↳ A REPRESENTATION*
- "Resistance" to suggestions simply indicates the need for more adequate rapport building, and for designing suggestions that pace the client's "map" and inner world more fully.
- People's actions are always motivated by a positive intention simply to meet their needs, as a system, as they identify those needs at the time. Their actions are based on the best choices available to them at the time, and expanding their choices can enhance their future actions. Another way of saying this is that every neural network in a person's brain was originally developed to assist meeting the goals of the brain itself.
- A person is in charge of their own internal images, sounds, sensations, tastes, smells and what they say to themselves. As a result, they are in charge of the emotional state generated by these "internal representations". This is as opposed to the belief that someone else, such as their family, or the therapist, is in charge of their state. In NLP, being in charge of one's own responses is often called being "at cause".
- People already have the resources they need, and the role of the consultant is to help them access these resources and apply them where they are needed. Using the neurological-network model, our task is to help people take skills and learnings stored in effective neural networks and connect them to neural networks where problem states are stored.

- Human beings are systems, where change in one part affects the whole. All change work needs to consider the ecological results on the person's body, psychological life, spiritual life and social life.
- All results, both "positive" and "negative", are useful feedback to enable you to adjust your next communication. In that sense, in NLP terms, there is no "failure", only feedback.
- Change is easy. It's not "changing" that takes time: it's "not-changing" that takes time.
- The expectations of the consultant profoundly affect what is possible for the client.

How do we summarise this attitude, which is at the heart of NLP? There is a word in English to describe helping which is based on:

- respecting the other person's model of the world
- seeking change that will be good for them as a whole human being
- believing that the person has basic good intentions
- believing that the person has the resources they need to change

That word is "love". The attitude of love is more important than the specific skills that the NLP practitioner draws on. Love cannot be faked therapeutically – our clients are far too perceptive for that to work. Love is not merely rapport, though effective rapport is an expression of love. Love is not merely the ability to focus on positive aspects of a client's exploration, though that too is an expression of love. Love is more than just an attitude, more than just a strategy or a Meta-program. It is the reason why most of us came into the therapy field in the first place. I begin every therapy session by remembering that.

Being a consultant

From an NLP perspective, there are risks with the traditional role of a "counsellor" or "psychotherapist". In their search for a term not tainted by the expectations of "counsellor" and "psychotherapist", Carkhuff and Berenson (1977) used the term "helper".

Their concern was based on some important research. For example, in 1951, E. Powers and H. Witmer published one of the most extensive and well-designed studies of the results of counselling and therapy, "An Experiment in the Prevention of Delinquency". In this study 650 high-risk boys aged six to ten were chosen and grouped into pairs based on various demographic variables. One of each pair was then assigned to counselling (either client-centred or psychoanalytic), and linked up to support services such as the YMCA. After an average five years of counselling, the boys were followed up. Counsellors rated two-thirds of the boys in their care as having "benefited substantially" from the counselling, and the boys agreed, saying it gave them more insight and kept them out of trouble.

Such is success, isn't it? Well, except for one detail. The treated boys were more likely to have committed more than one serious crime, had higher rates of alcoholism, mental illness, stress-related illness and lower job satisfaction than those left untreated. This remained true at thirty-year follow-up, and the researchers lamely suggest that there "must be" some positive benefits, but they were unable to find them. Just because counsellors believe that counselling "feels good", it doesn't mean it helps. This 1951 study demonstrates the risks of dependency-producing models of treatment in general. The boys and their therapists valued "their relationship", but it did not empower the boys to change: it disabled them (Zilbergeld 1983, pp. 132–4).

Often, when our clients come to us for "therapy", they are hoping that we can "rescue" them from their lives. Consider, as an example, depression. Others in the depressed person's life have tried to rescue them from depression. They may have tried to cheer them up, to give them gifts of time and objects, to take the load off their shoulders, to convince them that life is worthwhile, to defend them against those who demand more of them … But one human being cannot *make* another human being happy. In the end, these attempts only lead the rescuer to become more resentful, and the depressed person to feel worse. Rescue is a dangerous game, leading to increased risk of suicide as the depressed person seeks ever more frantically to indicate their need for more help, or to prove that the help has not worked. To repeat, one person cannot *make* another person feel good, even when that one person knows all the tricks of NLP. The depressed person's belief that they need another person to save them *is* depression. It is not a side effect. Cooperating with it would be keeping them depressed.

As another example, the anxious person wants to avoid anxiety. The "simple" solution to anxiety for the person with a spider phobia seems to be never to think about or come into contact with anything to do with spiders. For the person with anxiety about loss of self-control the "simple" solution would be never to be in a situation where loss of self-control was remotely possible. Of course these are impossible goals, but many people with anxiety clutch at the illusion of such solutions in the form of drugs, distractions, lifestyles totally organised around their fears and dependent relationships where the other person cannot be out of their sight or reach. What is usually called "secondary gain" (the accidental advantages that the problem brings to the person's life, in terms of sympathy, avoidance of challenges etc.) is really primary gain in anxiety conditions. It is often the immediate aim of the person who has anxiety. As an NLP consultant, I have to get clear first of all that my role is not to create such illusory solutions. One example of an illusory solution would be presenting NLP as a series of tools that will *automatically* solve the person's problem, regardless of what they do. Another example would be offering to be the person's total life-support system ("Call me any time!"). Being a "magician" can be very satisfying, but this satisfaction is small compared with the joy of empowering the anxious person to learn their own magic.

The depressed or anxious person is hiring me as a consultant (like a consultant in the business setting) to give them advice and support to put into action a plan that will change their life. If it is to work, this will be a collaborative relationship, in which they will need not only to "help", but also to follow experimentally the advice the consultant gives. I have no magic way of solving their problems for them. But, if they do the things I suggest, I believe that they will experience change. I often say, "NLP doesn't work. *You* work ... NLP just explains how you work, perfectly." The other side of this is that, if I am not hired as a consultant, I accept that. I do not carry on trying to "sell my services".

A consultant in a business context is hired to suggest strategies to enable clients to meet their goals. There are several implications to this arrangement, which I consider appropriate to the NLP setting:

- Consultants have some expertise in the area where they recommend changes, as well as some expertise in cooperating with clients.
- Consultants need to be "hired" either formally or informally. That is, they offer their expertise in response to a request. They are not just people who enjoy interfering in others' lives.
- Consultants elicit, clarify and work towards *clients'* goals, not towards their own.
- Clients are in charge of their own business. They are responsible for actioning all the consultants' suggestions – or not. Without this action, consultants' work is recognised to be of little significance.
- Consultants are paid for their work. They are expected to use time efficiently, particularly if they are paid an hourly rate.
- Consultants are in charge of the process of consulting; clients are in charge of the content of their business.
- Consultants operate with certain explicit professional guidelines, such as confidentiality, and avoidance of double relationships (e.g. combining a consulting relationship with a sexual relationship) with clients. In return they expect their clients to operate with some guidelines such as turning up to arranged meetings on time.

Adopting this consultant role is itself a therapeutic step. As I spell out for my clients what kind of relationship I want, I am modelling healthy relating for them. I am also treating them as if they are "at cause" in their life, rather than a helpless victim. The NLP attitude and the consulting role are conveyed very simply at the beginning of any encounter.

An example of resourceful state

As we explore the RESOLVE model, I want to give an example from the work of the NLP co-developer Richard Bandler. In this example session, Bandler works with Susan, who suffers panic attacks in which she imagines that people in her family may have died in a car accident (Bandler, 1984, pp. 1–31). Bandler begins the session much as Milton Erickson did in our previous example, by asking Susan to tell him what she wants him to do, and explaining that he is not a magician (p. 5).

Bandler says, "Okay, Susan. Now why don't you tell me what it is that you would like? I don't know. We just got brought here and wired up, so you have to give me a hint."

As Susan replies, she is accepting the roles Bandler has defined. She has begun contributing her share to the process of change. This simple statement by Bandler communicates much of the attitude of the NLP consultant, as described above.

2. Establish rapport

The developers of NLP noted that the chances that a helper would be able to lead someone to change their strategy were increased when the helper elegantly joined the person's reality first. "When you join someone else's reality by pacing them, that gives you rapport and trust, and puts you in a position to utilise their reality in ways that change it." (Bandler and Grinder, 1979, p. 81.) For example, one of the strategies that often help create anxiety is to make scary internal visual images. If I talk with the visually anxious person about what they can *see* as they sit beside me, there is an increased chance that, when I gradually shift my comments to talk more about kinaesthetic relaxation, the person will follow this lead into the new strategy of relaxation (Yapko, 1981). Examination of films and videotapes of therapy sessions and other conversations by communication researchers (Ivey et al., 1996, p. 60; Condon 1982, pp. 53–76; Hatfield et al., 1994) now confirms the significance of what researchers call "interactional synchrony" or "movement complementarity". This same process is variously referred to in the NLP literature (e.g. Bolstad and Hamblett, 1998, pp. 68–72) as "nonverbal matching", "pacing" or "rapport skills".

What are these nonverbal rapport skills? NLP developers propose that when conversation flows smoothly, people breathe in time with each other, and coordinate their body movements as well as their voice tonality and speed. The more this matching of behaviour happens, the more the other person gets a sense of shared understanding and at-one-ness or "rapport". Also, the more this matching happens, the more the other person will be open to useful suggestions, and adopt the emotional responses of the helper or therapist. All learning and change depends on this willingness of the client to be open to new responses.

William Condon has meticulously studied videotapes of conversations, confirming these patterns. He found that in a successful conversation, movements such as a smile or a head nod are matched by the other person within a fifteenth of a second. Within minutes of beginning the conversation, the volume, pitch and speech rate (number of sounds per minute) of the people's voices match each other. This is correlated with a synchronising of the type and rate of breathing. Even general body posture is adjusted over the conversation so that the people appear to match or mirror each other. Elaine Hatfield, John Cacioppo and Richard Rapson, in their book *Emotional Contagion*, show that matching another person's behaviour in these detailed ways results in the transfer of emotional states from one person to another. If I feel happy, and you match my breathing, voice, gestures and smiles, you will begin to feel the same emotional state. This is the source of empathy, and also of much therapeutic change.

What does this mean for us as consultants? First, it means that we benefit from developing the skills of breathing in time with clients, adjusting our voice tonality to match theirs, and adjusting our posture and gestures to match theirs. Second, it emphasises the importance, once the sense of rapport has been established, of having the flexibility to shift gradually back to a healthy and resourceful style of breathing, speaking and acting. The purpose of getting in rapport with our clients is then to assist them to move towards their goals – a process called in NLP "pacing and leading".

By revealing the nonverbal basis of rapport, NLP has been able to add considerably to the skills that a helper uses to convey empathy. Research identifying the effectiveness of *verbal* pacing (reflective listening, restating what the person said) first emerged in 1950, and a summary of the fifty years of continuing evidence for this core helping skill is presented by Allen Bergin and Sol Garfield (1994) in their *Handbook of Psychotherapy*. Building rapport in NLP terms also includes pacing the person's core Meta-programs and values as these are revealed. Clients have been shown, for example, to prefer a counsellor whose word use matches their own representational system (visual, auditory, kinaesthetic or auditory-digital) by a ratio of *three to one* (Brockman, 1980)! This means choosing whether you say, for instance, "So the way you see things ..." or "So it sounds like this experience is telling you ..." or "So your feeling is ...". Any emotional state can be described using metaphors from any of the sensory systems. Sadness can be acknowledged by saying, "Life looks pretty gloomy to you just now" or "The music seems to have gone out of your life just now" or "Life has been dragging you down just lately". An experience of anger can be acknowledged by saying, "You saw red" or "Something was screaming inside you" or "You felt like you blew a fuse".

Building rapport is also enhanced by the use of "artfully vague" language (i.e. use of the NLP Milton model patterns), and a study by Darrell Hischke showed positive effects on rapport from both representational system matching and nonspecific language. Chunking up verbally to generalised descriptions is the structure of agreement. When I talk in a generalised way, I am less likely to "mismatch" the client's own model of the world.

The process of building rapport, described here, is not merely a prelude to helping. It is by itself a therapeutic intervention. In a series of studies from the 1950s, Fred Fiedler (1951) showed that successful therapists from a number of different therapeutic orientations tended to use empathic restatement of the client's concern more than any other intervention. This marked them out from unsuccessful therapists so much that what they said had more in common with other effective therapists than with others in their own school of therapy. Five decades of research has tended to support Fiedler's conclusion (Lambert and Bergin, 1994, p. 181).

The type of reflective statement that will be useful varies depending on how fully the practitioner has succeeded in establishing rapport already. Early on, replies that match the client's conscious experience (as expressed in their words) will be most acceptable. Later on, replies that match the client's semiconscious values, beliefs and evolving sense of identity will be accepted and may be more powerful (Carkhuff, 1973). Consider the following client situation and statement.

A mother is talking about her relationship with her seventeen-year-old son. She has discussed his use of illegal drugs and her attempts to caution him about the dangers of these. She has teary eyes and looks down, shaking her head as she speaks. "He knows he can get away with it; that's the thing. If he just stays in his room and sulks for a couple of days, I just about go crazy with worry. Eventually, he gets whatever he wants – permission to go out with his friends, use of the car. In the end, I give in, and I know it's my own fault. I can hardly blame him, when I'm so inconsistent."

Reflective listening to this message could acknowledge:

- Key words stated by the client. Example: "Inconsistent" or "You worry".
- Simple facts reported by the client. Example: "So at the start you tell him he can't have what he wants, but if he continues, that concern leads you to give in and let him have it."
- The emotional state of the client as surmised from behaviour and statements. Example: "You feel so worried, and you feel upset and guilty; is that right?"
- The facts and the emotional state that they have triggered. Example: "You feel worried about what he's up to, and you feel disappointed in yourself for giving in to him too? Is that it?"
- A summary of the client's story so far. Example: "So there are several levels to this problem. There are things like the drug taking that you've been concerned about. And then there's the interaction between the two of you as you try to stop those other problems and end up giving in to him. Right?"
- The client's outcome. Example: "Are you saying you'd like to find some way that you can be more consistent, and less swayed by his behaviour?"
- Dilemmas or incongruities implied by the client's statements and/or behaviour. Example: "Let me check this, then. Sounds like an internal conflict. On the one hand, you worry about him and want him to be happy. On the other hand, you'd like to be more assertive and stick to your own decisions, even if that results in conflict. Does that make sense to you?"

- The deeper significance or meaning of the experiences reported by the client. Example: "I get the impression that the person that you feel *most* disappointed with at those times is actually yourself. The issue you're dealing with sounds like it's also about your taking charge of your *own* life and being more certain about what you want. Is that close?"

While the later replies in this list invite a deeper response, any of these replies has a good chance of communicating to the client that she is understood and that the NLP practitioner recognises her own positive intentions. The purpose of reflective listening is partially to reassure the person that they are not being blamed, judged or controlled by the consultant. This metacommunication creates a safe environment for the client to explore their dilemmas and begin to identify their own outcome (the next step of the RESOLVE model after this). At the same time, these replies are far from "nondirective". They all share a similar focus or "frame". Part of this "frame" is the focusing on the client's own responses, rather than the behaviour of other people (such as her son). A metacommunication of this client-centred focus is that the aim of consulting is to help her change her *own* responses, to take charge of her *own* maps and state, to be "at cause".

An example of establishing rapport

Richard Bandler, working in our example case with Susan, uses pacing statements and generalised language at the start of his interview, for example (Bandler, 1984, p. 7).

> Susan: It's a fear of losing friendships or close relationships. Even when I anticipate a loss that isn't even real I get a panic attack.

> Richard: The situation that you are worried about being in is the one of anticipating and thinking about the loss?

These simple checks assure Susan that Bandler understands her concern. This makes it safer for him playfully to challenge her later in the process of change.

3. SPECIFY *outcome*

Once rapport is established, chunking down to detailed plans becomes very significant. While using vague language helps to build a feeling of rapport, the ongoing use of vague language is part of the system by which many clients maintain their problem. For example, Thomas Macroy (1998) found that when family communication was analysed in terms of the NLP metamodel, those families who were most dissatisfied were also using the most deletions, distortions and generalisations in their language (especially deletions). Research on the Solution-Focused Therapy model (a model closely allied with NLP) confirms that clients improve after questions from their helper that focus on what outcome the client has. Also, the amount of discussion of solutions and outcomes in the first session is strongly correlated to the chances that the client will continue with the change process (Miller et al., 1996, p. 259). William Miller has done an overview of the research into successful psychotherapy, in which he identifies that enabling the client to set their own goal for therapy significantly increases their commitment to therapy and enhances the results (Miller, 1985).

There are two steps to this process. The first (sorting outcomes) involves identifying one outcome or more from the array of problem-based information the client presents. This sorting process includes asking solution-focused questions to shift their sorting from problems to solutions. It also includes checking which outcomes will be easiest or most significant to deal with first in this session.

Questions to discover and sort outcomes
Setting a successful outcome involves more active participation from the consultant than building rapport did. Whereas my focus in rapport building is on reflective listening (pacing), my focus in this section is on asking precise questions. Steve de Shazer, Insoo Kim Berg and others have developed a model of change called the Solution-Focused approach, based on this understanding (Chevalier, 1995). Following are some examples of their questions, which guide the person to identify what they want and how to get it. Where someone has an "adverse reaction" to the use of "official change techniques", I have used solution-focused questions as the

full consulting process. As de Shazer reports, this results in 75 per cent success over four to six sessions. That is to say, setting an outcome is itself a change process.

First, I help the person to clarify which is the most important issue to work with. For example, I might ask:

- "What is this problem an example of?"
- "What other examples are there of this larger issue?"
- "Which of these issues will, when you solve it, let you know that all the others can be solved?"
- "Which of these will be the easiest for you to change first?"

Second, I ask questions that help the client shift from thinking about problems to thinking about solutions. For example:

- "What has to be different as a result of your talking to me?"
- "What do you want to achieve?"
- "How will you know that this problem is solved?"
- "What would need to happen for you to feel that this problem was solved?"
- "When this problem is solved, what will you be doing and feeling instead of what you used to do and feel?"

It is also possible to guide someone into a solution or outcome framework by simply reflecting their problem statement as a goal. Simplistically, if a person says, "I'm hungry" I can restate with, "You'd like something to eat". Similarly, if they say, "I feel really lonely in my life; I don't get to meet new people and it seems like I'm always by myself" I could reply, "You'd like to learn new ways of meeting people and create a life where you feel more in contact". If the person responds to this statement by talking more about their problem, then I may simply accept that we have not completed the "Establish Rapport" phase yet. In NLP terms, any "resistance" to my leading onward is an indication of inadequate pacing or rapport.

Third, I ask about when the problem doesn't occur (the "exceptions"). For example:

- "When is a time that you noticed this problem wasn't quite as bad?"
- "What was happening at that time? What were you doing different?"

If the person tells me there are no exceptions, then I ask about hypothetical exceptions using the "miracle" question: "Suppose one night there is a miracle while you're sleeping, and this problem is solved. Since you're sleeping, you don't know that a miracle has happened or that your problem is solved. What do you suppose you will notice that's different in the morning, that will let you know the problem is solved?" After the miracle question, I can ask other follow-up questions such as:

- "What would other people around you notice was different about you?"
- "What would other people around you do differently then?"
- "What would it take to pretend that this miracle had happened?"

SPECIFYing the outcome

The second part of setting an outcome is to ensure that the person's goal is described in a way that enables it to be reached. For each goal that we decide to work with, I check that the outcome we are setting is "well formed". This is an NLP term meaning that it is described in sensory-specific terms, that its consequences for the rest of the person's life are known, and that the person is taking responsibility for initiating the process of change towards the goal. To summarise the list of possible questions, I use the acronym SPECIFY. While not all the aspects of this SPECIFY model need active questioning in each case, the practitioner has this model in mind as they assess the outcome being set. By identifying the first step the person would take to change, and by inviting them to access relevant resourceful states, the NLP practitioner is also beginning the process of change. Setting an outcome is not something we do *before* helping someone change. Setting an outcome and changing are better viewed as two aspects of the same system.

Sensory-specific. "What, specifically, will you see/hear/feel when you have this outcome?"

Positive language. "If you don't have the old problem, what is it that you will have?"

Ecological. "What else will change when you have this outcome?" "What situations do you want this outcome in and what situations do you not want it to affect?"

Choice increases with this outcome. "Does this outcome increase your choices?"

Initiated by self. "What do *you* personally need to do to achieve this?"

First step identified and achievable. "What is your first step?"

Your resources identified. "What inner resources do you have that will help you to achieve this outcome?"

Let me give you an example from my work with a client named Andrew. When Andrew came to see me, he said, "I want to stop getting anxious when I'm talking to a woman I find attractive."

A. SENSORY-SPECIFIC

First, I asked Andrew, "Exactly when do you plan to have achieved that goal?" That kind of surprised him. Many people still think of personal change as a hit-or-miss affair: "maybe in a year I'll be different", kind of thing. Andrew decided that "a month from now" would be better. Next I told him, "Step into your body a month from now, with this goal achieved. What do you see that's different? What do you hear? What do you feel differently?" Just answering this question caused Andrew to involve all his sensory systems. Right away he said he felt more confident that it could happen.

B. POSITIVE LANGUAGE

One of the things that Andrew said would be different was, "I don't have that voice telling me I'm a failure." Often when people set a goal, they say what they *don't* want. In the brain this doesn't work so well. Here's how I explained it to him: "Andrew, let me show you something about how the brain works. *Don't* think of a blue tree. Got that? *Don't* think of a blue tree. Keep not thinking of a blue tree. Now, what are you thinking of?" He laughed. "A blue tree!" he said.

"Right," I agreed. "If you want your brain to achieve your goal, the way to do it is to tell it what it *will* think of, not what it *won't*. If you tell it don't get anxious, in order to *understand* what you're saying it has to *think* about getting anxious. To get it to *stop*, you tell it, '*Do* get relaxed.'"

"OK," he said, "my goal is to feel relaxed when I'm talking to a woman I find attractive. And when I think of it in sensory-specific ways, I guess I hear my internal voice telling me how well I'm doing … Wow, *that's* weird. That's a whole new experience."

C. ECOLOGICAL

That was exactly what I wanted to check next. We needed to know that this goal was safe for Andrew in every way. What consequences that he might not have thought of could result if he changed. In NLP we call this being "ecological", using a metaphor from the consequences of environmental change. Before European settlement, 70 per cent of New Zealand was covered in forest. Enthusiastic settlers with powerful goals (personal wealth, farming lifestyles, national prosperity and so forth) have reduced this percentage to 22. It's an impressive example of the power of a dream with a use-by date. *And* the biggest petition ever presented to New Zealand's parliament was the 1977 Maruia declaration: 341,000 New Zealanders calling for a halt to the cutting of native forests (McVarish, 1992). They represent the concern about *the consequences of reaching our goals*. It's the same with internal goals.

I asked Andrew, "What other things will change if you achieve this goal? Especially, what benefits do you get from being anxious with those people that might be at risk if you change?"

"Hmm." He nodded. "I guess being anxious means I don't get into any close relationships with women. If I was relaxed, I might have to learn a lot about commitment and things like that."

"Is there any time you don't want to be relaxed with an attractive woman?"

He shook his head. "I don't think so. Maybe I'd still want to be careful about what I say. I mean, at least, being anxious, I don't make a fool of myself as much!"

"OK. So that's two things about the consequences which you want to incorporate into your goal. You want to still be careful to say appropriate things, and you'll be learning some new skills for dealing with the possibility of a relationship. Is that right?" He nodded.

D. CHOICE INCREASES

What I'm really checking with the questions about ecology is that choice increases with this goal. Some people have had the idea that change means getting rid of a bad choice: "How can I take away the choice of getting drunk?", for example. Instead, I believe that real change means increasing *good* choices, so the person simply won't bother using the old one. "How can you find some new choices for relaxing and having fun with people that are so exciting that the idea of getting drunk just bores you?" I want to check that Andrew is adding a new choice. He could always choose not to talk to a woman he's attracted to; he just has more options.

E. INITIATED BY SELF

Successful goal-setters work out what *they'll* do that's different, not what everyone else ought to do. Andrew can spend all day *wishing* that people he talks to would put him "at ease". The question is, what will *he* do to start things changing.

F. FIRST STEP IDENTIFIED AND ACHIEVABLE

How many times have you heard a smoker tell you they'll give up next year? It's a great goal, but what they need are small, achievable steps along the way. When someone sets a goal, I always ask them: "What small first step will you take *today*?" Andrew might ring up a friend and arrange to go out to a nightclub this weekend. He might take the time to identify what's different between his strategy for feeling relaxed with certain people and his strategy for getting anxious with others. He might contact a friend who seems to be really successful with this situation and find out how they do it. He might get a book from the library from which to get ideas. He might book another session with an NLP practitioner.

G. YOUR RESOURCES IDENTIFIED

As he thinks of each of the possibilities for a first step, what Andrew is also doing is identifying the resources he has to change. These include:

- strategies that work for him in other situations
- role models who have the skills he wants
- support systems: people who can give encouragement
- information sources
- personal change skills
- time and money he has available to put into the above things

An example of specifying the outcome

In his work with Susan's anticipatory anxiety, Richard Bandler checks carefully that she has a sensory-specific and ecological outcome. When she first tells him that fear is her problem, he asks her, "Is the fear appropriate?" This is checking the ecology of making this change (Bandler, 1984, p. 7). She tells him it's not, and says she wants some distance from her problem. He checks her outcome more fully to elicit a clear description of what it would be like for her to be changed (p. 16):

> Richard: If you were to have distance how would you know you had it?

> Susan: Well I believe I wouldn't feel those feelings. I'd have confidence, some self-confidence and I think I could say to myself, well, just because they're not here now doesn't mean that you've lost them and it really doesn't matter. Maybe something happened. And also you can go on. So what if they don't show up. You can go on.

4. Open up the client's model of the world

More of the "art" of changework happens at this next stage in consulting than at any other. The one core factor in the client's "personality" that reliably predicts how well they will respond to the change process is whether they experience themselves as having an internal locus of control. Clients who believe that they are in charge of their own responses ("at cause", to use the NLP jargon) do far better in numerous research studies with a variety of different models of therapy (Miller et al., 1996, pp. 319, 325). Furthermore, research shows that this sense of being in control is not a stable "quality" that some clients have and others do not. It varies over the course of their interaction with the helper. Successful therapy has been shown to result first in a shift in the "locus of control", and then in the desired success (Miller et al., 1996, p. 326). In their study of NLP psychotherapy, Martina Genser-Medlitsch and Peter Schütz in Vienna (1997) found that NLP clients scored higher than controls in their perception of themselves as in control of their lives (with a difference at 10 per cent significance level).

Dealing first with this Meta-level change dramatically increases your chances of enabling someone to change. There are three steps to putting someone "at cause" with their situation. These are (1) demonstrating the general possibility of change, (2) demonstrating the specific possibility of changing the client's current problem and (3) demonstrating the possibility of using a selected, specific change technique to change that problem. The first step is to give a concrete physical demonstration of change happening easily and quickly as a result of changing internal representations.

For example, I have every client do a visualisation exercise near the start of their session. They turn around and point behind them with their arm, and then come back to the front. Next they imagine themselves going further, and notice what they would see, feel and say to themselves if their body was more flexible and they could turn around further. Then, keeping their feet in the same place, they turn around again and notice how much further they can go, instantly and without any extra effort (Bolstad and Hamblett, 1998, p. 81). Another example of a simple demonstration of change is the lemon visualisation from near the start of the book. In this, you may remember, I say:

"Think of a fresh lemon. Imagine one in front of you now, and feel what it feels like as you pick it up. Take a knife and cut a slice off the lemon, and hear the slight sound as the juice squirts out. Smell the lemon as you lift the slice to your mouth and take a bite of the slice. Experience the sharp taste of the fruit.

"If you actually imagined doing that, you mouth is now salivating. Why? Because your brain followed your instructions and thought about, saw, heard, felt, smelled and tasted the lemon. By recalling sensory information, you re-created the entire experience of the lemon, so that your body responded to the lemon you created."

Loosening a strategy

To demonstrate the possibility of changing this client's specific problem, I want to show them that their problem has a strategy (a sequence of internal representations that creates the result they have been getting). I will access, elicit and experimentally alter the person's problem strategy:

a. *Pre-test the strategy.* Tad James (1995, p. 28) emphasised that the process of helping someone change (like all strategies) involves a test before the change intervention and a related test after the intervention. I ask, "When you think about it now, can you get back enough of a sense of that problem so you'd know if that changed?" Until they can, it would be risky to go on. After all, how will they know whether they've succeeded? Of course, some people say they get the problem only in a certain situation. I tend to say, with an air of conviction, "OK, let's go there now!" Once we have a pretested response from this comment, I can more easily check what's different later on, in our post-test, to verify the change.

b. *Elicit the strategy.* I say, "Wow! That's impressive. How do you do that? How do you know it's time to start?" These questions presuppose that the client "does" something. By answering them, the client has established that, if a change process didn't work, it's because they are still "doing" the old behaviour well enough to get the problem. The whole stage of opening up the person's model of the world is a process of reframing, of Meta-level change preparing for the simple shifting of the strategies, which happens next.

c. *Have the person dissociate from and experimentally alter the strategy.* I ask, "What if I changed that strategy in this small way. Would it still work?" Answering this question requires the person to rehearse a different strategy, and experimentally change their old way of behaving.

Preframing change techniques
The third step of this stage is to preframe the specific change techniques identified as useful by the consultant. This includes answering the question, "How does this technique relate to my problem and my outcome?", (in other words "Why are we doing this?"), and the question "Does this technique work?" Stories of other clients who have benefited from the change technique are an elegant way to answer both questions, as well as rehearsing the client through the process.

Each type of change technique is based on certain assumptions, which are discussed from the practitioner's point of view in Chapter 3. It is easy to assume that our clients share these assumptions, which we may easily take for granted after using the techniques so many times. For example, the following preframes are useful before making an intervention in each of the ten categories we saw at the beginning of Chapter 3. These may be introduced by demonstrations such as the pointing exercise, by metaphorical stories, by giving examples of clients' use of the process, by presupposing them, or by directly teaching them.

ANCHORING
- An anchor is a stimulus from any sense that evokes a whole experience
- Every emotional and behavioural response is anchored
- Anchoring is continuous and normal; everyone does it
- Anchors last until reanchored
- Everyone has positive states which can be accessed and anchored
- An anchor is best set when a strong state is being experienced
- An anchor needs to be unique and repeatable in the desired situation

INSTALLING A STRATEGY
- Emotional states are a result of the order of internal represen-tations we make
- Strategies are learned and can be changed quickly
- Once strategies are changed they tend to stay changed
- Strategies that work in one area of life can be transferred to another area
- Strategies run automatically once they are triggered
- Every strategy has a trigger
- Any repeated interruption to a strategy becomes part of that strategy

CHANGING SUBMODALITIES
- Emotional states are a result of the internal representations we make
- Submodalities are like a "bar code" of the brain
- Changing submodalities changes the "meaning" and feeling of experiences
- Everyone has positive states from which the submodalities can be elicited
- Certain submodalities have certain reliable results (e.g. associ-ation/dissociation)
- Once submodalities are changed, they tend to stay changed

TRANCEWORK
- Each person has an unconscious mind
- The unconscious mind communicates with every cell in the body
- It's OK for the unconscious to manage many things itself
- The unconscious mind is ideodynamic (ideas are expressed in actions)
- The unconscious mind is ideosensory (ideas are expressed in sensory experience)
- The unconscious can communicate using ideodynamic methods
- The unconscious mind aims to follow your "instructions" (ideodynamicism)
- You can trust that you have unconscious skills, understandings and resources

PARTS INTEGRATION

- "Parts" of the mind exist, often unconsciously, with their own intentions
- All parts are created within the one brain and so all were created by us
- Every part has a higher positive intention, which matches our own intentions
- If a part can find a better way to meet its own outcome, it will choose that way
- You can trust that you have unconscious skills, understandings and resources
- It's more useful for the brain to function as one integrated unit
- The unconscious mind is ideodynamic (ideas are expressed in actions)

TIME-LINE CHANGES

- You have an unconscious mind
- The unconscious mind is ideodynamic (ideas are expressed in actions)
- The unconscious mind is ideosensory (ideas are expressed in sensory experience)
- Emotions are coded based on the time perspective
- The unconscious mind has access to a "time line" where you store memories
- Memories are synthetic rather than 100 per cent real
- The meaning or emotional response to memories is especially synthetic
- Memories with similar emotions are connected by the brain
- Changing your memories changes your way of experiencing the present

LINGUISTIC REFRAMING

- Words trigger changes in the brain
- Events do not have meanings in themselves: *people* make meanings
- "The map is not the territory"
- Meanings that open up more choices are useful
- Changing meanings changes emotional states and behaviours

CHANGING INTERPERSONAL DYNAMICS
- Our behaviours exist only as arcs in systems that involve other people
- Changing the way we relate changes the way we feel
- People are always doing the best they can with the resources they can access
- The meaning of communication is the response you get
- Each person acts to meet their own needs/outcomes
- It is useful to be able to see, hear, feel and speak about sensory experience
- Conflicts are normal and can be resolved so everyone's needs are met

CHANGING PHYSIOLOGICAL CONTEXTS
- The mind and body are one system
- We can use feedback loops to alter brain functioning by altering physiology
- The brain attempts to heal itself naturally
- Changing physiology changes emotional responses

TASKING
- Change happens as a result of action, not as a result of hoping for it
- Each person is "at cause" in their own life
- The aim of consulting is to give the client, not the consultant, control
- We can learn from actions that do not, at the time, make conscious sense
- Any change causes the whole system to change

The client quite often believes that consulting is simply a conscious process of transmitting information. They may assume that if this information could be given more quickly, they would have changed more. To use a metaphorical example, nowadays all the sacred writings of the East are available for the beginning student to read. Does this mean more people experience the beneficial results of yoga or meditation? Occasionally, it does, but mostly it means that lots of people have "premature closure" about these subjects. They think they know them because they've read the book; and they've closed their mind to further learning. As Paul Watzlawick says, this is like a student musician saying, "Piano playing does not exist. I have tried it several times and nothing came of it."

The fact is that piano playing, meditation and any other new strategies are not learned merely consciously. That would be like transferring the text from computer to computer, and expecting the text to run without a program to run it. Or it would be like transferring a text from the old DOS operating system and expecting it to run in Windows 2000. All that "unconscious" backup (beliefs, values, Meta-programs and types of awareness) is essential to learning.

When clients try to pick up the information without getting the underlying *state* and the presuppositions that make the information work, they don't achieve their outcome. Effective consulting means ensuring clients receive these backups with the information. Whenever a client demonstrates that they have not taken on board part of this fundamental "operating system" the consultant's task is to guide them through some series of internal representations (visualising or looking at something, listening to sounds, feeling feelings, doing something physically, or talking to themselves, for example) which installs the backup, the "frame" within which the information makes sense. This process is sometimes called "reframing".

For example, when I use hypnotherapy, I use certain specific techniques for communicating with a client's unconscious mind. A client will occasionally ask me, "What do you mean by the term 'unconscious mind'? Unconscious means out to it, like in a coma. Either my mind is working, in which case I'm conscious, or it isn't, in which case I'm unconscious. I don't see how you can communicate with what is unconscious." When I hear this question, I'm aware that something of the backup for using hypnotherapy, the operating system, is missing. This backup includes certain beliefs about what is possible, and the opportunity to notice certain internal events. Among hundreds of choices, I might say, "Until I mention it now, you weren't conscious of the speed you were breathing, and the depth you were breathing to. But you can be conscious of that now, right? In fact, now that you're conscious of it, you can change the speed and breathe more slowly, or faster, more shallowly or more deeply. Check it out now. You can run your breathing with your conscious mind. Of course, if you do, then it's hard to get much else done. So being conscious of breathing may be useful for an athlete, but not necessary at some other times. So how were you deciding which speed to breathe at when you weren't conscious of it? That action of your brain that decided that is what I'm calling your unconscious mind. Now, when I play some classical music here, your breathing rate will tend to slow down, without your thinking about it consciously. That's what I mean by communicating with your unconscious mind. The music communicates with the part of your brain that is deciding how fast you'll breathe. So, in the same way, would it be useful to you to be able to communicate with the part of your mind that chooses what to memorise, or chooses how quickly you heal?"

This is a "reframe". It changes the *meaning* of "conscious" and "unconscious". The client said, " 'Unconscious' means nonfunctioning." I said, "To me 'unconscious' just means not being consciously thought about as it happens." The new meaning, as I note at the end, allows for lots of new learnings, new actions the person could develop skill with. To convey this new meaning fully, I took the person through a sequence of internal representations (noticing their breathing, varying its speed and depth, imagining how this was happening before they thought of it etc.).

Of course, the client may dispute my reframe. Because they already thought through their own conclusion (" 'Unconscious' means nonfunctioning"), they may find a way to fit my explanation into their map of the world. For example, by saying, "Well, when I'm not aware of my breathing, I'm *not* deciding how to breathe. It's happening automatically, just like water flows downhill. The water doesn't have a 'mind' that decides, 'Now I'll flow down here.' It just happens." Once again, this client frame doesn't support my hypnotherapy text very well. If I reply, we may well end up trading reframes for some time, and the person may then believe that the hypnotherapy model is "confusing", and consequently doubt their ability to use it.

Of course, this is a client who has chosen to use hypnotherapy. Their goal is to be able to use it as I use it. How could I more effectively assist them to meet that goal? For me, one central solution is to anticipate the objection and say my reframe *before* they express a contrary model. In that case, it is my experience that the contrary model will never even occur to the person. Because my model is plausible (it "could be true") they will accept it as an operating system, and move on from there. I will have *preframed* their understanding.

There is a way I can maximize the acceptance of my preframe. After stating it, I can focus attention on a particular issue that occurs once a person accepts the preframe. For example, particular issues that occur once we have accepted the reframe that says, "There is an unconscious mind that can be communicated with" include:

- What are we communicating to other people's unconscious minds already?
- Is it ethical to go on randomly communicating with other people's unconscious minds?
- Shouldn't everyone learn hypnotherapy so they can keep their communication tidy?
- Why do some people's unconscious minds respond so easily to communications such as music, while others' take longer?
- Should salespeople learn how to communicate with the unconscious or not?

Unless I'm working with a salesperson, all these issues are ones about which I'm quite happy for clients to have different opinions. As far as I can tell, their opinion about these issues will not affect their ability to use hypnotherapy. In raising such an issue immediately after my preframe, I'm offering people who enjoy disagreeing, people who like challenging my model, something to disagree with. Some people (in NLP terms, "mismatchers") sort their experiences by identifying mainly what is different, what doesn't fit, what they can disagree with. This is a perfectly useful skill, and essential to certain professional groups (such as lawyers and accountants, though they may disagree with me about that). Therapists often dread mismatchers, because they can use so much time and energy disputing essential points, and so on. I find that their energy is stimulating and valuable. And I like to help them use that energy in a way that meets their own goals.

By discussing the issue I've chosen, the client is accepting the key preframe, because, without that, what they're saying wouldn't make sense. You can't discuss whether salespeople should learn how to communicate with the unconscious, without deepening the belief that communication with the unconscious is possible. Or can you? Maybe it doesn't change the depth of your belief at all. You decide.

An example of opening up the client's model of the world
Working with Susan, the woman who experiences panic when her family are late home, Richard Bandler does a number of things to open up her model of the world and preframe the possibility of change. He asks her to explain to him the strategy she uses (1984, p. 9):

Richard: But how do you do it? How do you know, how do you get the panic?

Susan: Do you mean what feelings do I get?

Richard: Let's say I had to fill in for you for a day. So one of the parts of my job would be if somebody was late I'd have to have the panic for you. What do I do inside my head in order to have the panic?

Susan: You start telling yourself sentences like ...

Richard: I've got to talk to myself.

Susan: So and so is late, look they're not here. That means that they may never come.

Richard: Do I say this in a casual tone of voice?

Susan: No.

This pattern that Bandler is using has been modelled by Tad James and called the "Logical Levels of Therapy". James points out that, in doing this, Bandler has achieved, by linguistic presupposition, a number of shifts in Susan's experience:

- Susan agrees that she causes the panic: she is "at cause".
- Susan agrees that it takes a specific strategy to do so.
- Susan agrees she is expert enough to teach Bandler how to do it.
- Susan describes the process in second person, as if someone else does it.
- Susan, in order to answer Bandler's last question above, has to consider what would happen if she ran her strategy differently from the way she usually does.

In the transcript of Bandler's work with Susan, he continues asking her in similar detail about the visual aspects of her strategy for producing panic. He checks that, by bringing the pictures up close, she can bring on a feeling of panic, and then he compliments her on her success (pp. 16–17).

Richard: You've obviously mastered this. By the way, do you know that this is an accomplishment?

Susan: You mean to master the panic?

Richard: I bet you a lot of people here couldn't panic.

Susan: Probably not. Not like I do I'm sure.

Working with Susan, Bandler also preframes the change technique he will use. He shows her explicitly that, when she changes the submodalities of her experiences, she gets a different feeling inside. He tells her to take the pictures she frightens herself with and alter them (pp. 18–19):

Richard: Let me show you something else. Go back and look at it again from a distance. Now make the picture darker. Have you ever seen the brightness knob on the television? Turn the brightness down. What happens?

Susan: It creates more distance. Makes it fade away.

Richard: Makes it fade away. Turn the brightness up. Make it brighter. You do this real good. You're fast. And brighter. Now make it closer. What happens now as you make it closer and brighter at the same time?

Susan: I start getting feelings of tension and anxiety.

Richard: It works. Now the only difference is, is this time you did it deliberately.

In this section, Bandler has just pre-taught the actual "Swish" process that he will use as his change technique in the next stage of his work.

5a. Leading to desired state: models of change

By this stage, the NLP practitioner has elicited the client's key physiology styles, Meta-programs and values (while establishing rapport), their outcomes, their resources (while setting an outcome) and their old strategy for the problem. This provides an excellent base from which to select formal NLP change processes. The three variables that are relevant when choosing change techniques are:

1. **The consultant**. You will of course choose change processes that you are familiar with, and can facilitate congruently. This means that consultants choose change processes that they enjoy themselves!
2. **The problem**. This includes how clients frame problems and their desired outcome. A client with a phobia who says they need to get some "distance" on their anxiety is almost pointing at the phobia cure page in the NLP manual (the NLP phobia cure teaches the person's brain to distance itself or "dissociate" visually from disturbing memories). A client who says, "On the one hand ... and on the other hand ..." is already halfway through a parts-integration process (NLP processes in which two conflicting "parts" of the personality are fused into one).
3. **The client**. NLP practitioners usually discover that some people find that anchoring works really well for them, while others prefer submodality processes. Some people can fix anything as long as they use the NLP model called Time Line Therapy (James and Woodsmall, 1988), while others don't feel

right unless they do a parts integration. There is a structure behind these preferences, and I call this structure the Personal Strengths model. To understand how to choose techniques for each specific client, I will explain this model in a little more detail.

An example of leading

In his work with Susan, Richard Bandler guides her through the NLP Swish technique, discussed on page 57 of this book, as an example of a submodality shift. This technique begins with her using her ability to scare herself by seeing the picture of a car accident as if she were involved in it. The process gets her to alter this picture, rapidly shifting to what NLP calls a dissociated viewpoint (giving her the distance she has been asking for). Repeating this several times "installs" the new perspective in her brain. He says (Bandler, 1984, p. 21):

> Richard: Go ahead and make the picture bright and focus on it. Close your eyes again, move right in and as you approach very closely to it you begin to feel the panic. What I want you to do is to see in the small, lower left-hand corner a little tiny dark square that has a picture of you the way you would be if you had made this change. It's real darkened in the corner but suddenly the big picture begins to get darker and the other one begins to expand and become brighter until it fills the whole screen. But you can do it faster than that. There you go. Hurry up. Until you can see yourself the way you would be. Now I want you to do the exact same thing. I want you to do it five times real fast.

The Personal Strengths model

Milton Erickson, the hypnotherapist who was modelled by the developers of NLP, continually urged the identification and utilisation of clients' "problem" strategies in therapy. He says:

> This author has repeatedly stressed the importance of utilizing patients' symptoms and general patterns of behavior in psychotherapy. Such utilization renders unnecessary any effort to alter or transform symptomatology as a preliminary measure to the re-education of patients in relation to the crucial problems confronting them in their illness. [Erickson, 1980, Vol. IV, p. 348.]

In the following section, I provide a simple, easy-to-use format for NLP practitioners to identify quickly a client's "pattern of behaviour" and utilise it by providing NLP processes that pace it. I will show you how every client who enters your office is revealing their *strengths* by the very way they claim to have a "problem". My model is based on an earlier model developed by Carl Jung.

In developing the Meta-programs model of personality, NLP began with Jung's categories of Thinker, Feeler, Sensor and Intuitor. In Jung's model, the terms Thinker, Feeler, Sensor and Intuitor refer both to personality types and also to skills for living, which people develop to various extents. He explains (Jung, 1964, p. 49):

> These four functional types correspond to the obvious means by which consciousness obtains its orientation to experience. *Sensation* (i.e. sense perception) tells you that something exists; *thinking* tells you what it is; *feeling* tells you whether it is agreeable or not; and *intuition* tells you whence it comes and where it is going.

In NLP terms, four important analogues of Jung's skills are the ability to:

- **Dissociate** (distance oneself from experiences, seeing them from outside; corresponding to Thinker)
- **Associate** (step into experiences, feeling them from inside; corresponding to Feeler)
- **Chunk up** (be aware of the global "big picture"; corresponding to Intuitor)
- **Chunk down** (be aware of the specific details; corresponding to Sensor)

These four skills or Meta-programs (among others!) are essential for living an enjoyable life. They are also necessary prerequisites for all other internal processing, including the processing we call NLP techniques. To experience anchoring, for instance, you need to be able to associate into experiences. To run the phobia cure you need to be able to dissociate. To set a well-formed outcome you need to be able to chunk down, and to do the parts integration process you need to be able to chunk up.

When a client comes seeking change, they bring their own personal skills – skills they've developed over a lifetime. Certain upbringings support the development of skills for dissociating, encouraging the person to step out of their experience. Certain upbringings support the development of skills for associating into and fully "living" experiences. Some upbringings nurture both abilities. It's the same for chunking skills.

Anchoring processes require associating into a specific situation (stepping into an experience and feeling it from the inside). A client who is excellent at associating will generally be good at anchoring. They've been doing it already (possibly using it to create phobias, but the skill is intact). They may or may not have acquired the skill to dissociate that is presupposed in the phobia/trauma cure. If we use collapsing anchors before the phobia cure, or create a resource anchor first, we are utilising their strength (pacing) before leading them to new skills.

Submodality change processes require being able to dissociate somewhat from the experience for which you are eliciting submodalities. Some submodality processes (such as the phobia/trauma cure) specifically require making dissociated, constructed images. Time Line Therapy (in which the person imagines floating up above the time line of their life) requires dissociating from the experiences on the time line. A client who is excellent at dissociating will generally be good at Time Line Therapy (see James and Woodsmall, 1988). They may find checking an experience in the time line less convincing, but will experience the change from being way up above and before the problem event. Someone who "feels" cut off from their experience may appreciate healing their limiting decision (to be cut off) from above the time line before coming back and anchoring themselves to a powerful resource state.

It's the same with chunking. Using the detailed NLP questioning style called the metamodel or using solution-focused questions to clarify your thoughts and set specific goals requires chunking down. The person skilled at chunking down to the thousand details of their day and getting anxious may appreciate setting a sensory-specific goal before you do trancework and chunk up to some generalised "change". On the other hand, using the "artfully vague" language patterns developed by Milton Erickson to induce trance presupposes the ability to chunk up, as do techniques that ask for the purpose or "higher intention" of your behaviour. A client who gets depressed because "everything" is hopeless may find it easier to use parts integration before setting specific goals.

As an NLP practitioner, you'll discover that some techniques work better with certain clients. It's not random. Clients have strengths. This four-skill model is one method for "diagnosing" those strengths. Some clients can do everything you suggest easily; that's great – they have all four skills.

Figure E: Personal Strengths Model

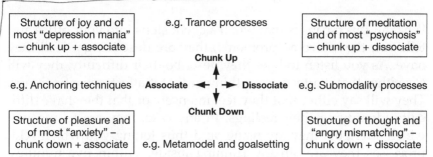

In a sense, every time you use an NLP technique with a client, you help them to develop the skills presupposed by it. In that way, it's not only the specific issue that changes. Your client develops the skills required by the technique, which are simultaneously the skills to live an enjoyable life. NLP techniques are training skills for life.

As Jung noted in his model, people generally utilise a pair of the basic skills most of all. In our model, for example, a person may use skills to associate into a chunked-up experience ("*Everything feels* like this"), which could be used to create euphoria or "depression". This person may benefit from developing their ability to chunk down and dissociate, using submodality processes and dissociated goal setting.

Someone who uses skills to dissociate in a chunked-up way ("*Everything I'm conscious of* is like this") could have used these skills to create a state of meditation or "psychosis". They could benefit from taking aboard techniques to chunk down and associate, such as strategy installation and associated goal setting.

If your client uses skills to associate into chunked-down experiences (*"These specific details feel like this"*), which can be used to generate pleasure or "anxiety disorders", they might benefit from learning how to chunk up and dissociate, with such trance techniques as Time Line Therapy.

Lastly, the person who uses skills to dissociate in a chunked-down way (*"These specific details I'm conscious of in this way"*) which support planning successful action or extreme mismatching (what in psychiatry might be called a borderline personality disorder) could benefit from developing the skills of chunking up and associating into life with parts integration, anchoring and trancework.

What all this means is that when a client steps into your office and tells you they have a "problem", they are describing a skill they have. As you listen to how they describe their difficulty, they will say either that it affects everything or that it affects specific things. They will say either that they feel intensely or that they have difficulty identifying their feelings. In any case, they are telling you which strengths they are using, and thus telling you which NLP processes they are already running inside. Within five minutes, you can identify which NLP processes are most likely to work for them as you help them change. This enables you to select, from the ten types of intervention we saw in Chapter 3, the most effective type to pace the person's current skills.

As I was developing this model, a client came to see me asking for NLP processes to help her create a sense of spiritual awakening. This, she said, was something she had never really had access to. I initially assumed that she wanted to experience processes such as "core transformation" (a process involving chunking up to a profound "core state"; see Andreas, 1992), but, as I attempted to lead her through this and other similar techniques, she continuously interrupted and disagreed with the instructions. In describing her goal, she had actually described in intricate detail what needed to change for her to achieve "spiritual awakening", but complained that while she could "think about it" the description had no feeling with it. As soon as I recognised her style as chunking down and dissociating, I offered to change to another technique. She was delighted to be introduced to the far more detailed and dissociated submodality belief change, which, she reported, gave her the real experience of spiritual opening.

This example emphasises that diagnostic terms such as "depression", "phobia" and "psychosis" only roughly correspond to the Meta-programs that we are sorting for here. I am interested in which strengths people actually demonstrate in relation to this particular challenge at this particular time, rather than which label someone has given them.

Finally, Jung's original model also contained another distinction that can be added to the Personal Strengths model. This is Extroversion–Introversion (Whitmont, 1991, pp. 139–140). Some clients will describe their problem in an introverted way ("This is what happens inside me") and some will describe their problem in an extraverted way ("This is what happens between others and me"). This is a third axis on the model, making it a three-dimensional chart. This distinction has been less significant in NLP consulting because most NLP processes are done internally. Nonetheless, some variation along this continuum does occur. Time Line Therapy is clearly a more introverted way of using the time line than Robert Dilts's re-imprinting on the time line, where the person actually walks along the floor. Dealing with relationships and setting tasks are two examples of more extraverted techniques used in the NLP context.

Figure F: Personal Strengths model with introvert–extravert axis

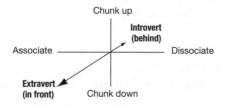

Robert Dilts's Unified Field model for NLP use
The NLP trainer Robert Dilts has developed a three-dimensional model for analysing the type of intervention that will assist someone to change. The three dimensions to be considered are time, "perceptual positions" and "neurological level".

TIME

Dilts encourages clients to check their issue from the perspective of the present, the past and the future. The Ericksonian therapist Michael Yapko points out that human distress is a consequence of "temporal rigidity". When a person is unable to live from all three temporal perspectives flexibly, they suffer. The person with anxiety is stuck looking towards the future. The person with depression is stuck looking towards the past (even when they think they are considering life "now"). The person with impulse disorders such as addictions is stuck in now. Yapko explains (1992, pp. 118–20):

> A temporal component is a part of virtually every experience … For example, a structural component of anxiety disorders is a future temporal orientation: the anxious individual anticipates (orients to) the future in such a way as to create images (or internal dialogue or feelings) about events that have not yet occurred … In contrast to anxiety disorders, in impulse disorders, the overwhelming emphasis is on the immediacy of experience – a present temporal orientation. The person is not particularly attached to either past tradition or future consequences. Rather it is the emphasis on here-and-now experience that governs the impulsive need for immediate gratification. In the case of depression, the emphasis is overwhelmingly on a past temporal orientation. The depressive is continually hashing and rehashing old traumas, including rejections, humiliations, disappointments, and perceived injustices – and in essence all the hurtful things from the past.

Health involves developing the flexibility to view life from multiple perspectives on the time line.

PERCEPTUAL POSITIONS

The NLP co-developer John Grinder points out that in an interaction between myself and another person, I can consider the interaction in three ways (DeLozier and Grinder, 1987, p. 323).

I can stay "in my own body", listening through my own ears and looking through my own eyes. This is called *first perceptual position*. It gives me useful information about my own opinions and choices. If I just "go with others' ideas" then I become unassertive, and I am unable to convey the understandings that I have. I need to be able to use first position because often I have important information (e.g. about my own needs) that others do not.

I can, in my imagination, step into the other person's body, and listen through their ears, and look through their eyes. This *second perceptual position* gives me more information about the effects of my actions on others. It also gives me a sense of where they are coming from. If I used only first position, I would not notice, for example, whether they understood me, because I'd be preoccupied with my own fascination with what I was saying. Second position helps me to know how to explain things effectively so that they make sense to this particular person. It also helps me to understand what it's like in their world, so I can help them meet their needs.

I can, in my imagination, step out of my body to a neutral spot, separate from both the other and myself. This *third perceptual position* gives me valuable information about the system of interaction between the other person and myself. I don't get caught up in conflicts or misunderstandings so easily here. I can monitor our relationship, and the consequences of my actions more objectively from here.

In Dilts's Unified Field model, he encourages clients to check their issue from all three perceptual positions – to get a "triple-description" of what is happening.

NEUROLOGICAL LEVELS

When a client says, "I can't seem to create the right state of mind to manage the pressure in my job", says Dilts, you could respond to this at a number of different "neurological levels" depending on which word or phrase in the sentence you attend to.

The final phrase, "in my job", refers to the *environment* where the problem happens. One way to create change is to change the environment (e.g. by finding a different job). Often this is the first level of change that clients themselves have tried.

The phrase "manage the pressure" refers to the specific *behaviours* that the client is unable to do. Change can be created at this level (e.g. by showing the client specific behaviours that will reduce the sense of pressure; by setting a resource anchor). Often this is the first level of change that consultants want to try.

The phrase "create the right state of mind" refers to the *capabilities* that the client would need in order to solve the problem. More profound change can be achieved at this level (e.g. by showing the client new strategies for creating useful states of mind in any circumstances).

The phrase "can't seem to" refers to the level of *beliefs and values*. It would be the same if the client said, "I don't want to have to create the right state of mind to manage the pressure in my job." The phrase "don't want to" is a beliefs-and-values-level issue. Fundamental changes can occur for clients when they resolve issues at this level (e.g. by changing their beliefs about what is possible using time-line processes).

The deepest level in the statement is the level of the word "I", the level of *identity*. At this level, change can occur by giving the client a new experience of who they are as a person (e.g. by using parts integration to integrate the part of them that becomes anxious with the part of them that knows they are capable of doing their job). Many of our attempts to get clients to change do not work because change needs to occur at this much more profound level.

There is a level before the person says anything, though. This is the level Dilts calls *spirit*, and involves the person's connection with greater systems of which they are a part (communities, the universe etc.). Great spiritual teachers often achieve change at this level by use of metaphor and profound reframing.

The important thing about using the neurological levels in change-work is that, as a generalisation, a problem at one level needs to be dealt with by a solution at a level at least one "higher" than the problem. For example, a person who gets panicky whenever they are in an elevator tends to think they have an "elevator" problem. This environment-level issue needs to be solved by a behaviour-level change (such as the NLP trauma cure). A person who cannot learn a new strategy for resolving conflicts in their relationships may think they have a problem of capability, but this capability-level issue needs to be solved by a beliefs-and-values-level change (such as reframing their beliefs about what conflict means and dealing with the disturbing event on the time line). Change at a "higher" level affects all the levels below it, virtually instantly. When a client changes their belief about anxiety, they find they can learn new ways to manage it, and they behave in different ways from previously.

Some clients specifically ask for change at a certain level. NLP practitioners often have their own preferences about which level they want to work at. It is useful to be able to accept, for example, that not every client comes in wanting spiritual transformation, or fundamental changes in their self-image. Sometimes a person just wants to get rid of their panic in the elevator. And, after all, once they have changed that, they may decide to learn a strategy that enables them to relax in any situation, and that may change their beliefs about what is possible.

Figure G: Robert Dilts's Unified Field model

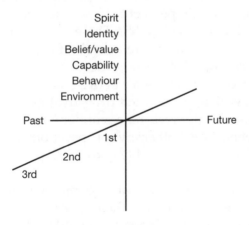

5b. *Leading to desired state: dealing with common issues*

In the book *The Structure of Personality*, Michael Hall, Bob Bodenhamer, Margot Hamblett and I discussed the application of NLP to a number of different personality-disordering processes. Here, I want simply to comment on some of the key issues people bring to NLP practitioners, discussing them in terms of the RESOLVE process, the Personal Strengths model, and the Unified Field model.

Depression

In the psychiatric manual *DSM-IV* (American Psychiatric Association, 1994), a major depressive episode is identified by the person having symptoms such as feeling sad or empty, experiencing lack of interest or pleasure, fatigue, feelings of worthlessness or guilt, inability to think, recurrent thoughts of death, insomnia or hypersomnia, weight loss or gain, and body agitation or slowing down. This is a life-threatening psychophysiological disorder. Studies show that people who score highly on these indicators of depression have lowered lymphocyte responsiveness and immunoglobulin levels in their blood – in other words, their immune systems are damaged and they are more likely to become ill (Thayer, 1996, pp. 30–1).

The rate of depression varies from social group to social group, and from time to time. Carefully adjusted studies (Seligman, 1997, pp. 64–5) show that the incidence of depression has increased more than tenfold in the last century. This has reached the point where, at any given time, 25 per cent of people are at least mildly depressed (Seligman, 1997, p. 55). These and other statistics indicate that most "depressions" are a result of experience, not genetics (Yapko, 1992, pp. 3–4). Alongside this apparent epidemic of depression has come an epidemic of drug usage to attempt to treat it. Studies show that, even when drug treatment is deemed successful, "relapses" (later recurrences of depression) are more common than when psychotherapy or psychotherapy plus drug treatment is deemed successful (Yapko, 1992, p. 4).

The very thinking styles that cause depression are used by the depressed person to convince themselves that they cannot or should not change. In fact, depression could be *defined* as the belief that a person cannot or should not change! Dr Martin Seligman, a professor of psychology, calls this belief a "permanent, pervasive explanatory style" (Seligman, 1997, pp. 40–8). He says it is part of the structure of "learned pessimism". In one of Seligman's studies (1997, pp. 78–9), he followed a group of 400 school students through several years of their life. Those who started out with a pessimistic style were the ones who, when an event such as a divorce happened, were likely to get depressed. The divorce (i.e. the life event) did not cause this depression by itself, and those with an optimistic style rebounded quickly from such events. What caused depression was the combination of painful life events plus a style of thinking. Because such events happen every so often, the person will appear to have a cyclical mood problem.

In NLP terms, the depressed person is using a characteristic pattern of strategies and Meta-programs. They chunk up, particularly in problem situations, claiming that "everything is going wrong, and always will" (what Seligman calls a "permanent pervasive explanatory style"). They associate into painful memories and are oriented towards the past – that is, they constantly think about unpleasant memories as if they were reliving them. In Personal Strength terms, then, they are chunking up and associating. In terms of the Unified Field model, they are past-oriented, stuck in first perceptual position (see above) and have an identity-level problem. They also slow down their body movements. Finally, they talk to themselves a great deal about how "everything is going wrong, and always will" (auditory-digital) and then check their feelings (kinaesthetic). They then tell themselves off for feeling bad (auditory-digital) and then check their feelings again (kinaesthetic). This repeated cycle is known in psychology as "ruminating" (Seligman, 1997, pp. 82–3) and in NLP as an Ad-K loop.

Using the client's personal strengths, we can begin changing this system by helping them relax and access memories of resourceful states (since they are already able to step into past memories, this might seem simple; bear in mind that they have actually dissociated past enjoyable memories, and will take time to access these again). We can use parts integration to integrate the part that generates depression with the part that wants to be happy. We can pace their interest in the past by using time-line processes. To alter the person's strategies, we then use solution-focused questions to help them chunk down to specific solutions, including identifying the specific structure of times when they have not been depressed (exceptions) and planning specific actions towards specific future goals. We can ensure they use their physiology effectively, making time to laugh and exercise every day. We can alter their auditory-digital strategies, for example using an auditory Swish process. The NLP trauma cure can be used to teach the person to recode painful memories as dissociated movies.

Suicide is a particular issue for some depressed people. As a consultant, you have a right to ask that, *during the period of your consulting,* the person will stay alive (otherwise your assistance is wasted). Make a "staying-alive contract" and check that they are congruently agreeing to this. Interestingly, depressed persons tend to keep such arrangements. The contract will include a method by which they can contact someone in a crisis. Decide whether that person is the consultant, a phone counselling service or a friend or relative. In the session, rehearse this crisis contact (e.g. have them actually phone the person). Have them "futurepace" any possible excuses they might make for not doing this ("What would make you decide not to keep this contract?") and build in reframes to ensure that even that situation leads to their contacting the person. If the client misses a session, has not notified you before and has been suicidal, contact them to reaffirm the staying-alive contract, or plan other interventions such as ringing a phone counselling service. Remind yourself that, as a consultant, you cannot ultimately *make* someone stay alive. The aim of this contract is just to maximize the chances that this will happen, so that they can learn to change the thinking style that created depression.

Anxiety

Thirty-three per cent of all people visiting their doctor have anxiety as a key complaint, and a similar percentage of the general population will develop a "clinically significant anxiety disorder" at some time in their life (Barlow, Esler and Vitali, 1998, p. 312). In the psychiatric manual *DSM-IV* (American Psychiatric Association, 1994) anxiety is described in three ways:

- **Prolonged anxiety** is described in terms of symptoms such as feeling restless, fatigued, keyed-up, irritable, suffering from muscular tension, and being unable to sleep or concentrate.
- **Acute anxiety** attacks (panic) are described in terms of even more intense responses, such as heart pounding, sweating, shaking, difficulty breathing, chest and abdominal pain, nausea, dizziness, and extreme fear (of death, insanity or loss of control).
- It is acknowledged that many people suffer from one of the above types of anxiety, but cope with it in ways that then become **other symptoms** – alcohol and drug use, extreme and

involuntary dissociation responses, eating disorders, compulsive rituals, violence and other behaviours designed to avoid the anxiety.

Twice as many women as men report anxiety as such, and this seems related to men's preference for certain of these other behaviours (Barlow, Esler and Vitali, 1998, p. 290).

Understandably, a plethora of medications such as Valium (diazepam) have been used to treat anxiety. There is little evidence that drugs, used alone, reduce the frequency and severity of anxiety, and users have been shown to exhibit the same level of fear and avoidance behaviour after the drug treatment as before (Franklin, 1996, p. 7). Again and again, though, cognitive NLP-style change processes have been compared to diazepam and related drugs and shown to be far more successful (Barlow, Esler and Vitali, 1998, p. 310). Unfortunately, the craving for a quick fix (such as pills seem to offer) is implicit in the very nature of anxiety. On the other hand, longer-term psychotherapy also feeds the nature of the problem, by creating dependency (Beck and Emery, 1985, p. 171). What works is what NLP offers: short-term change processes that give the person back control over their own state.

Anxiety is a physical response, and yet it cannot be generated without certain constructed internal representations (visual, auditory or kinaesthetic) of "possible" future events. A person seeing a spider may make a huge internal picture of a spider crawling towards them, and then feel the resulting fear (this is diagrammed in NLP terms as $V^c \searrow K^i$). Another person may create the sound of an entire hall of people laughing and shouting at their humiliation and feel the fear of that ($A^c \searrow K^i$). Another may create the feeling of slipping off a high place and falling so well that they feel as if they are falling, and feel the fear of that ($K^c \searrow K^i$). These are *synesthesias*: a representation in one sensory system is linked simultaneously to one in another system. The pictures, sounds or physical sensations simultaneously generate an internal set of sensations described by the person as "anxiety". The person increases the sensation of danger by magnifying the submodalities of the trigger experience, and reducing the submodalities of their own skills. They thus rate the risk of the danger as considerably greater than it actually is. Longer-term anxiety can be sustained by strategies that place A_d

(auditory-digital – self talk) in the sequence. A person may imagine failing an exam, talk to themselves about how terrible that would be, and pick up an increasing sense of panic about what they are saying ($V^c \leftrightarrows A_d \searrow K^i$).

The initial results of the original synesthesias can also be fed back into the system. A pounding of the heart resulting from thinking about the spider can lead to speculation about a heart attack, and thus to increased pounding ($V^c \searrow K^i \rightarrow A_d \searrow K^i$). Such physical escalation is the source of panic attacks, as opposed to longer-term anxiety. The person may also physically escalate the problem by attending to their in breath rather than their out breath, and by allowing less time than usual for rest and sleep. Like all anchored responses, the original trigger for anxiety may generalise to related situations. Research by cognitive psychologists (Beck and Emery, 1985, p. 94) suggests that the category of "generalised anxiety" or "free-floating anxiety" is mythological. Triggers always exist, but are not always consciously recalled by the person.

Using the client's personal strengths, we can begin changing the anxiety pattern in a similar way to the one suggested for depression – by having the person access and anchor resourceful states such as relaxation or trance. That is, we can use their skill with synesthesias to create positive synesthesias. We can use the person's focus on body sensations to introduce physiological change techniques such as the NLP Eye Movement Integrator or Thought Field Therapy. Teaching the person how they are triggering anxiety helps them reframe it as something changeable instead of an uncontrollable "visitation". Two important submodality shifts are the key to lasting change in anxiety. One is to alter the person's time orientation, so that they are able to float past the successful completion of the future feared event and look back at it (James and Woodsmall, 1988, p. 45). The other is the NLP phobia/trauma cure, which teaches the person's brain to step back from traumatic experiences and see them in a more detached way (Bolstad and Hamblett, 1998, pp. 109–12). Finally, NLP techniques that involve chunking up (such as parts integration) can be used to assist in reintegrating the old neural networks where the panic happened with the rest of the brain.

Schizophrenia

Schizophrenia is the most frequently discussed of the psychoses (disorders where the person is assessed by psychiatrists as out of touch with reality). Many psychiatrists consider that there may in fact be a number of different and overlapping syndromes that are being described under the one label of "schizophrenia" (Perris, 1989, p. 4). Perhaps one of the clearest areas of agreement, though, is that schizophrenia is a separate disorder entirely from split or multiple personality, with which it has previously been confused in the public mind. Schizophrenia is perhaps best described as a disorder of thought and perception. The *DSM-IV* (American Psychiatric Association, 1994) lists its symptoms as delusions, hallucinations, disorganised speech, disorganised behaviour or immobility, and loss of emotion or will. To be diagnosed, two of these symptoms need to be present in such a way as to damage achievement in social, career or self-care areas, over at least six months' duration.

In Canada (and probably elsewhere in the West) 8 per cent of all hospital beds are taken up by people with this diagnosis, using up more hospital beds than any other single disorder (Long, 1997). In US jails 6.2 per cent of prisoners have been diagnosed schizophrenic, and an estimated one in three homeless persons suffers from the condition (Kopelowicz and Liberman, 1998, p. 192). Schizophrenia is not often enjoyable. Depression and self-medication with drugs or alcohol are common among those diagnosed, and are associated with poorer chances of improvement. Twenty-five per cent of schizophrenics attempt suicide, and 10 per cent succeed (Kopelowicz and Liberman, 1998, p. 192).

Schizophrenia is associated with difficulty "chunking down" in NLP terms (Perris, 1989, p. 43, pp. 148–51, p. 157 and Arieti, 1948). The person with this problem is not identifying the distinctions between situations fully. Rather than chunk down to the sensory specific details of a problem event, they talk vaguely or metaphorically. One client, discussing this very problem with the authors, said, "Some days it hurts when I walk on the earth. I need to keep up in the air." This is a good example of metaphorical communication. I might say that same sentence metaphorically, but this young man experienced it as a sensory fact. The schizophrenic is often also unable adequately to *classify* situations from a metaposition (for example to distinguish a real memory from a hallucinated one, or an internal thought from an external voice). Many cognitive psychologists consider this the core of the disorder (see Jacobs, 1980). Interpersonally, the person diagnosed schizophrenic behaves much like someone unexpectedly placed in a totally foreign culture. Their attempts to communicate subtly mismatch the cultural norms. Often they mistakenly assume that others share their own unique sensory experiences, values, beliefs and Meta-programs. They may use "socially unexpected" gestures, body postures, proximity, facial expressions, voice tonality and phrasings, without apparently noticing that these metacommunications appear or sound odd to others. Many people working with schizophrenia note that their own way of diagnosing the condition is not primarily by the classical symptoms but by the very strange feeling that they get when they are with the person diagnosed this way – a feeling called "lack of affective resonance" (Perris, 1989, p. 5). In NLP terms, this refers to an awareness of the client's difficulty using socially normal rapport skills.

Because of this lack of rapport, the key issue in beginning work with someone diagnosed schizophrenic is to respect their map of reality adequately. Jeffrey Zeig identifies a sequencing in Milton Erickson's work with psychosis (Erickson, M. H., and Zeig, J., "Symptom Prescription for Expanding the Psychotic's World View" pp. 335–7 in Erickson, 1980). He explains:

> This pattern can be divided into three major elements, which occur in the following sequence: (1) meeting the patient where the patient is; (2) establishing small modifications that are consistent with, and follow from, the patient's behavior and understandings; and (3) eliciting behaviors and understandings from the patient in a manner that allows the patient to initiate change.

The person diagnosed schizophrenic often begins using a thinking style that is very chunked up and very dissociated (separated from sensory experience). Erickson's willingness to meet the person where they were extended to talking in similar vague style to his clients', assisting them to avoid hallucinated "dangers" and helping clients work towards goals that most therapists would have rejected as unrealistic. His small modifications would then involve altering the style of communication to become more normal, shifting the dangers so that they became irrelevant and having the person achieve more realistic successes "on the way" to their own more grandiose goals.

Three types of educational process then can be used to expand the person's own personal strengths. One is to teach the person how to use the metamodel to chunk down their own thought processes, questioning generalisations, mind-reading, premature assignation of meaning and tangential thinking (Perris, 1989, pp. 148–51; Hagstrom, 1981). Another is to teach the person how to code internal voices and fantasies in different submodalities from reality, so they can distinguish the two things (Bandler, 1993, pp. 7–9). Finally, the person can be taught the precise skills of building rapport and effective social relations.

Borderline personality disorder

In NLP terms the core characteristic of the person who gets diagnosed with BPD (borderline personality disorder) is a severe sequential incongruity (what they do/feel/believe at one time does not fit with what they do/feel/believe at another time). In external relationships this is expressed in swings from idolising another person and desperately wanting to be with them, to despising them and wanting to escape the relationship. In the person's relationship with themselves it is expressed in swings from apparent arrogant self-promotion to self-hatred and disgust. Cognitively, this means constant polarity responses: the person mismatches their own and others' experience continuously. Emotionally, this creates confusion about who they are and what they want, resulting in feelings of frustration, anxiety, depression, emptiness and hopelessness. The person with BPD is focused temporally on the present moment, as if neither memories of the past nor plans for the future can be trusted. They think in absolute, either-or terms, because they find it difficult to chunk up to an overall picture that can encompass two different details. The person's final behaviour may be deliberately self-destructive (e.g. suicide attempts, self-mutilation), destructive of others (e.g. physical fighting, smashing objects, explosive shouting) or dangerously impulsive (e.g. drug abuse, binge eating, reckless driving). It is as if they are at war with themselves, and with anyone else who gets in the way of this primary target.

Research so far rules out even a genetic *component* in the development of BPD (Crits-Christoph, 1998, p. 546). Neurological studies show that the BPD person has more right-brain activity (perhaps more emotional processing than logical processing) and an over-responsive noradrenaline system. But that's just another way of saying they're angry! The most significant thing known about the origin of the problem is that 70–79 per cent of these people have suffered severe physical or sexual abuse or endured serious trauma in very early childhood (Crits-Christoph, 1998, p. 545; Santoro and Cohen, 1997, p. 4).

Often, the person diagnosed with BPD comes for help at a time of crisis, when they may be severely depressed or anxious. Managing the relationship between the NLP practitioner and the client *is* the core therapeutic intervention here. This involves teaching the client to develop clear "first and second positions" (knowing when they are considering their own opinions and needs, and when they are considering yours). It involves confronting the issue of compulsive mismatching (continuous disagreement with you and with their own previous positions), and developing an understanding about how to deal with this. Mismatching is a choice that was valuable in this person's childhood, but has now become compulsive. Usually it will work better to have the person complete tasks and to take charge of the therapeutic processes themselves, rather than be "guided" through things by you.

A major aim of work with a person diagnosed with BPD is to generalise skills from areas of their life that are functional to areas where their unresourceful states are triggered (Layden et al., 1993, p. 38). The challenge is that even to begin talking positively is an art with the person who mismatches. Yvonne Dolan (1985, pp. 29–43) discusses a number of ways to do this without triggering mismatching behaviour. These include the use of interspersed embedded suggestions and presuppositional language. Teaching the person to sort for agreement and positive results is an important base from which change processes can actually work, rather than be incorporated into a long line of failures. Dolan explains (1985, pp. 50–7) how to convert a person's habitual "no" responses to "yes" responses by the careful use of restating the client's disagreement and concluding with a negative tag question. If the person says, for example, "I'd rather just give up on this", the NLP practitioner might reply, "You'd rather *not* be here?" or "There are lots of better places to be, are there *not*?"

Once these reframing processes have created a sense of contract, the person can use the NLP trauma-phobia cure to heal early life issues, and use parts-integration processes to create a more coherent sense of identity and wholeness.

Addiction

At any given time, 6–7 per cent of Americans show diagnostic signs of substance dependence (O'Brian and McKay, 1998, p. 127). In this research, substance is used in the strict sense of substances such as alcohol, cocaine, cannabis or opiates. The research excluded nicotine and caffeine dependence, as well as behavioural dependence such as compulsive gambling. Here, we will focus on substance use, but the same interventions will work with any addictive problem. There's no doubt the level of addiction in our societies is a serious problem. Alcohol alone is implicated in half of all driving fatalities, a quarter of all suicides, a third of all assaults, and in the medical cause of death for 100,000 Americans a year (Dorsman, 1997, p. 2).

In trying to define dependence, psychiatrists and others refer to more than just excessive use, and to more than a psychological sense of needing the substance (American Psychiatric Association, 1994, pp. 108–9). They refer to what counsellors call ambivalence (Miller and Rollnick, 1991, pp. 36–47) and what NLP practitioners would call sequential incongruity (Bandler and Grinder, 1982, pp. 179–88). The person accesses the part of their neurology that wants to use the substance, and then the part that doesn't want to use it, in an ongoing sequence. For example, they may take more of the substance than they originally planned to. They may make attempts to stop, or say they want to stop using the substance, and then carry on using it. They may abandon other activities that are important to them, as a result of using the substance. They may continue using the substance despite actually suffering persistent, painful problems as a result of this use. They may even have tried to stop using the substance, and experienced extreme discomfort (called withdrawal). In short, an addiction occurs where one part of a person wants them to stop, but (and that word "but" is used intentionally) another, apparently more powerful, part wants them not to stop.

The level of ambivalence about changing the addictive behaviour defines the appropriate response to assist a person with this type of problem. By knowing where you are in terms of the self-change model, you can decide which tasks the person is ready to undertake in changing (see Motivational Interviewing earlier in this chapter).

Often, the person's strategy for "using" will involve a sequential incongruity (e.g. telling themselves they shouldn't use the substance, and then adding to the stress until they feel they have "justified" giving in to their desire to use). Expressed in NLP strategy notation, and taking an example of someone who smokes cigarettes after each meal, the strategy might look something like this:
$$V^e \rightarrow V^r \searrow K^i \rightarrow A_d \searrow K^i \rightarrow K^i / K^i \rightarrow A_d \rightarrow K^e$$

Trigger	Operation	Polarity operation	Test (comparison)	Exit (A)	Exit (B)
V^e	$\rightarrow V^r \searrow K^i$	$p \rightarrow A_d \searrow K^i$	$\rightarrow K^i / K^i$	$\rightarrow A_d$	$\rightarrow K^e$
See meal finished	Remember cigarette and feel enjoyable feeling	Say to self, "It's wrong to smoke! This is terrible!" and feel guilty	Compare feeling of guilt to feeling of smoking	Say to self, "Damn it! Why should I have to feel bad?!"	Smoke cigarette

If the person is at the "action" stage, then you can assist them to alter the core strategies they have been using to respond to the addictive substance or behaviour. This can be done by using submodality changes such as the Swish, or simply by installing new behaviours that disrupt the old strategy. Milton Erickson might, for example, have the client agree to walk around the block once after their first cigarette, twice after their second, and continue doubling for each cigarette they have in a day; or he might suggest that they smoke no fewer than three cigarettes at a time, if they previously smoked only one at a time. Once the strategy is altered, parts-integration and time-line processes can be used to heal the internal incongruity, and new life skills can be taught to deal with the real-life issues that are associated with the incongruity.

Physical health issues
NLP as a therapeutic approach is not limited to purely psychological problems. Even in the case of serious physical illnesses with clear genetic components, such as many cancers, there are clear psychological factors at work. For example, two key psychological factors associated with the development of cancer are (1) loss of a crucial relationship perceived as a "reason for living" and (2) unexpressed hostility. In one study, 72 per cent of cancer patients were identified as having lost a crucial relationship recently as compared with 12 per cent of controls. In the same study, 47 per cent of cancer patients were rated as having unexpressed hostility, as compared with 25 per cent of controls. This enabled a researcher to predict which clients were likely to have cancer with 95 per cent accuracy, simply based on these two variables. The probability that this number of correct predictions would occur by chance was less than one in a thousand (LeShan, 1984, pp. 26–7).

Would NLP make a difference in such situations? Short-term educational psychotherapy can increase both the percentage of cancer-fighting T-cells and their activity, by teaching the person how to respond resourcefully (Fawzy et al., 1990, 1993). These improvements that are due to short-term therapy continue to intensify up to six months after the psychotherapy! Over the last century, health professionals in the West rediscovered the incredible power of the mind to heal the body. The first research demonstrating this in relation to cancer treatment was published by Dr Carl and Stephanie Simonton, from Dallas, Texas, in their book *Getting Well Again* (1978). Working with 159 people considered to have medically incurable cancer (average life expectancy: twelve months) the Simontons reported two years later that fourteen clients had no evidence of cancer at all, 29 had tumours that were stable or regressing and almost all had lived well beyond the twelve-month "limit" (pp. 11–12). Essentially, 10 per cent were cured and 20 per cent were curing themselves. The Simontons used a combination of biofeedback, visualisation, exercise, goal setting, resolving internal conflicts, letting go of resentment and engaging family support. They explained their success based on psychoneuroimmunology (the way the mind affects the nervous system, which in turn affects the immune system).

On the other hand, longer term, problem-focused psychotherapy may have a negative effect on survival in such cases. The psychologist Dr Hans Eysenck has warned of the dangers of traditional psychotherapy for some time. He describes a longitudinal study of 7,000 inhabitants of Heidelberg, from 1973 to 1986. This study was designed to discover the health effects of psychotherapy. Clients in psychotherapy were able to be matched by age, sex, type, amount of smoking etc. with controls. This study showed that cancer and heart disease were most prevalent in the group who had had two years or more of "therapy", less frequent in the group who had one year or more in "therapy", and least frequent in the group who had no "therapy" (Eysenck, 1992). Talking about what's wrong with life once a week for years is not healthy.

There are dozens of anecdotal NLP studies of cancer cure. The New Zealand NLP master practitioner Anthony Wightman (1999, p. 42) describes his successful treatment of his own skin cancer and of leukaemia with skills developed during his NLP practitioner training. He imagined a laser burning out the cancer cells, and filled his body with "a golden glow which imbued all cells with health and removed any unhealthy cells". He ran an imaginary hot iron over the inside of the vein next to the skin cancer to stop any spread and bleeding when it dropped out (which it actually did a week after he began visualising). Before treating his skin cancer, he had it diagnosed by three separate doctors, all of whom claimed after his cure that they must have misdiagnosed a solar keratosis. His haematologist had a somewhat more difficult job explaining the change in his leukaemia. Wightman says, "I believe we are only scratching the surface of our own capabilities and that the most promising area for research lies within our own minds, our own hearts, our own souls."

In other major causes of mortality and morbidity, such as heart disease, NLP interventions are also important. The evidence suggests that the mind is at least as powerful as surgery itself in predicting heart-surgery outcomes. In 1958, a study was done to evaluate the effectiveness of a new surgical treatment for heart disease (Cobb et al., 1959; Diamond et al., 1958; also reported in McDermott and O'Connor, 1996, pp. 75–6). The surgery has since been shown to be completely useless, but the effect for the patients in the study was wonderful. The patients were all told that their surgery would probably help, and indeed ten of the seventeen patients in the study reported great improvement. Their use of heart medication dropped to a third over the next weeks. What is most interesting is that only eight of these patients had actually been given the surgery. Nine of them simply had a skin incision made and sutured up again. Of those nine, five reported they felt much better, and reduced their medication to a third. When doctors expressed disbelief, another surgery team replicated the study, with even better results. But the healing effect of surgery is dependent on how it is presented by the surgeon and other health practitioners. The psychologist Henry Bennett has collected several hundred studies showing that preparing patients psychologically before surgery will markedly alter the surgical and post-surgical results. Simple changes in what the doctor says will reduce need for pain medication, reduce blood loss and result in fewer medical complications.

Consider an example. At the Department of Anesthesiology at the University of California, Bennett himself conducted a study on patients admitted for spinal surgery (Bennett, Bensen and Kuiken, 1986). Each patient received a fifteen-minute preoperative talk with a health practitioner from the centre. There were three subgroups. Group A received basic information about the procedure they were to go through. Group B received a brief training in how to relax their muscles before and after surgery. Group C were given an NLP-style intervention. The health professional pointed out that everyone has experienced blushing as a result of a few words said by someone else, so we know that the mind can cause blood to shift around in the body. They then explained that it would help if the person's blood moved away from the spine during surgery (to prevent blood loss), and then moved back afterwards (to promote healing). They then slowed down their voice and said, "Therefore, the blood will move away from the spinal cord during the operation. Then, after the operation, it will return to that area to bring nutrients to heal your body quickly and completely." The result of this simple conversation was dramatic. Patients in Group A and Group B lost, on average 900cc of blood, which is the normal level of blood loss over the course of this operation. Patients in Group C lost an average of 500cc of blood during the operation – only half as much.

There are two key principles to apply in working with health conditions using NLP. First, focus attention on all neurological levels, from spirit to environment. Dr Brendan O'Regan is a neurochemist who has collected a database of 3, 500 medically documented cases of spontaneous remission of cancer. Dr Charles Weinstock leads the New York Psychosomatic Study Group, and has commented on these cases:

> Within a short period before the remission, ranging from days to a few months, there was an important change, such as a marriage, an ordination, the birth of a grandchild, or removal of a relationship that was unwanted. There was a psychosocial rehabilitation of one sort or another, and then the cancer was healed. [Weinstock, 1997.]

Using parts integration, time-line work and interpersonal interventions is important for such change to be duplicated by our NLP sessions.

The other principle of such work is to utilise physical movement and expression. The person who has a physical health issue is demonstrating skill in expressing their internal state physiologically. To match that, it is appropriate to use physical interventions such as Thought Field Therapy and chi kung (a type of moving meditation developed in China). To date, the most dramatic clinical results of chi kung are reported by the Huaxia Zhineng Qigong Clinic and Training Centre near Qinhuangdao, China. I visited this centre in 1998. Founded by Western-trained physician, Dr Pang Ming, at that time it had over 600 staff, including 26 Western-trained doctors, and treated 4,000 to 7,000 people at any given time. Residents (called students because they are learning to use chi kung, rather than simply being "treated") were checked medically after each 24-day treatment period. Most of the people treated had been told that there was no orthodox treatment available for their condition. Most of them had inoperable cancers. Results at the Centre are classified as:

- Cured (no symptoms of illness, and no signs on EKG, ultrasound, X-ray, CT etc.)
- Very effective (almost no symptoms, and dramatic improvement on instruments)
- Effective (detectable improvements)

• Ineffective (no change, or even worsening symptoms)

In the centre's first published results (Huaxia Zhineng Centre, 1991; Chan, 1999, p. vii), data on 7,936 students showed that 15.2 per cent were cured, 37.68 per cent very effective, and 42.09 per cent effective. That is to say, after a month, 52 per cent were cured or almost cured, and overall 95 per cent had experienced some benefits. While the centre is using many NLP-style techniques (such as metaphor, trancework and reframing), clearly the physical movement involved in the chi kung exercises makes a significant contribution to their success.

6. Verify change

Whether the issues were about anxiety or depression, addiction or physical illness, as soon as the change process is complete in an NLP session, I ask the client to notice how they have changed. I want them to discover this change before they consciously "unpack it". Choosing my words so as to presuppose that they have changed, I may say, "Remember that problem you used to have. Try to do it now and notice what has changed." If they find they cannot now create the old problem, I say, "Try again, and find out how much you've really changed now!" You may remember that Milton Erickson, working with Miss X and her sweating hands, had her "try" to make a puddle on the floor and realise that she could not do it any more.

Solution-focused therapists have studied the difference in the way they ask about the results of change processes when the client returns to the next session. In studies replicated several times, they have found that if they ask questions that imply the possibility of failure (e.g. "Did the change process work?") they get a different result than if they ask questions that presuppose success (e.g. "How did that change things?"). When asked a question that presupposes change, 60 per cent of clients will report success. If the question presupposes failure, 67 per cent will report that their situation is the same as it was before (Miller et al., 1996, pp. 255–6).

One way to presuppose change is to ask the person to notice what else has changed, or even what else they *want* to change next. We

Muse
on
Context

may say, "A lot of people go away and only check for results with the things we were intending to change. In fact, when one aspect of your life changes, several other aspects tend to change, and it's a good idea to find out just what has happened. So, over the next week I'd like you to notice what else has changed in your life as a result of this process." This has the added advantage of directing the person's attention away from experimentally deconstructing their change.

Let's consider the situation where I have gone through an NLP process with a client and they tell me that it simply "didn't work". And let's assume it's a process that I know has been successful when used in my brain or someone else's brain. After all, if my process doesn't fit these criteria, I wouldn't use it. So, that process "worked" when I or someone else used it. That means that my "unsuccessful" client did something different from what I or the other successful user did. The process can still "work", but I need to find out what my client did differently. Actually, then, NLP doesn't "work": it's *people* who work. To claim that NLP works, regardless of the person, would violate the presuppositions of NLP. Each person is in charge of their own internal representations, and no system (including NLP) ever takes that ability away from them.

So, when someone tells me that a process "didn't work", they are only telling me what I knew all along. *How* the NLP didn't work – that is, *how* the person's brain worked in spite of NLP – is my immediate interest. If you really understand this, you'll never again have the experience that therapy "didn't work". Instead, you and your clients will discover more and more about how *what they do* works, and how to make it work in the way they want.

I may have forgotten to tell them some step of the process, or I may have assumed they would do something that they didn't do. One of my choices is always to search around for some NLP process that they already know how to do in the same way a successful person does it (which they already have the personal strengths to do well). I also have another choice, which is to "postframe" their experience of *this* technique from one of failure to one of success.

To do that I first want to find out *when* they did something differ-ent. Did they do something different during the technique (so that it never "worked" for them), or did they do something different afterwards, so that they now don't *remember* how it "worked" for them. Amazingly, the second situation is more common. Some clients do something different *during* the original NLP technique, so that it never worked for them. It still helps to find out what else has changed, but I do need an immediate response when the client says, "It didn't work." Such a client has somehow mismatched my instructions for the process, so I know that at some level they value being able to be different (being able to mismatch). My response is quite simple. I pace the person's comment, and connect it with the word "because" to an explanation that puts them in charge, and suggests that being different = doing it so it works. The structure is:

"That's right, it didn't work – because you didn't do the process the way I told you. Instead you did what you've always done – and the only way to get a different result is to do it the way I told you. Do you want to get that different result?" The most common thing that clients do that wasn't in the instructions is to sort for failure *while* the process is happening, usually using a critical internal voice. While they do the process, they tell themselves, "This prob-ably won't work." This is so common that I usually check for it with a client who doesn't get the result intended. We can then repeat the process, ensuring that the person relaxes their internal voice or gives it a useful task (such as repeating my instructions internally as we do the exercise).

The more common problem is that the person has not remembered how the process worked. Not noticing a change is an information-filtering (Meta-program) problem that underlies much of what our clients seek help with. Generally, our clients are filtering the infor-mation in their life, searching for evidence of problems. Part of the structure of depression, for example, is to go back over all the pos-itive experiences, seeing them as impermanent, and dissociating from them so they feel unreal, phoney or even nonexistent. The depressed person then goes through all the enjoyable experiences, sees them as permanent, and associates into them so they feel real. The structure of happiness involves noticing and associating into what is going well, what is enjoyable.

Martin Seligman explains his work with depressed children (Seligman, 1995, p. 88):

> No matter how many successes [the helper] recalls, [the depressed person] trots out why the successes were really failures. [The depressed person] is not being modest or shy, nor is [the depressed person] engaged in a random litany of complaints. At this moment, he truly believes that nothing will work out and it's because he has no talent. This is the standard thinking pattern of a depressed child. A pessimistic explanatory style is at the core of this kind of thinking. The bleak view of the future, the self, and the world stem from seeing the causes of bad events as permanent, pervasive and personal, and seeing the causes of good events in the opposite way.

Many times I have seen a client tell me that "nothing has changed" one minute, and then report that they have actually achieved every goal they set for our time together. What causes the shift? My willingness not to assume that their memory of events *is* reality, but instead to ask persistently, first, "So what has changed in your life (or in your experience of the situation that was a problem)? No matter how small the changes seem at first, what is different?" Then, second, I congratulate them genuinely: "Wow, that's great. How did you do that?" Then, third, I keep asking, "And what *else* has changed?" These three questions come from Solution-Focused Therapy (Chevalier, 1995). In asking them, I'm coaching the client to sort for solutions.

Milton Erickson emphasised that change is an unconscious process, and that the conscious mind needs reassuring that change has occurred. He says (Erickson and Rossi, 1979, p. 10):

> Many patients readily recognise and admit changes they have experienced. Others with less introspective ability need the therapist's help in evaluating the changes that have taken place. A recognition and appreciation of the trancework is necessary, lest the patient's old negative attitudes disrupt and destroy the new therapeutic responses that are still in a fragile state of development.

Here, Erickson refers to pacing a client's strategy for being convinced. In a similar fashion, in NLP terms, a client may need to be convinced by checking for the change only once, a number of times or over a period of time. They may even have a "consistent convincer" and never be fully convinced about anything. This Meta-program is called the "convincer strategy" in NLP. If the client has a period-of-time convincer, the consultant can ask them to go out into the future, past that time, and enjoy the changes. If they have a consistent convincer, the consultant may choose to reframe this, e.g. by saying, "Since you know you'll never be completely sure this has changed, you might as well accept it now."

An example of verifying change
In the example of Richard Bandler's work with Susan's anticipatory anxiety, he ensures that Susan is fully convinced that she has changed. He tells her (Bandler, 1984, pp. 24–5):

> Richard: You go ahead this time and go back and look at that panic. See if you can hold it. I want you to try as much as you can in vain.
>
> Susan: It's hard. I just keep getting white.
>
> Richard: What do you mean?
>
> Susan: I'm having trouble doing it.
>
> Richard: I thought you'd mastered that.
>
> Susan: I am a master at panic. Right now all I'm getting is white ...
>
> Richard: Try it once more. Just to be sure.
>
> Susan: I really just can't do it.

Once he has this clear, unequivocal statement verifying the change, Bandler moves on to "futurepacing" (planning for the future effects of the change).

7. Ecological exit

A number of studies have led helpers to recognise the importance of "futurepacing" the changes their clients initiate (having the client imagine themselves back in their actual life using their new skills). This process functions both to check out the appropriateness of their plans, the "ecology" in NLP terms, and also to install the expectation of success in the person's future (Mann et al., 1989; Marlatt and Gordon, 1985). Allen Ivey and others have their clients write a "future diary" of their success a year into the future. Alan Marlatt has clients step into the future and fully consider what might make them change their mind about their changes, and then has them plan to prevent that. Both approaches have been shown to deliver far more robust change than parallel programmes that skip this futurepacing stage. Of course, if any undesirable consequences of the change are detected at this stage, the process shifts back to clarifying outcomes.

Futurepacing involves having the client travel, mentally, into their future and look back to check how the change has occurred. I might say, "Think of a time in the future, when in the past you would have had that old problem, and notice how it's changed now." Or, "So, as you think of the future, is it OK for that to be changed in this way now?" I can also specifically ask the person to check the ecology of their changes, for example by asking, "Is there any way you could stop yourself automatically using the solution to your problem?" If they say, "I can't", I may say, "I guess you're stuck with the solution, then." If they tell me some potential problem, then that alerts me to some other changes that we need to make before we are completed. I am checking for "ecology issues", to use the NLP term.

In NLP, one of the assumptions we make is that there is an intention for each behaviour. So, if a client finds that after a certain time the problem "reappears", at least part of them must have some reason for reversing the change. If a person comes back and says that the change "didn't stick", I say, "That's right, it didn't work, and there may be a part of you that has a good reason why it wasn't OK yet to have it work; and, if you were to know what the intention of that part was, what would it be?" I am now beginning a parts-integration process with the person, to resolve the ecology issue they have raised.

An example of ecological exit
In Richard Bandler's work with Susan, once he has verified her change, he reminds her that she believed this would change her future. He says (Bandler, 1984, pp. 25–6):

Richard: You've got to keep your promise. You said it would change your whole life.

Susan: Yeah.

Richard: Now you have to keep your end of the bargain.

Susan: Well, I think if I don't have this problem that it is going to change. Because it's going to affect everything.

Richard: You're not going to be able to do it.

Susan: That would be wonderful.

Richard: Try it.

Susan: I've tried it.

Richard: Try it now.

Susan: I just can't get it. I just can't get it.

Richard: Well, if it was so easy before and it's so hard now, that's an indication. You can go try it in the real world. I tell you what. Why don't you go outside by the coffee machine and I'll meet you there in ten minutes?

Eight months later, Susan was interviewed by Michael Saggese about her experience. She told him (Bandler, pp. 28–30):

Susan: When I left the studio that day I knew I felt really good but I was still a little skeptical of what had happened because my panics are so bad and so painful to me. I went home that evening and the same situation occurred. Someone was supposed to come and they didn't show up for several hours. And I didn't get upset at all. I was able to lie down and take a nap. It didn't upset me at all. I was just truly amazed …

Michael: And that change is still holding up more than eight months down the road now.

Susan: Right.

Michael: How do you feel about that?

Susan: You don't know what a relief it is!

Summary: Using the RESOLVE Model

In summary, the RESOLVE model sequences a number of key tasks that research has suggested are an important part of effective changework. These tasks are:

Resourceful state for the practitioner
- Adopt the presuppositions of NLP
- Negotiate a consulting relationship
- Anchor yourself into a resourceful state
- Cultivate a quality of love

Establish rapport
- Pace (match) the client nonverbally
- Pace the client's sensory system use and other Meta-programs
- Use generalised language
- Verbally pace the client's dilemma (reflective listening)

Specify outcome
- Reframe problems as outcomes
- Sort outcomes
- Ensure outcomes are sensory-specific, and ecological
- Identify resource states and exceptions to the problem

Open up model of world
- Demonstrate the possibility of change (e.g. with the pointing exercise)
- Pretest the problem strategy
- Elicit the problem strategy
- Reframe the person as "at cause"
- Have the person dissociate from and experimentally alter the strategy
- Demonstrate the specific change techniques (preframe the change techniques)

Leading to desired state
- Select change processes based on the consultant's skills, the client's skills and the client's outcome
- Run the change processes

Verify change
- Ask questions presupposing change
- Use the client's convincer strategy to confirm change

Ecological exit
- Futurepace any changes
- Check for ecology issues
- Futurepace past any "relapses"

At the end of our NLP practitioner course, we have our practitioners run through some full sessions using the RESOLVE model on issues for which the client has no particular intervention in mind. We also have them take challenging sessions from their experience and review them using the RESOLVE model to identify important choice points and generate more options, in a peer-supervision format. That's a way you could use the model right now, to expand your awareness of its usefulness. The RESOLVE model suggests a logical sequence in a reality that may be neither logical nor sequential. There are five ways your actual NLP session could well seem different from the map.

1. The actual use of skills is cumulative rather than sequential. Once rapport is established, you will of course maintain it throughout the other steps. Once you've begun using the metamodel, you will often challenge metamodel patterns at later stages as well.
2. The real process of therapy may end successfully at Step 2, 3 or 4. Just eliciting a strategy may cause it and the problem to disappear. It's tough, but life's like that – easier than you expect.
3. You may cycle through the RESOLVE model several times, or run through it as a subroutine of one step in a larger RESOLVE process.
4. It is likely that occasionally you will successfully leap several steps at a single bound, or apparently reverse steps. No generalisation is ever totally true (including this one).
5. Once you know a town, you don't carry a map every time you leave home. But it sure helps the new immigrants; and everyone knows how handy it is to have a map in the glovebox for those unexpected side trips. In the same way, the RESOLVE model is only a model. Once what you are doing is working, keep doing that!

Another example: Case study

In the following example, I have applied the RESOLVE model bearing in mind these cautions.

John came to see me after reaching a crisis in the management of his "psychiatric condition". He explained that he had a double diagnosis, as both schizophrenic and depressed. His doctor wanted to add Prozac to the cocktail of antidepressants and antipsychotics he was already taking. He told his doctor to give him four weeks to decide. "If you can fix me by then, I won't take the Prozac," he explained to me as he walked in the door.

Alerted to the fact that he was undergoing psychiatric treatment already, I asked John what help he had used previously to deal with his problems. He listed a number of psychotherapeutic models. He had been to three other NLP practitioners, five different hypnotherapists, a Rational Emotive therapist, a Transactional Analyst, a Gestalt therapist, a Rebirther, and several other helpers. It was an impressive list. I asked him, "So, what helped in all that?"

"Nothing," he replied. "Nothing helped at all."

I nodded. "Well," I said, "I need to tell you right now: NLP doesn't work." John flushed red and sat down. I paused. "*You* work," I continued, "and NLP is just a way of explaining *how* you work."

"OK." He agreed. "I can accept that."

In terms of the RESOLVE model, I had just made clear both my confidence in his ability to change, and my refusal to play a game where I tried to "rescue" John from his own behaviour (Resourceful State). I had also paced his own experience – after all, he had just finished telling me that NLP didn't work (and nor did Rational Emotive Therapy. Transactional Analysis, Rebirthing, hypnotherapy or Gestalt).

But I was puzzled. I asked John why, when nothing worked, he kept going to see therapists. He explained that, when he was with a therapist, it gave him a feeling of hope. That felt good. Also, he said with a laugh, by seeing so many therapists, he was learning a lot about psychotherapy. He had even considered that this might be a future career direction for him. We chatted about the possibilities in terms of NLP and hypnotherapy training, laughing at his crafty new method of research.

Next, John explained to me what the problems were that he needed to deal with. There were, he said, two issues. First, he was depressed, and, second, he was socially awkward. I asked him to be a little more specific about the depression issue. He said that what he did (his strategy) was to hear his father's voice shouting at him through his left ear, and telling him he was no good. After doing this for thirty minutes or so, he felt really bad, and this was what he called depression. I told him that, as he was describing it, I had checked out that strategy and I thought I myself could get depressed in much less than thirty minutes by doing that. We laughed.

Focusing on the other problem, I asked him what he meant by his being "awkward". He said, "Well, I never knew I was awkward until I was referred by my GP to a psychiatrist first. I opened the referral letter on my way, and it began, 'Dear sir, I am referring you this awkward man ...' And that's when I realised I was awkward." I apologised to John, and explained that I was trying hard to find his awkwardness, but I'd been having a lot of fun chatting and laughing with him, and I couldn't find it. Maybe we would have to accept that it didn't exist any more.

Clearly, as we discussed these problems, I was not just building rapport. I was also opening up John's model of the world, and eliciting his strategy for the "problems" he had experienced. I asked him what he would like to have instead of being depressed (eliciting an outcome) and he said he would like to feel happy, to be able to complete things he started and to be able to build friendships. These seemed like useful goals, but there was one clear ecology issue with all of them. If John succeeded in getting these things, he would lose his ability to create hope by seeing psychotherapists. And where would he go to learn about therapy?

I told him that I had decided that I didn't want to be his psychotherapist. However, I explained, I was willing to be a consultant. That meant that, so long as he did the things I suggested, he could hire me to make some recommendations. However, if he did-n't want to use those recommendations, I'd prefer to finish our work. I said that initially I'd like to work with him for six sessions, because I believed that it could take that long for him to be sure that he was getting the changes he wanted. He agreed to this.

I had John stand up and I explained that I was going to show him why I didn't want to be his therapist. I gently pushed him from one side asking him to stay in the same place. As I pushed, I asked, "Are you doing anything to stay in the same place?"

"Yes," he replied, "I'm tightening the muscles on the other side."

"OK." I thanked him, and went around to push from that other side. "Are you doing anything to stay there now?"

"Of course." he acknowledged. "I'm tightening muscles again."

"The same muscles?"

"No. The ones on the other side."

I next pushed him from behind, and then from in front, checking each time that he was tightening different muscles each time. "So you were able to use different muscles each time to stay in one place," I said admiringly. "You're pretty flexible, then. If you weren't, you'd have moved with one of my pushes, right?" He nodded. "And if you weren't so flexible, and adaptable, you'd have changed when you visited one of the psychotherapists you've seen."

I also had John do the pointing exercise described in Paragraph 3 of the section "Open Up the Client's Model of the World" above. I emphasised that the internal representations he made created the state of mind he experienced, and that there were two important tasks I wanted him to do between this session and his next meeting with me. One was to read a chapter of an NLP book. I selected a book he had not yet read and gave it to him, explaining that next week I would discuss with him what he agreed with and what he disagreed with in the author's claims. Second, I told him that every morning, before he got out of bed, he was to identify three things he was looking forward to in that day's activities. Leaning over near his left ear, I pointed out to him that I had had previous clients who were given this task and claimed it made them feel bad. "When I asked them," I said, "it turned out that they didn't actually do the task I had set them. Instead, they struggled to think of one thing they were looking forward to; and then they told themselves that the task was too hard. Then they felt hopeless about that, and didn't try again. That's not doing the task! If you want me to be your consultant, you need to follow the instructions very precisely. You *will* feel much better, if you *do the task as described*. Agreed?" He nodded and smiled.

Why did I give John these two tasks to do? First, I wanted to choose an intervention that left the responsibility with him, and tasking is the clearest way to do that. Second, I chose my tasks to match the ecology issues John had identified. The two things he got from visiting therapists were learning about psychotherapy, and a sense of hopefulness. You do not need to pay a psychotherapist money to get those things! All you need to do is start every day by feeling hopeful, and read some good books! In terms of this one session with John, setting these tasks served both as a "Leading" technique and as a futurepacing process.

Next, I explained to John that he was obviously really good at having voices come in through his left ear and change his state of mind. I suggested we hijack that skill and use it to create the kind of state he wanted. I had him imagine himself in a situation where he usually started hearing his father's voice. As he heard that voice, I had him turn down the volume and shift the voice far out to the horizon. Meanwhile, I had him bring a resonant, confident-sounding version of his own voice in towards that same ear, increasing in certainty and comfortable loudness as it came closer. The new voice affirmed that he was capable and worthy of respect. Having done this, I had him close off all internal sound, and then run the same process again. We repeated this "auditory Swish" five times, and John reported that the changeover was now happening automatically whenever he imagined himself in that situation. Next, we repeated the process for another type of situation which had previously created "depression". This was the only official NLP change technique we did at the Leading stage of the RESOLVE model.

John confirmed that he felt a lot better, and that he was looking forward to trying the two tasks at home. But, as he was getting ready to finish our first session, he turned to me and said, "You know, six sessions is a long time. Milton Erickson was a really great therapist, wasn't he?" I agreed, surprised, because it was usually I who told Milton Erickson stories to clients! "Yes," John continued, "no six sessions for him! Do you know the story about when the young man who had been violent came to visit Milton? And Erickson said to him, 'How surprised will you be when you find out next week that you've totally changed?' And the boy said, 'I'll be bloody surprised.' And Erickson said, 'That's right, you will. Goodbye.' And that was all the therapy he did. The boy changed after one session. One session!"

This comment seemed to me to be a comment with two levels in it. At one level it was simply a story about Erickson, and at another it was a criticism of my "needing" six sessions to "fix" John's problem. In terms of futurepacing, this was an important issue. I decided to respond with the same type of two-level comment. "Yes," I agreed, "Milton Erickson was an amazing guy. Do you know the story about the guy who was depressed and came to see Erickson when Erickson was in a wheelchair?" John shook his head.

I continued, "Erickson explained that they would do some relaxation processes, so it would be best for the man to take off his shoes first. A little puzzled, the man complied. 'And now,' said Erickson, 'I'd like you to take off your socks also.' Well, what was the man to do? He had already taken off his shoes, so he was halfway there. He took his socks off. 'And now,' said Erickson, 'I'd like you to roll my wheelchair up onto your foot.' This was obviously a bizarre request, but who was the man to complain? He was already sitting there in bare feet! So he did it. And Milton compassionately said, 'And does that hurt?' The man nodded. 'A little bit, yes.' Milton leaned forward and added, '*It wouldn't hurt if you didn't do it!*' "

John burst into laughter, and we were still laughing as he left.

We had four sessions altogether, and, at the end of that time, John had completed several home tasks successfully. Each morning he was identifying three things to look forward to. Each evening he was identifying three things he was grateful for. He had run the auditory Swish on himself in a number of situations. And he had read plenty of NLP. He had also restarted and completed a training course that he had abandoned several years before. And, when that course ended, the trainer working with him invited John and some others out to a bar for a celebratory drink. John said it was the first time in his entire life that he had been out to a bar with a friend. He was as excited about that achievement as he was about passing the course. After the fourth session, John thanked me and said that he felt that he had solved the problems he came to deal with. He had decided not to bother with the Prozac. He also said that he felt that, if he had any further problems, he knew how to solve them using the skills he had been practising. "I think I can manage on my own from here," he said with a smile.

That was our final futurepacing.

Conclusions

In the history of Neuro-Linguistic Programming, there has often been a focus on the pyrotechnics – the seemingly magical techniques that have been developed by NLP trainers. There have been few attempts to make links between these NLP techniques and those used in other models of psychotherapy. One of the most successful was the Ericksonian therapist Steve Lankton's book *Practical Magic*, published in 1980.

In the more than twenty years since Lankton's book, both NLP and psychotherapy have evolved. The solution-focused brief therapy approaches emerged out of the same milieu as NLP, and have shaped much of the change in psychotherapy (see Chevalier, 1995; Miller et al., 1996). Other brief psychotherapy approaches have emerged over this period, offering techniques closely paralleling those from NLP (e.g. EMDR, see Shapiro, 1995). NLP has important contributions to make to this ongoing evolution, offering a series of fresh perspectives on such new techniques. To contribute in this way, NLP itself will need to acknowledge that its methods are part of the wider search for successful change techniques. In Chapter 3, I reviewed the main types of NLP intervention, noting the beginnings of research into them, and suggesting the links between them and interventions in many other psychotherapies. Under their own labels, most psychotherapists use anchoring, strategy installation, submodality shifts, trancework, parts integration, time-line changes, reframing, tasking and interpersonal and physiological methods. While, as an NLP practitioner, I value the NLP frames for explaining these interventions, they have been with us under other names for over a century.

NLP itself, like most other models of therapy, has often lacked a coherent explanation of its results in terms of the actual events occurring in the brain. Ernest Rossi is one of the few NLP and Ericksonian therapists who have grounded their clinical work in actual neurological research (Rossi, 1986, 1988, 1996). The study of state-dependent neural networks has advanced dramatically in the last decade (see Carter, 1998). In Chapter 2, I expanded Rossi's explanation of this field to encompass the NLP notions of sensory modalities, submodalities, strategies, states and parts. This gives us a working metaphor for what is happening in psychotherapy generally, as well as an encompassing explanation of what NLP has discovered.

Perhaps the most frequent criticism levelled at NLP in psychotherapy has been that it fails to understand the importance of the therapeutic relationship. I believe that, on the contrary, NLP psychotherapy has its foundation in a new and innovative framing of this relationship. It is educative and consultative rather than "therapeutic". Its focus is on empowering rather than nurturing, transforming rather than merely "holding".

I believe that the structuring of this relationship by the NLP practitioner is one of NLP's most original contributions to psychotherapeutic theory. The resourcefulness of the NLP practitioner is the beginning place for this person-to-person interaction, summarised in Chapter 4 with the RESOLVE model. The practitioner then includes their client in this resourcefulness through the process of rapport. Only then are they able to set precise outcomes by which their work together can be evaluated. The pivotal time of NLP psychotherapy emerges once these outcomes are set, as the practitioner opens up the client's model of the world and demonstrates the possibility of change. It is only in this context that the NLP change processes themselves have their "miraculous" effect. Finally, success is not complete until the *client* has verified it and planned for its safe, ecological expression in their future life.

Even within the "Leading" section of the RESOLVE process, the NLP practitioner does not blindly "hurl" NLP "explosives" at a passive client. In fact, together they design a learning process that matches and expands the client's own personal skills (chunking up or down, associating and dissociating), the client's own time orientation and their focus in terms of neurological levels.

Having discussed so systematically the *structure* of NLP psychotherapy, it remains to remind you that this is the analysis of an extraordinary human adventure. To restate a point made at the start of Chapter 2, an understanding of the chemistry of paint does not account for the beauty of a great painting. Virginia Satir, one of the original models studied in the development of NLP, said:

> Using oneself as a therapist is an awesome task. To be equal to that task, one needs to continue to develop one's humanness and maturity. We are dealing with people's lives. In my mind, learning to be a therapist is not like learning to be a plumber. Plumbers can usually settle for techniques. Therapists need to do more. You don't have to love a pipe to fix it … In my teaching, I focus in depth on the personhood of the therapist. We are people dealing with people. We need to be able to understand and love ourselves, to be able to look, listen, touch and understand those we see. We need to be able to create the conditions by which we can be looked at, listened to, touched and understood. [Satir and Baldwin, 1983, pp. 227–8.]

In the frontispiece of his book, "Is There Life Before Death", Steve Andreas quotes a beautiful poem by Sister Mary Corita Kent. It says:

> *Choose life –*
> *Only that*
> *And always*
> *And at whatever risk.*
> *To let life leak out*
> *To let it wear away*
> *By the mere passage of time*
> *To withhold giving it and spreading it*
> *Is to choose nothing.*

I believe that the RESOLVE model of NLP psychotherapy is an expression of the choice of life. But, however skilful our psychotherapy becomes, it is *life* that we are choosing, not psychotherapy. If this book contributes to that choosing of life, it has met my own outcomes.

Bibliography

Adler, R, "Crowded Minds", *New Scientist*, Vol. 164, No. 2217, December 18, 1999, pp. 26–31.

American Psychiatric Association, *Diagnostic Criteria From DSM-IV*, American Psychiatric Association, Washington, DC, 1994.

Andreas, C, *The Aligned Self*, audiotape set and book by NLP Comprehensive, Boulder, Colorado, 1982.

Andreas, C, *The Aligned Self: An Advanced Audiocassette Program* booklet, NLP Comprehensive, Boulder, Colorado, 1992.

Andreas, C and Andreas, S, *Heart of the Mind*, Real People Press, Moab, Utah, 1989.

Andreas, S, *Is There Life Before Death?*, Real People Press, Moab, Utah, 1995.

Andreas, S, *NLP Eye Movement Integration*, videotape from the Milton Erickson Foundation, Phoenix, Arizona, 1993.

Andreas, S, *Virginia Satir: The Patterns of her Magic*, Science and Behavior Books Inc, Palo Alto, California, 1991.

Andreas, S, "What Makes a Good NLPer?", *Anchor Point*, Vol. 13, No. 10, October 1999, pp. 3–6.

Andreas, S and Andreas, C, *Change Your Mind and Keep the Change*, Real People Press, Moab, Utah, 1987.

Andreas, S and Andreas, C, "Neuro-Linguistic Programming" in Budman, S H, Hoyt, M F and Friedman, S, *The First Session in Brief Therapy*, Guildford Press, New York, 1992, pp. 14–35.

Andreas, S and Faulkner, C (eds), *NLP: The New Technology of Achievement*, Nicholas Brealey, London, 1996.

Arieti, S, "Special logic of schizophrenic and other types of autistic thought", *Psychiatry*, 11, 1948, pp. 325–38.

Assagioli, R, *Psychosynthesis*, Penguin, Harmondsworth, England, 1976.

Bacon, S C, "Neurolinguistic Programming and psychosomatic illness: a study of the effects of reframing on headache pain", Dissertation Abstracts International, Vol. 44 (7), University of Montana, 110 pages, Pub. = DA8326959, p. 2233-B.

Bandler, R, *Magic In Action*, Meta Publications, Cupertino, 1984.

Bandler, R, *Using Your Brain For a Change*, Real People Press, Moab, Utah, 1985.

Bandler, R and Grinder, J, *Frogs Into Princes*, Real People Press, Moab, Utah, 1979.

Bandler, R and Grinder, J, *Patterns of the Hypnotic Techniques of Milton H Erickson, M.D.*, Vol. 1, Meta Publications, Cupertino, California, 1975.

Bandler, R and Grinder, J, *Reframing: Neuro-Linguistic Programming and the Transformation of Meaning*, Real People Press, Moab, Utah, 1982.

Bandler, R, Grinder, J and Satir, V, *Changing With Families*, Science and Behaviour, Palo Alto, California, 1976.

Barlow, D H, Esler, J L and Vitali, A E, "Psychosocial Treatments for Panic Disorders, Phobias and Generalised Anxiety Disorder", in Nathan, P E and Gorman, J M, *A Guide To Treatments That Work*, Oxford University Press, New York, 1998.

Baxter L R, "Positron emission tomography studies of cerebral glucose metabolism in obsessive compulsive disorder", *Journal of Clinical Psychiatry*, 1994, Number 55 Supplement, pp. 54–9.

Beck, A T and Emery, G, *Anxiety Disorders and Phobias: A Cognitive Perspective*, Basic Books, New York, 1985.

Bennett, H L, Bensen, D R and Kuiken, D A, "Preoperative Instruction for decreased bleeding during spine surgery", *Anesthesiology*, Number 65, p. A245, 1986.

Bergin, A and Garfield, S, *Handbook of Psychotherapy and Behavior Change*, Wiley & Sons, New York, 1994.

Bisiach, E and Luzzatti, C, "Unilateral Neglect of Representational Space", *Cortex*, Volume 14 , Number 4, 1978, pp. 129–33.

Blackerby, D, *Rediscover the Joy of Learning*, Success Skills, Oklahoma, 1996.

Blakemore, C and Cooper, G, "Development of the Brain Depends on the Visual Environment" *Nature*, Number 228, 1970, pp. 477–8.

Blatner, A, *Acting In: Practical Applications of Psychodramatic Methods* Springer, New York, 1988.

Bolstad, R, "Carl Rogers Covert NLP Influencing Skills", in Anchor Point, Vol. 9, No. 9, September 1995, pp. 24–33.

Bolstad, R, "NLP: The Quantum Leap", *NLP World*, Vol. 3, No. 2, July 1996, pp. 5–34.

Bolstad, R. "R.E.S.O.L.V.E.: An NLP Model of Therapy", in Anchor Point, Volume 9, Number 8, August 1995 (B), pp. 12–14.

Bolstad, R and Hamblett, M, *Communicating Caring*, Longman Paul, Auckland, 1992.

Bolstad, R and Hamblett, M, "Developing NLP Based Treatment Programs for Fast Resolution of Psychological Trauma", *NLP World*, Vol. 7, No. 1, March 2000, pp. 5–22.

Bolstad, R and Hamblett, M, "Preventing Violence in Schools: An NLP Solution", *Anchor Point*, Vol. 14, No. 9, September 2000, pp. 3–14.

Bolstad, R and Hamblett, M, *Transforming Communication*, Addison-Wesley-Longman, Auckland, 1998.

Bolstad, R and Hamblett, M, "Visual Digital: Modality of the Future?", *NLP World*, Vol. 6, No. 1, March 1999.

Briggs-Myers, I, *Manual: The Myers–Briggs Type Indicator*, Consulting Psychologists Press, Palo Alto, California, 1962.

Brockman, W P, "Empathy revisited: the effects of representational system matching on certain counselling process and outcome variables", *Dissertation Abstracts International* Volume 41, Number 8, 3421A, College of William and Mary, 1980, p. 167 ff.

Cairns-Smith, A G, *Evolving the Mind*, Cambridge University, Cambridge, England, 1998.

Callahan, R J, *Tapping the Healer Within*, Contemporary Books, Chicago, 2001.

Carkhuff, R R, *The Art of Helping*, Human Resource Development, Amherst, Massachusetts, 1973.

Carkhuff, R R and Berenson, B G, *Beyond Counselling and Therapy*, Holt, Rinehart and Winston, New York, 1977.

Carter, R, *Mapping The Mind*, Phoenix, London, 1998.

Chan, L, *101 Miracles of Natural Healing* Benefactor Press, West Chester, Ohio, 1999.

Cheek, D, "Awareness of Meaningful Sounds Under General Anaesthesia", *Theoretical and Clinical aspects of Hypnosis*, Symposium Specialists, 1981.

Chevalier, A J, *On the Client's Path*, New Harbinger, Oakland, California, 1995.

Clarkson, P, *Gestalt Counselling In Action* Sage, London, 1989.

Cobb, I A, Thomas, G I, Dillard, D H et al., "An evaluation of internal-mammary-artery ligation by a double blind technic", *New England Journal of Medicine*, No. 260, 1959, pp. 1115–1118.

Condon, W S, "Cultural Microrhythms", in Davis, M. (ed.), *Interactional Rhythms: Periodicity in Communicative Behavior*, Human Sciences Press, New York, 1982, pp. 53–76.

Craldell, J S, "Brief treatment for adult children of alcoholics: Accessing resources for self care", *Psychotherapy*, Vol. 26, No. 4, Winter, 1989, pp. 510–13.

Crasilneck, H B and Hall, J A, *Clinical Hypnosis: Principles and Applications*, Allyn and Bacon, Boston, 1985.

Crits-Christoph, P, "Psychosocial Treatments for Personality Disorders", in Nathan, P E and Gorman, J M (eds), *A Guide To Treatments That Work*, Oxford University Press, New York, 1998, pp. 544–53.

Day, M, "An Eye Movement Phenomenon Relating to Attention, Thoughts, and Anxiety", *Perceptual Motor Skills*, 1964.

DeLozier, J and Grinder, J, *Turtles All the Way Down*, Grinder, DeLozier and Associates, Bonny Doone, California, 1987.

Diamond, E G, Kittle, C F and Crockett, J E, "Evaluation of internal mammary artery ligation and sham procedure in angina pectoris", *Circulation*, No. 18, 1958, pp. 712–13.

Diamond, M, *Enriching Heredity: The Impact of the Environment on the Brain*, Free Press, New York, 1988.

Dilts, R, *Modelling With NLP*, Meta Publications, Capitola, California, 1998.

Dilts, R, *Roots of Neuro-Linguistic Programming*, Meta Publications, Cupertino, California, 1983.

Dilts, R, *Sleight of Mouth*, Meta Publications, Capitola, California, 1999.

Dilts, R, Grinder, J, Bandler, R and DeLozier, J, *Neuro-Linguistic Programming: Volume 1 The Study of the Structure of Subjective Experience*, Meta Publications, Cupertino, California, 1980.

Dilts, R, Hallbom, T and Smith, S, *Beliefs: Pathways to Health and Wellbeing*, Metamorphous, Portland, Oregon, 1990.

Dilts, R B, *Strategies of Genius, Volume I, II, and III*, Meta Publications, Capitola, 1994–95.

Dilts, R B and Epstein, T A, *Dynamic Learning*, Meta Publications, Capitola, 1995.

Dolan, Y M, *A Path With a Heart*, Brunner/Mazel, New York, 1985.

Dorsman, J, *How To Quit Drinking Without AA*, Prima, New York, 1997.

Egan, G, *The Skilled Helper*, Brooks/Cole, Monterey, California, 1975.

Einspruch, E L and Forman, B D, "Neurolinguistic Programming in the Treatment of Phobias", *Psychotherapy in Private Practice*, Vol. 6, No. 1: 1988, pp. 91–100.

Ellis, A, "The History of Cognition in Psychotherapy", in Freeman, A, Simon, K M, Beutler, L E and Arkowitz, H (eds), *Comprehensive Handbook of Cognitive Therapy*, Plenum Press, New York, 1989.

Ellis, A, *The Sensuous Person*, Signet, New York, 1972.

Erickson, M H, *The Collected Papers of Milton H. Erickson, Vol. I–IV* (ed. Rossi, E L), Irvington, New York, 1980.

Erickson, M H, *Experiencing Hypnosis*, Irvington, New York, 1981.

Erickson, M H, "The therapy of a psychosomatic headache", *Journal of Clinical and Experimental Hypnosis*, No. 4, 1953, pp. 2–6.

Erickson, M H and Rossi, E L, *The February Man*, Brunner/Mazel, New York, 1989.

Erickson, M H and Rossi, E L, *Hypnotherapy: An Exploratory Casebook*, Irvington, New York, 1979.

Eysenck, H, "The outcome problem in psychotherapy", in Dryden, W and Feltham, C (eds), Psychotherapy and its Discontents, Open University, 1992, Milton Keynes, England, p. 100–23.

Fawzy F I, Fawzy N W, Hyun C S et al., "Malignant Melanoma: effects of an early structured psychiatric intervention, coping and affective state on recurrence and survival 6 years later", Archives of General Psychiatry, 1993, 50:681–689.

Fawzy F I, Kenieny M E, Fawzy N W et al., "A structured psychiatric intervention for cancer patients. 11 Changes over time in immunological measures", Archives of General Psychiatry 1990, 47:729–735.

Fiedler, F E, "Factor analysis of psychoanalytic, non-directive and Adlerian therapeutic relationships", *Journal of Consulting Psychology*, No. 15, 1951, pp. 32–8.

Franklin, J A, *Overcoming Panic*, Australian Psychological Society, Carlton, Victoria.

Freud, S, "Project for a Scientific Psychology", *The Standard Edition of the Complete Psychological Works of Sigmund Freud*, Hogarth Press, London, 1966.

Freud, S, "Recommendations to Physicians Practising Psychoanalysis", in Goleman, D and Speeth, K R (eds), *The Essential Psychotherapies* Mentor, New York, 1982, pp. 4–12.

Freud, S, "Two Encyclopaedia Articles: (A) Psycho-analysis", *The Standard Edition of the Complete Psychological Works of Sigmund Freud, Vol. 18*, Hogarth Press, London, 1923.

Freud, S (trans. Sprott, W J H), *New Introductory Lectures on Psychoanalysis*, W W Norton & Co., New York, 1933.

Freud, S and Breuer, J, *Studies on Hysteria*, Penguin, Harmondsworth, England, 1974.

Genser-Medlitsch, M and Schütz, P, *"Does Neuro-Linguistic psychotherapy have effect? New Results shown in the extramural section"*, ÖTZ-NLP, Vienna, 1997.

Glöser, C, "Testing the effectiveness of NLP's Six-step reframing Model with subjectively obese clients", University of Bielefeld, Department of Psychology, Master Thesis, Bielefeld, Germany, 1991.

Gordon, D, *Therapeutic Metaphors*, Meta Publications, Cupertino, California, 1978.

Gordon, D and Meyers-Anderson, M, *Phoenix: Therapeutic Patterns of Milton H. Erickson*, Meta Publications, Capitola, California, 1981.

Greenough, W T , Withers, G and Anderson, B, "Experience-Dependent Synaptogenesis as a Plausible Memory Mechanism", in Gormezano, I and Wasserman, E (eds), *Learning and Memory: The Behavioural and Biological Substrates*, Erlbaum & Associates, Hillsdale, New Jersey, 1992, pp. 209–229.

Grinder, J and Bandler, R, *Frogs Into Princes*, Real People Press, Moab, Utah, 1979.

Grinder, J and Bandler, R, *The Structure of Magic*, Science and Behavior, Palo Alto, California, 1975.

Grinder, J and Bandler, R, *The Structure of Magic II*, Science and Behavior, Palo Alto, California, 1976.

Grof, S, "The Shamanic Journey: Observations from Holotropic Therapy", in Doore, G (ed.), *Shaman's Path*, Shambhala, Boston, 1988, pp. 161–76.

Hagstrom, G C, "A microanalysis of direct confrontation psychotherapy with schizophrenics: using Neurolinguistic Programming and Delsarte's system of expression", from California School of Professional Psychology, 1981, available in *Dissertation Abstracts International*, Vol. 42, No. 10, 4192-B.

Hall, L M and Bodenhamer, B G, *Mind Lines: Lines For Changing Minds*, ET Publications, Grand Junction, Colorado, 1997.

Hall, M, "The New Domain of Meta-States in the History of NLP", *NLP World*, Vol. 2, No. 3, November 1995, pp. 53–60.

Hart, J T and Tomlinson (eds), T M, *New Directions In Client Centred Therapy*, Houghton Mifflin, Boston, 1970.

Hatfield, E , Cacioppo, J and Rapson, R, *Emotional Contagion*, Cambridge University Press, Cambridge, England, 1994.

Hischke, D. "A definitional and structural investigation of matching perceptual predicates, mismatching perceptual predicates, and Milton-model matching", *Dissertation Abstracts International*, Vol. 49, No. 9, p. 4005.

Hoffman, D D, *Visual Intelligence*, W W Norton & Co., New York, 1998.

Holden, R, *Laughter: The Best Medicine*, Thorsons, London, 1993.

Huaxia Zhineng Centre, *A Summary of Zhineng Qigong's Healing Effects on Chronic Diseases*, Huaxia Zhineng Clinic & Training Centre, Zigachong, 1991.

Ivey, A E, Bradford Ivey, M, and Simek-Morgan, L, *Counseling and Psychotherapy* Allyn and Bacon, Boston, 1996.

Jablensky, A, Sartorius, N, Ernberg, G, Anker, M, Korten, A, Cooper, J E , Day, R and Bertelsen, A, "Schizophrenia: manifestations, incidence and course in different cultures. A World Health Organisation ten country study", *Psychological Medicine*, Supplement 20, 1992, pp. 1–97.

Jacobs, B, Schall, M and Scheibel, A B, "A Qualitative Dendritic Analysis of Wernicke's Area in Humans: Gender, Hemispheric and Environmental Factors", *Journal of Comparative Neurology*, Vol. 327, No. 1, 1993, pp. 97–111.

Jacobs, L, "A cognitive approach to persistent delusions", *American Journal of Psychotherapy*, 34, 1980, pp. 556–63.

James, T, "General Model for Behavioural Intervention" in *Time Line Therapy® Practitioner Training* (manual, Version 3.1), Time Line Therapy Association, Honolulu, 1995.

James, T and Woodsmall, W, *Time Line Therapy and the Basis of Personality*, Meta Publications, Cupertino, California, 1988.

James, W, *The Principles of Psychology*, Dover, New York, 1950.

Janov, A, *Primal Man: The New Consciousness*, Abacus, London, 1977.

Jensen, E, *Brain-Based Teaching and Learning*, Turning Point, Del Mar, California, 1995.

Jung, C (ed.) *Man and His Symbols*, Dell, New York, 1976.

Kalat, J W, *Biological Psychology*, Wadsworth Publishing, Belmont, California, 1988.

Kernberg, O, *Object Relations Theory and Clinical Psychoanalysis*, Jason Aronson Inc., Northvale, New Jersey, 1986.

Kipper, D A, *Psychotherapy Through Clinical Role Playing*, Brunner/Mazel, New York, 1986.

Kopelowicz, A and Liberman, R P, "Psychosocial Treatments for Schizophrenia", in Nathan, P E and Gorman, J M, *A Guide to Treatments That Work*, Oxford University Press, New York, 1998, pp. 190–211.

Krumboltz, J D and Thoresen, C E (eds), *Counselling Methods*, Holt, Rinehart and Winston, New York, 1976.

Laborde, G, *Influencing With Integrity*, Syntony, Palo Alto, California, 1987.

Lambert, M and Bergin, A, "The Effectiveness of Psychotherapy", in Bergin, A. and Garfield, S, *Handbook of Psychotherapy and Behavior Change*, Wiley, New York, 1994.

Lane, J, "Improving athletic performance through visio-motor behavior rehearsal", in Suinn, R (ed.), *Psychology In Sports Methods and Applications*, Burgess, New York, 1980.

Lankton, S R, *Practical Magic*, Meta Publications, Cupertino, California, 1980.

Layden, M A, Newman, C F, Freeman, A and Byers Morse, S, *Cognitive Therapy of Borderline Personality Disorder*, Allyn and Bacon, Boston, 1993.

LeShan, L, *You Can Fight For Your Life*, Thorsons, Wellingborough, Northamptonshire, 1984.

Levitsky, A and Perls, F S, "The Rules and Games of Gestalt Therapy", in Goleman, D and Speeth, K R, *The Essential Psychotherapies*, Signet, New York, 1982, pp. 142–54.

Liberman, M B, "The Treatment of Simple Phobias with NeuroLinguistic Programming Techniques", *Dissertation Abstracts International*, Vol. 45, No. 6, St Louis University, 1984, p. 86 ff.

Lowen, A, "What is bioenergetic analysis?", *Energy and Character*, Vol. 2, No. 3, 1971.

Lowen, A, *Depression and the Body* Penguin, Harmondsworth, England, 1972.

Lowen, A and Lowen, L, *The Way To Vibrant Health: A Manual of Bioenergetic Exercises*, Harper & Row, New York, 1977.

Lund, H, "Asthma Management", *Time Line Therapy Association Journal*, Vol. 5, Summer 1995.

Luria, A R, *Higher Cortical Functions In Man*, Basic Books, New York, 1966.

Macroy, T D, "Linguistic surface structures in family interaction", *Dissertation Abstracts International*, Vol. 40, No. 2, 926-B, Utah State University, Order = 7917967, 1978, p. 133 ff.

Malloy, T E, "Cognitive strategies and a classroom procedure for teaching spelling", Department of Psychology, University of Utah, 1989.

Malloy, T E, Mitchell, C and Gordon, O E, "Training cognitive strategies underlying intelligent problem solving", *Perceptual and Motor Skills*, No. 64, 1987, pp. 1039–1046.

Mann, L, Beswick, G, Allouache, P and Ivey, M, "Decision workshops for the improvement of decisionmaking: Skills and confidence", *Journal of Counselling and Development*, 67, 1989, pp. 478–481.

Marlatt, G and Gordon, J, *Relapse Prevention: Maintenance Strategies in the Treatment of Addictive Behaviours*, Guilford, New York, 1985.

Marsh, A "Smoking: Habit or Choice?", *Population Trends*, Vol. 37, No. 20, 1984.

Marshall, I, "Consciousness and Bose–Einstein condensates", *New Ideas in Psychology*, 7, 1989, pp. 73–83.

Masson, J, *Against Therapy*, HarperCollins, London, 1993.

Masters, B J, Rawlins, M E, Rawlins, L D and Weidner, J, "The NLP Swish Pattern: An innovative visualising technique", *Journal of Mental Healthy Counselling*, Vol. 13, No. 1, January 1991, pp. 79–90.

Maturana, H R and Varela, F J, *The Tree of Knowledge*, Shambhala, Boston, 1992.

McDermott, I and O'Connor, J, *NLP and Health*, Thorsons, London, 1996.

Miller, G, Galanter, E and Pribram, K, *Plans and the Structure of Behaviour*, Henry Holt & Co., 1960.

Miller, J, "Going Unconscious", in Silvers, R (ed.), *Hidden Histories of Science*, Granta, London, 1995.

Miller, S D, Hubble, M A and Duncan, B L, *Handbook of Solution Focused Brief Therapy*, Jossey-Bass, San Francisco, 1996.

Miller, W, "Motivation for treatment: a review with special emphasis on alcoholism", *Psychological Bulletin*, Vol. 98 (1), 1985, pp. 79–90.

Miller, W R and Rollnick, S, *Motivational Interviewing*, The Guilford Press, New York, 1991.

Mitchell, D, Osbourne, E W and O'Boyle, M W, "Habituation under stress: Shocked mice show non-associative learning in a T-maze", *Behavioural and Neural Biology*, No. 43, 1985, pp. 212–17.

Moine, D, "A psycholinguistic study of the patterns of persuasion used by successful salespeople", *Dissertation Abstracts International*, Vol. 42, No. 5, 2135-B, University of Oregon, Order = 8123499, 1981, p. 271 ff.

Moreno, J, *Psychodrama: First Volume* Beacon House, New York, 1977.

Moreno, J L, "Hypnodrama and Psychodrama", *Group Psychotherapy*, Vol. 3, No.1, 1950, pp. 1–10.

Moreno, J L, *Une Demonstration de Psychodrame*, Le Service de la Recherche de l'ORTP et les Analyses Cinématographique, Paris, 1964.

Muss, D, "A New Technique for Treating Post-Traumatic Stress Disorder", *British Journal of Clinical Psychology*, No. 30, 1991, pp. 91–2.

Muss, D, *The Trauma Trap*, Doubleday, London, 1991.

O'Brien, C P and McKay, J "Psychopharmacological Treatments of Substance Use Disorders" p. 127–155 in Nathan, P E and Gorman, J M, *A Guide To Treatments That Work*, Oxford University Press, New York, 1998.

O'Connor, J and Seymour, J, *Introducing Neuro-Linguistic Programming*, HarperCollins, London, 1990.

O'Connor, J and Seymour, J, *Training With Neuro-Linguistic Programming*, HarperCollins, London, 1994.

O'Connor, J and Van der Horst, B, "Neural Networks and NLP Strategies: Part 2", in *Anchor Point*, Vol. 8, No. 6, June 1994, pp. 30–8.

Olinick, S L, *The Psychotherapeutic Instrument*, Jason Aronson, New York, 1980.

Pavlov, I P, *Conditioned Reflexes: An Account of the Physiological Activities of the Cerebral Cortex*, Oxford University Press, London, 1927.

Peele, S, *Diseasing of America*, Houghton Mifflin, 1989, Boston.

Perls, F, *Gestalt Therapy Verbatim*, Real People Press, Moab, Utah, 1969.

Perls, F, Hefferline, R F and Goodman, P, *Gestalt Therapy*, Julian, New York, 1951.

Perris, C, *Cognitive Therapy with Schizophrenic Patients*, Cassell, London, 1989.

Podolsky, E, *The Doctor Prescribes Colors*, National Library Press, New York, 1938.

Ragge, K, *The Real AA: Behind the Myth of 12 Step Recovery*, See Sharp Press, Tucson, 1998.

Rainey, J M, Aleem, A, Ortiz, A, Yaragani, V, Pohl, R and Berchow, R, "Laboratory procedure for the inducement of flashbacks", *American Journal of Psychiatry*, No. 144, 1987, pp. 1317–19.

Reckert, H W, "Test anxiety … removed by anchoring in just one session?", *Multimind*, NLP Aktuell, No. 6, November/December 1994.

Reich, W, *The Invasion of Compulsory Sex-Morality*, Penguin, Harmondsworth, England, 1971.

Rogers, C, *Client Centred Therapy*, Constable, London, 1973.

Rogers, C, *Encounter Groups*, Penguin, Harmondsworth, England, 1974.

Rogers, C, *A Way of Being*, Houghton Mifflin Co., Boston, 1980.

Rose, S, *The Making of Memory*, Bantam, New York, 1992.

Rossi, E L, *The Psychobiology of Mind–Body Healing*, W W Norton & Company, New York, 1986.

Rossi, E L, *The Symptom Path to Enlightenment*, Palisades Gateway Publishing, Pacific Palisades, California, 1996.

Rossi, E L and Cheek, D B, *Mind-Body Therapy*, W W Norton & Company, New York, 1988.

Sacks, O, "Scotoma: Forgetting and Neglect in Science", in Silvers, R (ed.), *Hidden Histories of Science*, Granta, London, 1995.

Samuels, M and Samuels, N, *Seeing with the Mind's Eye*, Random House, New York, 1975.

Santoro, J and Cohen, R, *The Angry Heart: Overcoming Borderline and Addictive Disorders*, New Harbinger, Oakland, California, 1997.

Satir, V and Baldwin, M, *Satir Step By Step*, Science and Behavior, Palo Alto, California, 1983.

Schachter, S, "Recidivism and self-cure of smoking and obesity", *American Psychologist*, No. 37, 1982, pp. 436–44.

Schachter, S and Singer, J E, "Cognitive, social and physiological determinants of emotional state", *Psychological Review*, Vol. 69, No. 12, 1962, pp. 379–99.

Seligman, M E P, *Learned Optimism*, Random House, Sydney, 1997.

Seligman, M E P, *The Optimistic Child*, Random House, Sydney, 1995.

Shapiro, F, *Eye Movement Desensitisation and Reprocessing*, Guilford Press, New York, 1995.

Shostrom, E (ed.), *Three Approaches to Psychotherapy* (Film No. I), Psychological Films, Orange, California, 1965.

Simonton, O C, Mathews-Simonton, S and Creighton, J L, *Getting Well Again*, Bantam, New York, 1980.

Smith, E L and Laird, D A, "The Loudness of Auditory Stimuli Which Affect Stomach Contractions In Healthy Human Beings", *Journal of the Acoustic Society of America*, No. 2, 1930, pp. 94–8.

Solomon, P and Patch, V D, *Handbook of Psychiatry*, Lange Medical, Los Altos, California, 1974.

Southwick, S M, Krystal, J H, Morgan, A, Johnson, D, Nagy, L, Nicolaou, A, Henninger, G R and Charney, D S, "Abnormal noradrenergic function in post-traumatic stress disorder", *Archives of General Psychiatry*, No. 50, 1993, pp. 266–74.

Starr, A, *Psychodrama: Rehearsal for Living*, Nelson/Hall, Chicago, 1979.

Sterman, C M (ed.), *Neuro-Linguistic Programming In Alcoholism Treatment*, Haworth Press, New York, 1990.

Stewart, I and Joines, V, *TA Today*, Lifespace, Nottingham, 1987.

Suhd, M M, *Positive Regard: Carl Rogers and Other Notables He Influenced*, Science and Behaviour Books, Palo Alto, California, 1995.

Thalgott, M R, "Anchoring: A 'Cure' For Epy" *Academic Therapy*, Vol. 21, No 3, January 1986, pp. 347–52.

Thayer, R E, *The Origin of Everyday Moods*, Oxford University Press, New York, 1996.

Trimpey, J, *Rational Recovery*, Simon & Schuster, New York, 1996.

Van der Kolk, B A, "The body keeps the score: Memory and the evolving psychobiology of post-traumatic stress", *Harvard Review of Psychiatry*, Vol. 1, No. 5, 1994, pp. 253–65.

Van der Kolk, B A, McFarlane, A C and Weisaeth, L (eds), *Traumatic Stress*, Guilford, New York, 1996.

Walters, C and Havens, R A, "Good News For a Change: Optimism, Altruism, and Hardiness as the Basis for Erickson's Approach", in Zeig, J. (ed.), *Ericksonian Methods: The Essence of the Story*, Brunner/Mazel, New York, 1994, pp. 163–81.

Weinstock, C, "Notes on spontaneous regression of cancer", *Journal of the American Society of Psychosomatic Dentistry and Medicine*, Vol. 24, No 4, 1977, pp. 106–10.

Whitmont, E C, *The Symbolic Quest: Basic Concepts of Analytical Psychology*, Princeton University, Princeton, New Jersey, 1991.

Wightman, A, "Cancer, The Mind, Science and the Abyss", Trancescript, Transformations, Christchurch, No. 16, 1999, pp. 41–2.

Wilhelm, F A, "Submodality change and nail chewing. Empirical test of an imaginative method ('Swish')", Masters Thesis, Department of Psychology, Phillips University, Marburg, 1991.

Williams, A, *The Passionate Technique*, Tavistock/Routledge, London, 1989.

Wolpe, J, *Psychotherapy by Reciprocal Inhibition*, Stanford University Press, Palo Alto, California, 1958.

Yapko, M, "The Effects of Matching Primary Representational System Predicates on Hypnotic Relaxation", *American Journal of Clinical Hypnosis*, No. 23, 1981, pp. 169–75.

Yapko, M D, *Hypnosis and the Treatment of Depressions*, Brunner/Mazel, New York, 1992.

Zeig, J K, *A Teaching Seminar with Milton H. Erickson*, Brunner/Mazel, New York, 1980.

Zilbergeld, B, *The Shrinking of America*, Little Brown & Co., Boston, 1983.

Index

Addiction, 10, 51, 114–115, 171, 177

Alcoholism, 73, 125, 207, 210

Anaesthetics, 175

Anchors, 46–47, 49–50, 102, 106, 142, 154

Andreas, Connirae,5, 12, 55, 57, 60, 82, 102, 106, 197

Andreas, Steve, 4–5, 8, 12, 55, 57, 60, 82, 102, 104, 106, 111, 195, 197

Anxiety, 7, 15, 34, 46, 50–51, 57–58, 60, 72, 77, 119, 122, 126, 128, 139, 151, 156, 158, 161, 164–166, 169, 177, 181, 198, 200, 208

Assagioli, Roberto, 50, 79, 197

Associate/Dissociate, 61, 153

Auditory sense, 13, 24–25, 27, 30

Auditory–digital sense, 23

Bandler, Richard, 4–5, 9, 18, 25, 46, 51, 57, 66–67, 72, 90–91, 96, 102, 127–128, 132, 139, 149–152, 169, 171, 181–183, 198, 201, 203

Borderline personality, 50, 156, 169, 205

Bosnia-Herzegovina, iii, 8, 43

Breathing and state control, 105–106

Callahan, Roger, 103–104, 199

Cancer, 173–174, 176, 202, 210

Carkhuff, Robert, 8–9, 11, 113, 122, 124, 130–131, 199–200

Cheek, David, 6, 38–39, 66–67, 200, 208

Chi kung, 176–177

Chunk up/Chunk down, 153

Client centered therapy, 4, 56, 65, 71, 81, 88, 96, 102, 109, 199, 208, 210

Cognitive behavioural therapy, 2, 5, 72, 103, 112

Consulting, 127, 132, 134, 140, 145–146, 157, 164, 184, 199, 202

Counselling, 29, 71, 97, 103, 112, 122, 125, 164, 199–200, 205–206

Dendrites, 36–37, 41

Depression, 7, 15, 30, 32, 49, 51, 58, 93, 105, 115, 125–126, 155, 157–158, 162–164, 166–167, 169, 177, 179, 187, 189, 206

Diclemente, Carlo, 114, 116

Dilts, Robert, 3–4, 25–26, 29–30, 32–34, 51–52, 73, 83, 92, 123, 157–161, 201

Dissociate/Associate, 61, 153

Ecological outcomes/Ecology, 137, 182

Ellis, Albert, 5, 55, 201

Erickson, Milton, 4–5, 50, 66–67, 71–72, 89–92, 102, 104, 106–107, 117–122, 128, 152, 154, 168, 172, 177, 180, 190, 197–198, 201–203, 210–211

Extravert/Introvert, 157

Eye accessing cues, 27, 29

Eye Movement Desensitisation and Reprocessing, 103–105, 193, 209

Freud, Sigmund, 4, 13, 39, 64, 70–71, 76–78, 87, 105, 109, 111, 202

Gestalt therapy, 11, 49, 64, 88, 95, 101, 205, 208

Grinder, John, 4–5, 9, 25, 46, 51, 66–67, 72, 90–91, 96, 102, 128, 158, 171, 198, 200–201, 203

Hall, Michael, iii, 33, 35, 66, 71, 99,
    161, 165, 200, 203, 209
Hamblett, Margot, iii, 1, 8–9, 11,
    26, 61, 84, 98, 128, 140, 161, 166,
    199
Health problems, 173–177
Hypnosis, 66, 69–72, 87, 89,
    200–201, 211

Ideomotor signals, 67
Interpersonal dynamics, i, 44, 96,
    99, 101, 145
Introvert/Extravert, 157

James, Tad, 4, 9, 83, 85, 95, 141,
    149, 151, 154, 166, 204
James, William, 18–19, 24–26, 105,
    166, 204
Jung, Carl, 4, 49, 70, 78, 87, 95, 97,
    109, 153, 155, 157, 204

Kinaesthetic sense, 13, 24–25, 27,
    30

Laughing, 165, 187, 190
Learning, 12, 26, 29, 36–39, 46, 49,
    51–52, 55, 66, 77, 89, 92,
    119–120, 122, 129, 138, 145–146,
    156, 176, 186, 189, 194–195, 198,
    201, 203–204, 207
Love, 16, 34, 79, 85, 124, 184, 195
Lowen, Alexander, 49, 55, 70,
    79–80, 88, 96, 105, 109, 206
Lund, Hanne, 83–84, 206

Meta states, 35
Metamodel, 90–93, 101, 133, 154,
    169, 185
Meta-programs, 97, 129, 146, 151,
    153, 157, 163, 168, 184
Milton model, 67, 91–93, 130
Moreno, Jacob, 70–71, 79, 207
Motivational Interviewing, 113,
    116–117, 119, 172
Muss, David, 8, 58, 207

Neural networks, iv, 36–41, 43, 49,
    66, 76, 82, 94, 103, 117, 123, 166,
    193, 207
Neurological levels, 159–160, 176,
    194
Neuro-Linguistic Programming
    (NLP), iv, 1–15, 18, 21, 23–33,
    39–41, 43–46, 49–52, 54, 56–58,
    60–61, 66, 72, 77–83, 88–89, 90,
    94, 96–99, 101–105, 111, 117,
    122–130, 132–135, 137, 139–140,
    148, 151–158, 160–161, 163,
    165–174, 176–182, 184–189, 191,
    193–195, 197, 199, 201, 203,
    206–208, 210

Object Relations theory, 205
Obsessive compulsive disorder,
    39, 198
O'Connor, Joseph, 33, 54, 102, 174,
    207
Opening up model of world, 140
Outcomes, 41, 116, 133, 145, 151,
    174, 182, 184, 194–195

Parts integration, iv, 44, 72–73, 76,
    83, 94, 144, 152–153, 155–156,
    160, 163, 166, 176, 193
Pavlov, Ivan, 31–32, 39, 45–46, 71,
    208
Perception, iv, 7, 14, 16–17, 22, 40,
    65, 89, 140, 153, 167
Perceptual positions, 157–159
Perls, Fritz, 4, 64–65, 70, 80–81, 88,
    95, 101–102, 109, 205, 208
Personal Strengths model, 152,
    157, 161
Personality disorders, iii, 77, 200
Physiological contexts, ii, 44, 102,
    104–105, 145
Preframing, 142
Presuppositions of NLP, 178, 184
Pre-test, 141
Prochaska, James, 114, 116
Psychoanalysis, 2, 39, 49, 55, 70,
    76–77, 101, 109, 202, 205

Psychodrama, 5, 49, 56, 64–65, 70–71, 88, 102, 109, 111–112, 207, 209
Psychosis, 155, 157, 168
Psychosynthesis, 50, 79, 197

Rapport, 9, 69, 96, 120, 123–124, 128–130, 132–134, 151, 168–169, 184–185, 187, 194
Rapport, basis in matching, 128–130
Rational emotive therapy, 5, 55, 186
Reflective listening, 97, 101, 129, 131–133, 184
Reframing, i, 43–44, 66, 72–73, 90, 94–96, 141, 144, 146, 160–161, 171, 177, 193, 198, 203
Reparenting, 49
RESOLVE model summaries, 9–10, 119–122, 184–185
Rogers, Carl, 4, 56, 65, 71, 81, 88, 96, 102, 109, 199, 208, 210
Rossi, Ernest, 38–39, 66–67, 70, 89, 105–106, 119–120, 180, 193, 201–202, 208

Sarajevo, 1–3
Satir, 4, 35, 80–81, 90, 96, 102, 194–195, 197–198, 209
Schizophrenia, 115, 167–168, 204–205
Sensory accessing cues, 27–28
Sensory representational system, 27, 29
Shapiro, Francine, 103, 193, 209
Sleight of Mouth, 93, 201
Solution-focused questions, 133, 154, 163
SPECIFY model for outcomes, 135–136
Spelling strategy, 29, 52
Spirit, 160, 176

State dependent memory, 38
State dependent neural networks, 37–40
States, i, 13, 33–35, 37, 39, 47, 49, 51, 65, 71, 77–79, 87, 123, 129, 135, 142–144, 160, 163, 166, 170, 184, 194
Strategies model, 30
Submodalities, i, 18–24, 28, 40, 44, 56–61, 64–65, 143, 150, 154, 165, 169, 194
Surgery, 115, 119, 174–175, 198

Tasking, ii, 44, 106–107, 109, 145, 189, 193
TFT, 103–104
Thought Field Therapy (TFT), 103, 166, 176
Time Line, 82–89, 117, 144, 151, 154, 156–158, 161, 204, 206
TOTE model, iv, 31–33
Trancework, i, 44, 66–67, 69, 71, 143, 154, 156, 177, 180, 193
Transactional Analysis, 4, 12, 49, 55, 77, 87, 102, 186
Transforming Communication, iii, 98, 199
Trauma process (NLP), 7–8, 57–58, 61

Unified Field model, 157, 159, 161, 163

Vision, colour 16
Vision, recognition of objects colour, 16–18
Visual sense 30
Visual cortex, 14–20, 22
Visual digital sense, 26

Yapko, Michael, 29, 72, 115, 128, 158, 162, 211

Now you've read the book, see Dr Richard Bolstad in action!

RESOLVE: The Complete Workshop
Videotape Set
by Dr Richard Bolstad

This cutting-edge visual resource skilfully guides therapists and counsellors through the process of applying the RESOLVE model to help solve clients' real life problems. Using in-depth case studies, and drawing on extensive research on human change, this training resource offers an invaluable insight into making that essential breakthrough with your clients.

Utilising the methodology and practice of *RESOLVE*, the book, you will see Dr Bolstad explain:

● NLP models of how the brain works
● An overview of NLP in changework
● How to use your clients' personal strengths to promote self-change

Also, how the RESOLVE model can be used in the treatment of a variety of disorders including:

● Anxiety   ● Addictions
● Psychoses   ● Personality disorders

This latest work is sure to create a paradigm shift in the application of NLP in therapeutic settings, and has direct applications to other areas of change as well.

Running Time: 3 ½ hours, 2 videotapes – PAL Format

Available in the UK and Europe from: The NLP Video Library, Crown Buildings, Bancyfelin, Carmarthen, SA33 5ND, UK.

Tel: +44 (0)1267 211880   Fax: +44 (0)1267 211882
                Website: www.nlpvideos.com

Available in the rest of the World from Dr Richard Bolstad, *Transformations International*, Consulting & Training Ltd, 26 Southampton Street, Christchurch 2, New Zealand.

Tel: +64-337-1852   Fax: +64-337-1852
        (in New Zealand it is 0800-FOR-NLP; 0800-367-657)

The Structure of Personality
Modeling "Personality" Using NLP
and Neuro-Semantics
L. Michael Hall PhD, Bob G. Bodenhamer DMin,
Dr Richard Bolstad & Margot Hamblett

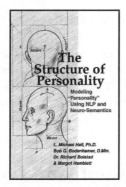

Personality is not a 'thing', it is a process. When we discuss personality, what we are talking about is a system of responding and relating or, more precisely, a set of *behaviours*. This is good news for those who deal with, or suffer with, personality problems. What it means is that personality can be *reordered* and *reprogrammed* in a way that is both beneficial and liberating.

The Structure of Personality begins by exploring how we actively 'pattern' experience. Guiding us through the cognitive system of internal representation, it examines the contexts and environments in which such patterning arises, and the higher levels at which we produce beliefs and values that determine our behaviours. Once it has identified the process of 'producing a personality', it presents strategies that will alter those behaviours and reprogram personality, targeting each stage of personality production – and in particular, the stage at which the client forms *core beliefs*.

Coaching the reader in a number of effective and specially adapted NLP techniques, *The Structure of Personality* includes reordering strategies such as The R.E.S.O.L.V.E. model – that ingeniously sequences a number of key tasks that form an important part of change work, and the Personal Strengths Model – that determines which NLP techniques will be useful for you or for your client. Addressing general and specific behaviour problems, such as schizophrenia, paranoia and addiction, it is an essential reference for counsellors, therapists and NLP practitioners, presenting effective solutions to personality disorders.

HARDBACK   496 PAGES   ISBN: 1899836675

USA & Canada *orders to:*

Crown House Publishing
P.O. Box 2223, Williston, VT 05495-2223, USA
Tel: 877-925-1213, Fax: 802-864-7626
www.crownhouse.co.uk

UK & Rest of World *orders to:*

The Anglo American Book Company Ltd.
Crown Buildings, Bancyfelin, Carmarthen, Wales SA33 5ND
Tel: +44 (0)1267 211880/211886, Fax: +44 (0)1267 211882
E-mail: books@anglo-american.co.uk
www.anglo-american.co.uk

Australasia *orders to:*

Footprint Books Pty Ltd
101 McCarrs Creek Road, P.O. Box 418, Church Point
Sydney NSW 2105, Australia
Tel: +61 2 9997 3973, Fax: +61 2 9997 3185
E-mail: footprintbooks@ozmail.com.au